CLIFFORD ODETS

LITERATURE AND LIFE: AMERICAN WRITERS

Selected list of titles in the series:

LOUIS AUCHINCLOSS	*Christopher C. Dahl*
SAUL BELLOW	*Robert F. Kiernan*
TRUMAN CAPOTE	*Helen S. Garson*
RACHEL CARSON	*Carol B. Gartner*
STEPHEN CRANE	*Bettina L. Knapp*
THEODORE DREISER	*James Lundquist*
WILLIAM FAULKNER	*Alan Warren Friedman*
F. SCOTT FITZGERALD	*Rose Adrienne Gallo*
ROBERT FROST	*Elaine Barry*
LILLIAN HELLMAN	*Doris V. Falk*
ERNEST HEMINGWAY	*Samuel Shaw*
JOHN IRVING	*Gabriel Miller*
THE NOVELS OF HENRY JAMES	*Edward Wagenknecht*
THE TALES OF HENRY JAMES	*Edward Wagenknecht*
KEN KESEY	*Barry H. Leeds*
JACK LONDON	*James Lundquist*
MARY MCCARTHY	*Willene Schaefer Hardy*
JAMES A. MICHENER	*George J. Becker*
ARTHUR MILLER	*June Schlueter and James K. Flanagan*
ANAÏS NIN	*Bettina L. Knapp*
JOHN O'HARA	*Robert Emmet Long*
THE PLAYS OF EUGENE O'NEILL	*Virginia Floyd*
EDGAR ALLAN POE	*Bettina L. Knapp*
J. D. SALINGER	*James Lundquist*
JOHN STEINBECK	*Paul McCarthy*
WILLIAM STYRON	*Judith Ruderman*
LIONEL TRILLING	*Edward Joseph Shoben, Jr.*
MARK TWAIN	*Robert Keith Miller*
NATHANAEL WEST	*Robert Emmet Long*
THORNTON WILDER	*David Castronovo*
EDMUND WILSON	*David Castronovo*
RICHARD WRIGHT	*David Bakish*

Complete list of titles in the series available from the publisher on request.

CLIFFORD ODETS

Gabriel Miller

A Frederick Ungar Book
CONTINUUM • NEW YORK

1989

The Continuum Publishing Company
370 Lexington Avenue
New York, NY 10017

Printed in the United States of America

Library of Congress Cataloging-in-Publication Data

Miller, Gabriel, 1948–
    Clifford Odets / Gabriel Miller.
    p.   cm. — (Literature and life series)
    Bibliography: p.
    Includes index.
    ISBN 0-8044-2632-5
    1. Odets, Clifford, 1906–1963—Criticism and interpretation.
I. Title.   II. Series.
PS3529.D46Z75 1989
812'.54—dc19   87-28799
                                                                              CIP

For
Lauren Jessica

Contents

Preface

American drama is a stepchild of American literature, rarely acknowledged and even more rarely subjected to serious study. Anthologies of American literature pay scant attention to drama: the 1979 edition of the *Norton Anthology of American Literature* contains not a single play; the 1985 revision has three, including Odets's *Waiting for Lefty*. Even scholars of American drama who should be formulating a canon rarely write about anyone except the "big three," O'Neill, Miller, and Williams. (Edward Albee sometimes swells the pantheon to four.) This parsimony of critical recognition owes something, certainly, to the exigencies of publishing, but probably more to a hesitancy on the part of many academics to go beyond what has been "officially" accepted. It is doubly surprising, therefore, that a discipline in search of subjects and in need of a canon should ignore one of this country's most talented playwrights, Clifford Odets. The neglect of Odets derives, in part, from an unfortunate tendency to label him an interesting "thirties" writer, or, worse, a revolutionary playwright, and this critical condescension is underscored by his continual association with *Waiting for Lefty*—the only one of his plays generally to be anthologized—which is perhaps representative of thirties theater but not of Odets's major work. And, because he was a cooperative witness before HUAC and because he spent too much time in Hollywood, even writing an Elvis Presley movie and some television shows, much of the intellectual establishment has never forgiven him, and so he has been confined to a critical limbo whence he awaits redemption.

This study is an attempt to present Odets as a playwright who experimented with dramatic form while giving voice to significant thematic and social concerns that evolved over the course of his career, transcending the narrow perspective of Depression politics. I hope to reopen the career of an important playwright to more serious discussion and consideration. I deal primarily with Odets's eleven published plays, but make reference also to four unpublished pieces and to Odets's film and television scripts.

As of this writing, only one book-length study of Odets is in print: Gerald Weales's *Odets: The Playwright,* a reprint of his 1971 book. Of the four published full-length studies of Odets, Weales's is the most complete and penetrating, although it directs more attention to the life than to the works. Margaret Brenman-Gibson's first volume of a mammoth biography ends in 1940; volume two has not yet appeared. While her work provides a wealth of valuable material, the critical focus is psychoanalytic rather than literary. Mine is the first critical study to treat all of Odets's work in detail.

A final note: after this book was finished and had already been copy-edited, I received the galleys of Odets's 1940 journal from Grove Press. Rather than attempt to restructure an entire book, I have added a short chapter on it as an afterword which focuses less on the biographical information found in the journal than on its relationship to Odets's writing.

There remain some thank yous. First to Dorothy Swerdlove, curator of the Billy Rose Theatre Collection of the New York Public Library at Lincoln Center, for her cooperation, patience, and kindness, and to her staff for their assistance as well. Also to Walt Bode of Grove Press for being so prompt about sending the galleys for the 1940 journal. I also want to thank the Graduate School of Rutgers University, Newark, for two grants that helped me in the preparation of this book. Grateful acknowledgment is also made to Mr. Walt Odets for permission to quote from the published and unpublished writings of Clifford Odets.

Lizzie and Jessica did nothing to speed up the completion of this book, but did make the time away from it priceless. My greatest debt, as always, is to Kathy, my "country girl," who has proofread these chapters and has done the most to reduce the number of errors they contain. I can never sufficiently acknowledge her patience and generosity.

Chronology

1906 Born July 18, in Philadelphia, to Pearl Geisinger Odets and Louis Odets.

1908–16 Family makes three moves: to the Bronx, NY, to Philadelphia, and back to the Bronx. Sister, Genevieve, born in 1910; sister, Florence, born in 1916.

1921–23 Attends Morris High School in the Bronx.

1929–30 Understudies Spencer Tracy in Broadway production of *Conflict;* an extra with Theatre Guild touring company.

1931 Group Theatre formed; Odets a charter member.

1932 Understudies Luther Adler in John Howard Lawson's *Success Story;* begins writing *I Got the Blues* (to become *Awake and Sing!*).

1934 Writes *Waiting for Lefty* in Boston; it wins *New Theatre* magazine play contest.

1935 (January) *Waiting for Lefty* presented at benefit performance; Odets hailed as a major new talent.

   (February) *Awake and Sing!* opens at Belasco Theater; writes *Till the Day I Die.*

   (March) *Waiting for Lefty* and *Till the Day I Die* double bill opens at Longacre Theatre.

   (April) Publication of *Three Plays by Clifford Odets* by Covici-Friede.

(May) Death of his mother; "I Can't Sleep."

(July) Trip to Cuba, where he is arrested and deported.

(December) *Paradise Lost* opens at Longacre Theater.

1936   Goes to Hollywood; writes screenplay for *The General Died at Dawn*.

1937   Marries Luise Rainer; *Golden Boy* opens at Belasco Theater.

1938   London opening of *Golden Boy; Rocket to the Moon* opens at Belasco Theater in November; *Time* magazine cover story, December 5.

1939   Odets and Luise Rainer separate; publication of *Six Plays of Clifford Odets* by Random House.

1940   *Night Music* opens at Broadhurst Theater.

1941   Dissolution of the Group Theatre; *Clash by Night* opens at Belasco Theater.

1942   Goes to Hollywood; later returns to New York to adapt Simonov's *The Russian People,* produced by the Theatre Guild.

1943–44 Marries Bette Grayson; goes to Hollywood to write *None But the Lonely Heart,* which he also directs.

1945   Daughter, Nora, born.

1946   Writes screenplay for *Deadline at Dawn;* coauthors screenplay for *Humoresque.*

1947   Son, Walt Whitman, born.

1948   Returns to New York.

1949   *The Big Knife* opens at National Theater.

1950   *The Country Girl* opens at Lyceum Theater.

1951   Divorced from Bette Grayson.

1952   Questioned by House Un-American Activities Committee in May.

1954   *The Flowering Peach* opens at Belasco Theater.

1955   Returns to Hollywood.

1957   Coauthors screenplay for *The Sweet Smell of Success*.

1960   Writes and directs film, *The Story on Page One*.

1961   Writes screenplay for *Wild in the Country;* receives Award of Merit Medal for Drama from American Academy of Arts and Letters.

1962–63 Story editor for NBC-TV series, "The Richard Boone Show," for which he also writes three teleplays, of which two are produced. Dies of cancer on August 14, 1963, in Los Angeles.

1988   *The Time is Ripe: The 1940 Journal of Clifford Odets* published by Grove Press.

1

The Whirl and the Terror

I want to find out how mankind can be helped out of the animal kingdom into the clear sweet air.

—Clifford Odets, 1935

Clifford Odets's parents, Pearl Geisenger and Lou (later changed to Louis) Odets, were immigrants. Pearl had come to America with her sister, Esther, from Rumania at the turn of the century; they were from a poor family of twenty-eight children (from two marriages), most of whom died young. Esther was married first, to a Russian Jew, Sroul (Israel) Rossman, who agreed to house Pearl as well. *Tante* Esther and Uncle Israel would become for Clifford Odets substitute parents, as he was to spend countless hours in their house, receiving there the familial nourishment he craved but could not get from his own parents. The future playwright would later model Noah and his wife (whom he named Esther) on his favorite uncle and aunt in his final play, *The Flowering Peach*.

A shy, quiet, and rather melancholy person, Pearl was also sickly and emotionally vulnerable. Exhibiting a typical immigrant's fear of the American city, she kept mostly to her apartment. She never learned English very well and was ashamed of her illiteracy.[1] Pearl was, in fact, the antithesis of the domineering, outspoken, and abrasive women who appear in many of her son's plays; Odets's portrayals of his "fictional" mothers more closely resemble his father.

Lou Odets came from Russia, though he would later claim that he was born in Philadelphia. His father was an Old World Jew, a scholarly man with a white beard and a strong love of music, and although Clifford never met his grandfather, he probably served as a

1

model for Jacob in *Awake and Sing!* In stark contrast to his wife, Lou was garrulous, loud, and sociable, priding himself on his natty appearance. Like many first-generation immigrants, he had an overwhelming desire to shed his ethnic identity and to be a success, a "big shot." After his mother died, he forbade anyone to visit her grave lest they see the name on the gravestone. The family name was Goredetsky, but he always vehemently denied it. (One branch of the family changed the name to Gordon, which Odets used in *Paradise Lost*.)

This ill-matched pair was married on March 6, 1905, and moved in with the Rossmans, whom Lou despised for their pronounced ethnicity, in their row house at 207 George Street, Philadelphia. There, on July 18, 1906, after not quite eight months of pregnancy, Pearl gave birth to their first child, named Clifford because Lou thought the name had a nice ring. The couple would have two more children: Genevieve, born in 1910, and Florence, in 1916.

When Clifford was born, his father worked for the Curtis Publishing Company, where he was a printer. Determined to succeed and escape Pearl's family, Lou moved his family to New York City when Clifford was two, but was unable to make a living. Humiliated, he moved back to Philadelphia and back in with the Rossmans. Then, in 1912, when Clifford was six, Lou Odets lost his job and decided again to move his family to New York. They settled in the Bronx, at 747 Southern Boulevard. There Lou Odets made friends with Louis Rosenberg and Harry Horowitz, who introduced him to the Hell Hole in Greenwich Village (also frequented by Eugene O'Neill). There Lou would drink and play cards after attending evening classes in advertising at New York University. Later that year, after a murder, it was discovered that his card partners were "Gyp the Blood" and "Lefty Louie," notorious at the time as two of the "Four Gunmen." Young Clifford was fascinated by the tales of such gangsters, who would be incorporated into his early plays as Moe (*Awake and Sing!*), Kewpie (*Paradise Lost*), and Fuseli (*Golden Boy*).

In 1916, when Clifford's youngest sister was born, the family moved again, this time to a nicer building in the Bronx, at 783 Beck Street. The neighborhood was primarily an ethnic mix of Jewish and Irish, and here Clifford experienced anti-Semitism for the first time. Briefly attending parochial school there, he formed an attachment to the Bible. He also joined a gang called "The Beck Street Boys," impressing his fellow members with his generosity, his voracious appetite for reading, and his writing ability (he helped his friends with their school writing assignments). Also, at Public School 52, Clifford Odets made his stage debut, playing the Prince in *Cinderella*.

At the outbreak of World War I and the economic boom in America, Lou Odets, now known as L. J. (The L for Louis, the J just for class) had his own printing plant, with a growing list of clients. He was now prosperous enough to send his family to the country for the summer, and soon he would buy one of the first phonographs. Music thus became an important part of Clifford's life, and later he liked to tell interviewers that he should have been a composer. As a boy he listened to the Red Seal recordings of the *William Tell* and *1812* Overtures, and the singing of Enrico Caruso. Remaining one of his passions, music would become a central symbol in his plays; a recording of Caruso singing "O Paradiso" would play a central role in his first full-length play, *Awake and Sing!*

When Clifford was thirteen, his father made plans for an elaborate and expensive bar mitzvah ceremony, an unusual concession to religious observance. He decided to attend a High Holiday service at a wealthy Reform temple and sent Clifford to a rabbi for lessons, but Clifford did not take to the rabbi, L. J. apparently lost interest, and the bar mitzvah was never celebrated.

Clifford spent much of his time as a teenager going to the movies and reading books, often a dozen a week. One of his formative reading experiences was provided by Victor Hugo's *Les Miserables*. Like Hugo, whom he idolized, Clifford aspired to champion the outcast, and he would later recall his enthusiasm for Hugo in *The Big Knife,* having Charlie Castle say, "Hugo said to me: Be a good boy, Charlie. Love people, do good, help the lost and fallen, make the world happy, if you can!"

As the family's fortunes continued to improve, L. J. moved them again to 830 East 163rd Street in the Bronx. In 1921, at the age of fifteen, Clifford was enrolled as a freshman at Morris High School. He was an indifferent student, in two years failing five subjects and doing only borderline work in four others, including English. However, he won the Declamation Medal with his recitation of Robert

Service's "The Spell of the Yukon," and he devoted himself to the activities of the Junior Dramatic Club, performing in a number of plays. Some of Clifford's teachers, including the head of the drama club, who felt he was talented, tried to persuade him to apply himself more to his studies, but his grades continued to be poor. This failure in school aggravated his already strained relationship with his father, who felt that his son was turning into a bum and that his interests in writing and theater were getting him nowhere. Clifford dropped out of Morris High School in 1923.

Despite his father's opposition, Clifford pursued his interest in acting. In 1923 he discovered an amateur acting company, the Drawing Room Players, which was willing to give him small parts, and sometimes he played roles in plays produced by the local library or the Heckscher Foundation, a child settlement house. His desire to act even led to his deceiving an English teacher at Dewitt Clinton High School: pretending to be a student there, he auditioned for and won the lead part of François Villon in the school production of *If I Were King*. After a few days he confessed his deception to the teacher, who quickly enrolled him in two courses to keep him in the play, but even that was too much for Clifford, who was forced to withdraw from the school and the play.

His brief career at Dewitt Clinton ended, Clifford got himself hired as a "ringer" elocutionist by the Moss Vaudeville Circuit office. Appearing as an amateur, he would recite such standards as "The Face on the Barroom Floor," "The Shooting of Dan McGrew," and "Fleurrette," for which he was guaranteed three dollars in addition to any prize money he could win (the first prize was ten dollars). For these occasions Clifford would round up the Beck Street Boys to give him the loudest and longest applause, thus assuring him the additional prize money.

During this time Clifford was also persuaded by his father to train as a copywriter for the Odets Company at 235 Fifth Avenue. As indifferent an employee as he had been a student, Clifford was regularly late to work and careless in the performance of his duties, which further aggravated the relationship between father and son. L. J. publicly abused Clifford, who soon left his employ. Clifford confronted his anxiety about the conflict between his artistic desires and his inability to succeed in the world and in the eyes of his father by writing a novel, which he later burned because it seemed excessively melodramatic. The novel dealt with the pianist whose career is cut short by an accident to his hand. As early as 1924, at the age of eighteen, Clifford's artistic preoccupations thus began assuming embryonic form, here evidenced in his use of music as a central image and the fatal conflict of the artist/idealist with the world. The image of the mutilated musician would continue to haunt Odets: he returned to it in *Till the Day I Die,* wherein the protagonist, a violinist and revolutionary, loses a hand in an episode of Nazi torture, and in *Golden Boy,* where Joe Bonaparte, also a violinist, breaks his hand in the boxing ring.

Thereafter, Clifford held a series of jobs, working in the bookkeeping department of a piece-goods factory, at the Commercial Investment Trust, and then in the bookkeeping department of L. Bachmann & Co. He found all of these jobs tedious and longed to fulfill himself as an actor or writer. His central outlet was writing long, passionate letters to friends in which he discussed his plans, his need for love and companionship, and the dissatisfaction he felt with his failure to succeed at anything. After a brief stint as a Fuller Brush salesman in 1925, Clifford determined to be more aggressive in pursuit of acting jobs. He ordered business cards printed up, featuring the name Clifford L. Odets (the initial borrowed from his father), and listing in the corners what he considered his most marketable talents: "actor, elocutionist, drama critic." He also wrote squibs advertising himself as "the Roving Reciter," available to perform anywhere at anytime for a modest fee. This self-promotion produced a number of jobs at small radio stations where Clifford would recite poetry.

During this period, in 1924, Clifford met Harry Kemp, an intellectual and resident of Greenwich Village, who organized The Poet's Theater, performing in St. Mark's-in-the-Bouwerie Church at Fourth Street and Avenue A. Clifford felt privileged to be a part of this group, which performed mostly poetic English dramas, even though he wasn't paid; in one production he played the Ghost in *Hamlet.* Meanwhile he was also appearing in some productions of the Drawing Room Players. For a brief time he felt successful, though he was earning little money, because he was working in the theater world he so desperately wanted to belong to.

In 1926, with his confidence on the rise, Harry Kemp fired Clifford from The Poet's Theater for his displays of egotism and for his ignorance of the works of Percy Bysshe Shelley. However, he continued winning numerous bookings on the radio as an elocutionist, and he also landed a job at radio station WBNY as a kind of disc jockey. Suggesting that the station develop a program offering popular and classical selections on the air, interspersed with commentary that he would provide, he had new business cards printed, advertising himself as a "dramatic critic." Walter Winchell mentioned Odets in his column as New York's "youngest critic." After finishing his job at WBNY, Clifford would use his passes to see Broadway shows.

That year he also wrote two radio plays, "Dawn" and "At the Water Line," both dealing with men in spiritual crisis who are saved by women from their pasts. "At the Water Line" was broadcast on station WFBH in New York on January 13, 1926, and later in Philadelphia, with Odets in the lead. The play takes place on a ship, where the stoker tells a friend that he is in despair over a woman he once loved who has married another man. The ship runs aground just as a group of tourists is exploring the stokehold, and one of them turns out to be the stoker's lost love. Rejuvenated, and stirred to action by his concern for her safety, this hero arranges a breathtaking rescue. Her husband having conveniently died in the wreckage, the stoker and his love are then reunited as they are able to escape through an ash expeller.[2]

Odets next returned to Philadelphia, where he joined Mae Desmond and her husband Frank Fiedler, who ran a company at the William Penn Opera House. This company's productions were mostly melodramas featuring Miss Desmond, who had achieved a reputation as an actress before World War I. Odets made his debut with the Desmond Players in a small part in *Tess of the Storm Country,* listed in the program as Mister Audette—his name was variously spelled as Odette, Odettes, and Odetts between 1927 and 1931. For that company he also appeared in *Way Down East, Uncle Tom's Cabin,* and *What Price Glory.* In 1928 he appeared in *Three Weeks* by Elinor Glyn, *The Hunchback of Notre Dame,* and as Judge Josh Billings in *Over the Hill to the Poorhouse.* Mae Desmond was apparently not much impressed with Clifford Odets as an actor, as he remained in small parts.

In the cataclysmic year of 1929, a decade of economic expansion abruptly came to an end with the stock-market crash. Odets, who had not shared in the nation's success during the twenties, was to find his voice during the next decade of turmoil and suffering and so emerged as America's leading playwright. The seeds of this dramatic reversal were sown, ironically, in the final year of the twenties. Odets's last work with the Desmond Players was on a play, *Madame X*, presented in Camden, New Jersey. The company was suffering financially at the time and, although the play required a courtroom scene, was unable to afford to put a full jury on stage. Odets suggested making the audience the jury and then proceeded to write the lead-in speeches for a new jury scene. Six years later, in *Waiting for Lefty*, he would write a play of his own that formally dissolved the distance between actor and audience.

At the suggestion of an agent, Odets met in New York with playwright Vincent Lawrence, who needed an actor to play a small part and understudy the lead in his play, *Conflict*, which deals with the decline of a World War I flying hero. Cast as the prohibition agent and also as understudy for Spencer Tracy, Clifford Odets made his Broadway debut on March 6, 1929. Unfortunately, the play was a failure, lasting only thirty-seven performances, and since Spencer Tracy did not miss a performance, Odets never got to play the lead.

Despite the play's failure, Odets's career was helped when he befriended another actor in the cast, Albert Van Dekker (later Albert Dekker), who was instrumental in getting him a job with the Theatre Guild. The Guild's casting director, Cheryl Crawford, who would soon become one of the directors of the Group Theatre, hired Odets to play walk-on parts at forty dollars a week. He played one of the "other robots" in the road company production of *R.U.R.*, which was directed by Rouben Mamoulian (later to direct the film version of *Golden Boy*). He was a member of the crowd in Eugene O'Neill's *Marco Millions* when the Guild toured with that play in January 1930. He stayed with both plays when they ran in New York in February and March. He was also one of the sailors in *Roar China* in October. In December he finally got a speaking part in

Claire and Paul Sifton's *Midnight,* which dealt with the need for juries to understand the circumstances surrounding a murder case before determining the guilt of a defendant. Odets was paid the handsome sum of one hundred dollars every Friday for this show, which, however, closed after forty-eight performances.

1931 was a momentous year for Clifford Odets, for it marked the birth of the Group Theatre, perhaps the most influential theater group of the Depression decade. Throughout most of its term of operation, the fate and success of the Group was to be intertwined with the playwright who would emerge from its ranks in 1935 to become its biggest star. By the time of its collapse in 1941, the Group had presented twenty-three plays, seven of them by Odets, including *Golden Boy,* which was its greatest financial success. Prior to 1935 he was a bit actor for the Group (though he started writing plays seriously in 1932), appearing in most of its productions.

The genesis of the Group occurred in 1928 when Harold Clurman, then working for the Theatre Guild, and Lee Strasberg, employed by the American Laboratory Theater, gathered together a group of young actors who were troubled by the lack of contemporary ideas on the American stage. Among this group were Sanford Meisner, Franchot Tone, and Morris Carnovsky, all of whom became leading members of the Group Theatre. They envisioned a self-contained theater with a permanent acting company and a specific, recognizable style. The job of the director was to be more extensive than that commonly prescribed on the commercial stage: not only was he to help the actors rehearse a particular play, but he was also to be a teacher who strove to develop the actor's craft. The actor, in turn, was not only to fill his role, but to study his part in relation to the play as a whole and to understand the play's application to society as well. As Harold Clurman wrote:

A technique of the theatre had to be founded on life values. The whole bent of our theatre, I reiterated time and again, would be to combine a study of theatre craft with a creative content which that craft was to express. To put it another way, our interest in the life of our times must lead us to the discovery of those methods that would most truly convey this life through the theatre.[3]

He went on:

Theatrical experience was, for the greater part, the antithesis of human experience; it bespoke a familiarity with the clichés of stage deportment rather than experience with direct roots in life. It seemed to us that without such true experience plays in the theatre were lacking in all creative justification. In short, the system was not an end in itself, but a means employed for the true interpretation of plays.[4]

For Clurman and Strasberg the purpose of the Group's productions was to analyze the structure and re-create the feel of modern society. Although the Group was considered by some a Communist organization (and some of its members were Party members), its aims were liberal rather than radical. Its objectives were not doctrinaire, proposing to alter the social establishment, not to overthrow it.

The Group formulated other ideas that became part of the communal philosophy, among them: "The writer himself was to be no star either, for his play, the focus of our attention, was simply the instrument for capturing an idea that was always greater than the instrument itself."[5] The play was seen as only one element of the total theater experience and therefore the actors and director should work with the playwright during production in rewriting and revising it. (Paul Green's *The House of Connelly* and Odets's *Awake and Sing!* were changed substantially in this way, for they were perceived initially as too pessimistic.) The American playwrights who worked with the Group proved amenable to the demands of the unit.

In developing their acting technique, the actors adopted the process developed by Constantin Stanislavsky at the Moscow Art Theatre. The Method was introduced in America in 1924 when Stanislavsky's company appeared in New York; Strasberg then studied with Maria Ouspenskaya and Richard Boleslavsky, members of the Moscow troupe who stayed in New York to teach at the American Laboratory Theater. In teaching the Method himself, Strasberg emphasized improvisation and exercises in "affective memory" or "memory of emotion," during which,

the actor was asked to recall the details of an event from his own past. The recollection of these details would stir the actors with some of the feeling involved in the original experience, thus producing "mood." These "exercises" were used to set the mechanism of the actor's emotion rolling, so to speak. When the actor was in the grip of this mood—although that is not what we called it, nor was it the purpose of the exercise to capture it directly—the actor was better prepared to do the scene calling for the particular mood that the exercise had evoked.[6]

The actors were thus to inhabit their roles and live them.

Clurman and Strasberg eventually invited Cheryl Crawford, the casting director for the Theatre Guild, to join them in founding the Group. They recruited actors, and between November 1930 and May 1931 held Friday night lecture series with them. In the spring of 1931 they formed their own production unit, and with donations from the Theatre Guild and from friends, they went to Brookfield, Connecticut, to rehearse for their first season.

In 1931 the Group's first two productions were listed as "under the auspices of the Theatre Guild," but by 1932 the Group had broken with that organization. The plays chosen for production reflected the Group's concerns: they were critical of American society, displaying some dark overtones, but balancing them with a basically optimistic, forward-looking spirit. Generally, the plots featured either the testing and triumph of individuals of superior morality or the destruction of avaricious, ambitious characters whose attitudes are shown to be dangerously antisocial. Mordecai Gorelik, who designed many of the Group's productions, often said that the Group's favorite theme was "What shall it profit a man if he gain the whole world and lose his own soul?"[7]

The first work produced by the Group, *The House of Connelly* by Paul Green (1931), deals with a man who defies his selfish landowning family, marries the girl he loves despite family opposition, and restores the family farm, which has been mismanaged. This play was one of the Group's few successes; in it Odets played Uncle Reuben. Later, he had small parts in Claire and Paul Sifton's *1931,* a play about a laid-off shipping room worker that included documentary scenes of Depression unemployment, and in Maxwell Anderson's *Night Over Taos,* which chronicled the destruction of a dictator. He understudied Luther Adler in the leading role in John Howard Lawson's *Success Story* (1932), a play about a radical who succumbs to the success ethnic and rises to the top, only to lose his soul and the woman he loves. Although it was a critical and commercial failure, this play, with its realistic street dialogue, was to influence Odets as a playwright.

Odets also played Mr. Houghton, a member of the hospital board, in Sidney Kingsley's *Men in White* (1933), which was the Group's longest-running show (351 performances) and which won the Pulitzer Prize. This play, focusing on an idealistic doctor, prefigures the "Intern" episode in *Waiting for Lefty*. Odets also played two roles in Melvyn Levy's *Gold Eagle Guy*, which opened in 1934 and ran until Odets's own emergence as a playwright. That play, like *Success Story*, chronicles the rise and fall of a businessman, this time a shipping magnate, whose career is traced from 1862 up to his death in 1902. Odets's last acting stint, then, was to be his appearance as Doctor Benjamin in *Waiting for Lefty* when the play moved to Broadway.

The Group presented most of Clifford Odets's plays, bringing four of them to Broadway in 1935: *Waiting for Lefty, Till the Day I Die, Awake and Sing!* and *Paradise Lost*. These were followed by *Golden Boy* (1937), *Rocket to the Moon* (1938), and *Night Music* (1940), performed in the Group's final season, along with Irwin Shaw's *Retreat to Pleasure*. The success of Odets's works cemented the Group; it was the company's disengagement from his play *Clash by Night* in 1941 that formally marked its end.

The principal cause of the Group's failure was its inability to secure the kind of financial independence that would have afforded it the artistic independence its lofty ambitions required. Harold Clurman summed up the reasons for the Group's collapse in an article for the *New York Times* in 1941:

The basic defect in our activity was that while we tried to maintain a true theatre policy artistically, we proceeded economically on a show-business basis. Our means and our ends were in fundamental contradiction. Our past—the past which brought forth what I strongly believe was the most important theatrical accomplishment of the thirties—has shown what could be done in the worst circumstances. The compromise (running the Group on an unsound basis) was forced on the Group for ten years. But it is a compromise I no longer desire to make.[8]

Despite its brief tenure the Group's accomplishment was impressive, its legacy considerable. Focused exclusively on social drama, the company produced quite a few works of importance. It gathered together and trained more actors of distinction than any other organization in the American theater: a partial list of those nurtured by the Group includes Elia Kazan, Luther Adler, Stella Adler, Lee J. Cobb, Franchot Tone, John Garfield, and Morris Carnovsky. Its three directors carried on distinguished careers even after their Group Theatre days. Perhaps the Group's greatest contribution to the history of the American theater, however, was Clifford Odets, unquestionably the thirties' most significant playwright.

It is important to recognize the reciprocal nature of this relationship, for while Odets was largely responsible for the Group's success, his career was, in a sense, created by the company that supplied both inspiration and foundation for his work. Odets's plays make clear that he was a man in search of a home; as he said in 1940:

When I was a boy the whole promise of American life was contained for me in Xmas cards which showed a warm little house snuggled in a snow scene by night; often little boys and girls were walking up the path of the door and carrying bundles of good things. This represented protection, a home and hearth, goodness and comfort, all things which become increasingly more difficult to attain.[9]

Odets was to develop this image most fully in *Clash by Night,* though it suffuses all his plays. For Odets, the Group was a home, an extended family with a shared aesthetic and a sense of social mission. As Clurman wrote, "From an experiment in the theatre we were in some way impelled to an experiment in living."[10]

This feeling of belonging became a primary force in enabling Odets to express his vision. His wider impetus derived from the Depression itself, which dispossessed millions of Americans of their homes and their psychological roots. Odets responded emotionally to their plight because he identified with their loss and he recognized their pain. Just as he had responded, as an adolescent, to the works of Victor Hugo, with an elevated and heartfelt romanticism, he persisted as an adult in the desire to be a champion of the dispossessed and disinherited not only because of a personal sympathy, but because of a deep-seated need to combat actively the suffering he saw in the social upheaval of his time.

He came to Marxism for much the same reason. Odets was not an intellectual, and his acceptance of Marxist ideology did not entail study or rigorous thought, but emotional, romantic empathy. Radicalism was in the air in the thirties, and Odets breathed it in, like many other artists receiving it as a humane alternative to a system that had collapsed. Odets was attracted particularly by his perception of Marxist society as a brotherhood, an ideal community; none of his plays displays any deep commitment to its political ideology. Jacob's pronouncements in *Awake and Sing!* are mostly a collection of homespun pieties, and at the end of the play it is revealed that Jacob has never even opened, let alone read, most of the political texts in his room. *Waiting for Lefty,* Odets's most doctrinaire work, actually displays little specific policy, and it is interesting that the play's most overt Marxist scene was cut out when the play moved to Broadway and omitted from the published version in *Six Plays of Clifford Odets* in 1939. *Waiting for Lefty* was simply a call to action, a rallying cry for all kinds of people to rise up and give voice to their despair. Thus the combination of greater and smaller environments, of the Depression and the Group, nurtured Odets's growth as an artist, supplying him with a human context of ideas and ideals to which he could relate his life and dedicate his art.

Because Odets's concept of Marxism was so romantic and idealistic in nature, it is difficult to pinpoint his motives for leaving the party in 1935. Probably more was involved than his anger at the treatment he received while heading a delegation to Cuba in that year (see chapter 7). Having been attracted emotionally by the Marxist vision of universal brotherhood, it is likely that he felt betrayed by it on the same level. Even after abandoning the party itself, he did not entirely reject its ideals: the Marxist metaphor continued to infuse his plays throughout the thirties and early forties, not in any doctrinal sense, but in a mystical, Whitmanesque tone of democratic utopianism. The connection remained emotional and spiritual rather than formal.

It is no accident that Odets's most despairing play, *Clash by Night,* was written as the Group Theatre began to fold. A play essentially about homelessness, its atmosphere is pervaded by forebodings of

the world war that would engulf America shortly after its opening
and end the decade that gave rise to Odets's best-known work. *Night
Music,* too, is permeated by an aura of gloom and fatality. Here
Odets strove to dispel it through magic and romance, enlisting the
aid of a guardian-angel figure, Rosenberger, to control what seems
out of control. This optimism, however, remains unconvincing, for
it is predicated on nothing more than nostalgic faith in the power of
love to overcome a catastrophic environment. Odets's despondency,
in fact, anticipates Frank Capra, whose communal ideal was also to
be tested by history and who also would require a deus ex machina
to save the protagonist from his own despair (and Capra's) in *It's a
Wonderful Life* (1946).

After 1941 Odets spent most of his life in Hollywood, writing for
the movies and then for television. His loss of the dual supports of a
spiritual home and a sustaining myth is apparent in that he was able
to write only three more plays in the remaining twenty-two years of
his life: *The Big Knife* (1949), *The Country Girl* (1950), and *The
Flowering Peach* (1954). His appearance before the House Un-
American Activities Committee in 1952 and his willingness to coop-
erate with its inquisitorial activity probably also contributed to his
creative decline, for it marked a formal and public break with the
ideal of community that had inspired him. Without it he floundered.

Odets's work was never, in any real sense, reformist. It might be
more accurately termed personal; at times it was even confessional,
an examination of the self. His artistic impetus was, in fact, a
profound moral idealism that he struggled to find or to impose, both
on his world and within himself. His work emerged from a peculiar
sensitivity to external pressures placed upon the individual spirit,
from his attempt to reconcile public myths with private imperatives.
Odets's early plays vividly re-create the parameters of the social
world his characters inhabit, articulating in dialogue—unsurpassed
in the naturalism of its tone, texture, and rhythm—the tensions
produced in the individual who harbors within himself the impulses
and energies of that world's competitive materialism and social
injustice. In an obituary essay on Odets, Harold Clurman wrote,
"His central theme was the difficulty of attaining maturity in a world
where money as a token of success and status plays so dominant a
role."[11]

Again, despite his membership in the Communist Party, the plays do not explore its ideology because Odets himself never really grasped it. What his plays do explore is the struggle of an elusive poetic spirit (for which Odets primarily uses the metaphor of music) to emerge in a debased world polluted not only by materialism, but also by human mediocrity. What Odets longs for is a communal ideal, a restored Eden that ultimately is only imaginary, as intangible as music itself. Odets's protagonists can dream about it, visualize it, and, sometimes, even articulate it, but they cannot achieve it. As the thirties recede, social realism, once a distinguishing aspect of his plays, is replaced by the more magical landscape of *Night Music,* which still makes reference to the real world outside, and then by the insular worlds of Charlie Castle's "playroom" in *The Big Knife,* the theater in *The Country Girl,* and biblical myth in *The Flowering Peach.* Reality gradually recedes before Odets's pursuit of symbolic and psychological complexity.

By the end of the thirties, and thereafter throughout his playwriting career, Odets was intrigued by the possibilities of romance. Indeed, in *Rocket to the Moon* and *Night Music* a romance world seems to exist side by side with the real one. The grip of the real proves too strong in *Rocket,* defeating Ben Stark's attempt to transcend it, whereas in *Night Music* Odets managed to suspend reality by bringing on a magical figure to banish it temporarily. His last two plays frame the dramatic conflict in even more artificial environments. *The Country Girl* restricts them to the theater itself, where the outside world does not intrude upon the interaction of the three main characters. In *The Flowering Peach,* Noah's family creates a private world on the ark when the real one has been destroyed. Thus Odets's poetic imagination could conceive a realization of the musical ideal where no external forces might overwhelm it. Just as Shakespeare's Prospero revels in the control of the magical world of his island and ultimately breaks the spell only grudgingly, as if doubtful of the fate of his charges in the world of reality, so Odets's last two plays dissolve their unreal communities with a hint of regret, leaving some lingering questions. The reconciliation of Georgie and Frank in *The Country Girl* represents an unusually harmonious merging of Odets's poetic images with his characters' desires, and yet the play ends in the theater, casting some doubt, considering Odets's other work, as to whether that magic can be sustained outside it. *The Flowering Peach* is Odets's most optimistic play, featuring characters who do achieve growth and spiritual renewal by the end of the play, but again Odets projects his vision of transcendence at the expense of realism, for the outside world has by then been destroyed, and the lessons learned by Noah's family will be tested not in a recognizable social context but in a landscape that has been purged and washed clean. If the Bergers of *Awake and Sing!* have been replaced by Noah's family, and the tenement by the ark, the outside world has been conveniently transformed into a garden where the rejuvenated family will have only themselves to deal with. The communal ideal seems possible only in such contrived circumstances, but perhaps that is enough: Odets at least allows some sense of "mystery," and a little wish fulfillment as well.

Because Odets's social vision was essentially romantic, class definition plays no important role in his plays; the proletariat, as such, was not central to his themes. Envisioning a world where man could be at one with his surroundings, where he could truly belong, he portrayed the restrictive influence of environments like the tenement, the boxing ring, a Hollywood mansion. All his characters long for space, both literally and figuratively, but such liberation is only to be realized in the earlier plays in the imagination, through Caruso's records, the image of Cleo Singer, a violin duet. Here the protagonists are ultimately defeated by the atmosphere of restriction that cripples their souls: Jacob by the tenement, Joe Bonaparte by the boxing ring, Charlie Castle by Hollywood; they can escape only through death. In some of the later plays, however, the characters succeed in actually inhabiting a kind of imaginary space, where "unheard melodies are sweet" and peach trees can flower.

Odets's characters struggle not only against the world, but against themselves as well. Some, like their creator, succumb to the lure of success. Joe Bonaparte and Charlie Castle reflect Odets's own torment at his more-than-occasional acquiescence to easy money. Read autobiographically, *The Country Girl,* too, represents the cry of a once-prominent actor (read playwright) for guidance and support in saving a foundering career. Like Frank Elgin, the later Odets could have used a Georgie and a Bernie Dodd to restore his creative discipline, as Clurman and the Group had done in the thirties. In these plays Odets recognizes that society is not solely to blame for the failure and suffering of his world. If he celebrated man's possibilities, he was in turn appalled at the propensities for weakness and compromise he saw in humankind as well as within himself, and his plays detail his anguish and his anger at a spoiled civilization whose values infected all within its reach. His despair maintained a precarious balance with his persistent idealism, giving rise to a desperate need for affirmation. Odets's despair is captured in his realistic portrayals of the tenement and the beleaguered family, rendered in a dramatic idiom few playwrights can match. His dream of transcendence is realized in images less tactile and specific, but when his poetic imagery is allowed to grow out of the material at hand rather than being imposed arbitrarily, it can be as provocative and mesmerizing as his ability to capture reality.

It is often difficult to separate Odets the success story from Odets the playwright. After his sudden and spectacular debut, he became a celebrity, his every move and association catalogued in gossip columns. Clurman recalled those days in *The Fervent Years:*

The lion hunters were on the trail. Actresses, publicists, bankers, novelists, editors, wanted to meet the boy wonder. . . . Odets was regarded by many as the dramatic find of the day, he was in addition that new phenomenon, a radical, a revolutionary, a Red.

An interest in an important new playwright was altogether normal for people like Tallulah Bankhead, Ruth Gordon, Beatrice Lillie, Helen Hayes, Charles MacArthur, Clare Boothe (Luce). But when Bernard Baruch began to examine him, when Edna Ferber asked that he be invited to a party that she might simply "take a look" at him, when Walter Winchell sought him out to have him explain the meaning of Communism . . . we were confronted with a sign of the times as significant as it was comic.

Odets was in a whirl, pleasant at first no doubt, a little terrifying later.[12]

The "whirl" and the "terror" were to remain a part of his life until he died. Like anyone who attains celebrity in the arts in America, Odets became a target for those who were waiting to knock him down, and because he himself was not immune to the success syndrome, the critical reception of his early work colored the critics', the audiences', and Odets's own attitude toward his subsequent efforts. At the end of his life, Odets had placed two issues of *Time* magazine by his typewriter, one containing the cover story from 1938 wherein he is hailed as America's premier playright, the other from 1962 in which the television page features an article entitled "Credo of a Wrong Living Man," which berates Odets for becoming a TV writer. Never allowed to outlive his early label as a bold revolutionary playwright, he was mercilessly disparaged whenever he went to Hollywood to work on projects that others considered beneath him. Sadly, Odets himself acquiesced in this judgment. At the height of his success, he told the *New York Times*, "I am the most talented young playwright in the business." Two years before his death he wrote, "I may well be not only the foremost playwright manqué of our time but of all time. I do not believe a dozen playwrights in history had my natural endowment. . . . Perhaps it is not too late."[13]

In spite of this private sense of defeat and disappointment, Odets's career does not reflect the stereotypical pattern of promising genius unfulfilled, for he produced a substantial body of work that remains a lasting contribution to the American theater. Possessing enough intuitive confidence in himself as a playwright to write from his own experience, he achieved a measure of realism that vividly communicates the experience of his time. He was also a poet, and when the subjective and objective perspectives merged artistically, Odets's vision transcended reality, making of his struggle a powerful version of America's wider dilemma. In his best plays Odets succeeded in fusing the contemporary with the poetic, realistic dialogue with symbolic force, anger and despair with warmth, tenderness, and compassion, to forge a unique and remarkable dramatic idiom. He is surely one of America's preeminent playwrights.

2

Early Self-Portraits
"910 Eden Street" (1931)
"Victory" (1932)

It is work, work, work . . . and one must not falter.

—Clifford Odets, 1932

The early thirties marked the real beginnings of Odets's search for his voice as a playwright, and two incomplete drafts from this period provide instructive glimpses of the seeds of themes and character types that he would struggle with all of his life. When Odets began working on these plays, he was morose, depressed, nearly suicidal, for he was not succeeding as an actor, and a novel he had started was going nowhere. No money was coming in and he was under increasing harrassment by his father; Odets had a desperate need to prove himself, especially to his father and his family, but nothing seemed to be working out.

The earlier work, dated 1931, is "910 Eden Street"; two previous titles, "The Melancholic Gorillas" and "One of These Days," are crossed out.[1] This play takes place in a rundown Philadelphia rooming house, where a group of struggling artists is found, including a poet, a dancer, a pianist, and an artist who is discussed, though he never appears, and whose suicide is discovered at the end of the first scene. This work displays Odets's marvelous ear for dialect and dialogue, particularly the Yiddish speech patterns (here evident mostly in the character of "Tiny" Manishevitz) which he would exploit so effectively in *Awake and Sing!* and *Paradise Lost* and then,

19

unfortunately, abandon until his final play, *The Flowering Peach*. Basically he is concerned here with the relationship of art and the self, but this primary theme is never to be satisfactorily resolved, for the young playwright is still groping for an appropriate form in which to contain his subject. Emotionally and intellectually Odets was moving in several directions at once, and the resulting struggle and confusion are mirrored in the play. Indeed, Odets's conflicts with himself and with his identity as a writer are precisely what invest this embryonic attempt with a certain significance.

The central character, and the one who most closely resembles Odets himself, is a poet named Mark Berke (orginally Berkowitz), who wants to be a serious artist and at the same time impress people with his seriousness. His dedication to his art and his ability to produce it, however, are frustrated by his search for love and his inability to reconcile himself to his past, his father, and his Jewishness. Odets hints at, but never openly explores the possibility that the division within Mark may have been caused by the rejection of his Jewishness that is symbolized by the name change, which is commented on a number of times. In Odets's finished plays there is little evidence that he thought much about his Jewish identity, but some degree of absorption of the culture is demonstrated here in his ability to delineate accurately the character of "Tiny" and his knowledge of rituals such as "Kaddish," the Hebrew prayer for the dead. Mark's abandonment of his identity is voiced by Berenson, a store owner who comes to collect money Mark owes him for soda:

I couldn't believe a Jewish boy would do such a thing. But I know, I know, he's a goy. He's ashamed anyone should speak a Jewish word to him in the store. I tell you I'm ashamed for his father.

Mark's apostasy is made evident, also, in his pursuit of Linda, a non-Jewish blonde who was once even in a convent—a detail Odets uses again in his early drafts of *Awake and Sing!* to emphasize the distance between Ralph and his girl friend Blanche. Odets cut this detail from the final version of the later play; here, Nick, Mark's friend who represents another aspect of Odets, advises him to forget about Linda and "Look homeward, Jew."

Mark, who never emerges as a very likable character, is given to making broad declarations such as, "There's no God, there's only a cosmic pimp. Some people call him biology," and "I despise people who make compromises with life." Odets is simply writing himself here, exploiting his own conflicts of identity: his family name had been changed, from Gorodetsky, and his father, who detested his own Jewishness, berated him for not being a good Jewish boy. Odets, too, longed to be an artist and indulged romantic notions about the artist's life and his struggles, but he also craved a home and rootedness, which he considered incompatible with the artist's life.

Mark links his art and his yearning for love to Linda, an insecure, frigid woman who fears the physical but is attracted to Mark because he writes poems to her. Linda shares an apartment with her very protective cousin Irma, who seeks to discourage this attachment: "love is something people write and think about. Romantics. It's not that way in real life." Linda's hesitancy leaves Mark to look for sex with other women and to self-loathing, for he is appalled by his physical needs. Insistently aspiring to some higher ideal, he implores Linda, "Pull me out of this mud, to make me see things as they are, to be at one with the world."—a rather Strindbergian line, and yet representative of Odets's own ambivalent response to the energies of the spirit and the body. Linda's reluctance to commit herself to him at length suggests to Mark that she resists him because he is Jewish. However, when Irma calls him a "filthy, unprincipled Jew"—oddly recalling his own desire to transcend the "mud"—Mark's reaction is to laugh, and he leaves vowing to "go back where I came from."

Odets's more practical side is embodied in the character of Nick, a boxer, who advises Mark that "Reality is the prize ring—cash." The interplay between the opposed natures of these two friends is highlighted early on, when Nick berates Mark for his idealism, in words that echo Odets's father: "Life ain't an arithmetic problem to me, or some high sounding phrases or sitting on your ass playing music all night. It's real!" Mark's reply—"The real thing . . . The real thing's malodorous, gorilla. Stinks, if you like."—provides, on the other hand, an echo of O'Neill's *The Hairy Ape*, wherein is made a similar association of the real with man's animal nature, creating a like sense of alienation. Nick, however, is no simple materialist, since he insists that he is looking not for a career, but for "people with hearts," elaborating, "I like to think of a time when men'll live in little groups

again, with hearts . . . believing in something." He thus represents
also the communal aspect of Odets's vision, the need to be responsible to someone and something beyond the self. (Mark, the intellectual, interestingly, is the one who mocks the communist ideal.) Late
in the play Nick again berates Mark for wallowing in self-pity and
indulging his romantic fantasies, remarking that he is "doing
nothing and dying by inches." They are preparing for Mark's
twenty-sixth birthday party—this protagonist is the same age as
Odets, who no doubt shares Mark's sense of frustration and uncertainty at this stage of his career. Nick's present is to tweak Mark's
nose and slap him around, finally advising his friend to leave Philadelphia and go to New York.

This tension is to be resolved in melodramatic fashion. At the
party Mark goes into a room with Edith, a struggling pianist who
loves him, and asks her to play for him. A major subplot has been
developing the story of Edith and her ex-husband Joe, whom she left
to pursue her musical career; Joe still loves her and wants her back.
Prior to the final scene he has told her that he is dying of cancer,
precipitated by his smoking—at twenty-six Odets, who was complaining even then of ruining his health by smoking too much,
presaged his own death from cancer—and asked that she spend his
final year with him. She refused, but acquiesced to a request to play
the piano for him. While she did so, he fingered his gun, but was
unable to use it to commit suicide. In the final scene at the party,
while Edith is playing for Mark, Joe enters the room and kills Mark
instead. The play in which the first scene involves a suicide thus
climaxes upon a murder.

The personal dilemma that Odets the fledgling playwright shares
with his troubled protagonist thus yields no solution but death.
Odets is indulging here in some wish fulfillment, having con-
templated suicide himself, and he obviously remains uncertain how
to combine his artistic aims with his desire for success and love. This
early attempt also demonstrates the novice's awkward formal grasp:
the concept of interrelated lives converging in a rooming house is a
sound one, but the young playwright is unable to shape an action
whereby disparate elements and themes may be resolved. Art and life
merge unfortunately here, as they would do so often later in Odets's
career.

Nevertheless, the seeds planted in "910 Eden Street" were to blossom in different shapes in *Awake and Sing!, Golden Boy,* and *Night Music,* even generating a mirror ending in *Clash by Night.* This early work, too, like the early drafts of *Awake and Sing!* and *Paradise Lost,* displays Odets's tendency to regard human conflict as fundamental and unresolvable, and so to conclude his dramatic dilemmas in an atmosphere of pessimism and, often, violence. Even the overtly political plays, *Waiting for Lefty, Till the Day I Die,* and the unpublished "The Silent Partner" and "The Cuban Play" regularly end in violent death. Odets's desire to be a voice of the oppressed and his need to invest his art with social significance invariably conflicted with his more personal depression, causing some awkward disjunctions in his art and painful ambivalence within himself.

Odets showed "910 Eden Street" to Harold Clurman, hoping for his new friend's approval and a certification of his talent as a writer. Clurman, however, was not encouraging, offering instead a bluntly accurate assessment of the play:

I hardly thought of it as a play, or of its author as a potential playwright. It was a personal document, such as others brought to me from time to time. . . . What I said, as far as I can remember now, had to do with only one aspect of the play. It gave evidence of an internal injury in the writer, I said. Something in his past life had hurt him. He was doubled up in pain now, and in his pain he appeared to be shutting out the world. His perception was disturbed because everything was seen in relation to his hurt. He had to learn to stand up straight and see the world more objectively.[2]

Another incomplete work, dated 1932, is "Victory""—originally entitled "The Beethoven Play"—which also concerns the artist's posture of conflict with self and society. Beethoven, an early hero for Odets, remained for him the quintessential artist figure. Margaret Brenman-Gibson described the recollections of Ivan Black, Odets's roommate in 1931:

Black, acutely aware of Odets' preoccupation with suicide, would look at his grim face and listen to him at four in the morning play again and again at top volume the funeral music in Beethoven's "Eroica." It seemed to Black that Clifford was dying to be a genius but that, as he listened to Beethoven, he knew he could not create anything of that magnitude. . . . Odets' hopeless identification with Beethoven appeared to Black more than romantic, actually pathological. . . . Believing that Beethoven was a "true genius," Odets labelled himself to his friend as "a lesser breed."[3]

Odets even began a file marked "Beethoven," wherein he listed the similarities between himself and the composer: both, he felt, were "shy, suspicious, essentially homeless, poor, and parentless—negative elements that Beethoven had changed into a positive but embattled idealism. . . . In his creative work he embraced the entire world . . . making it the home he had never had."[4]

Odets began to make entries about a Beethoven play in a journal he kept during 1932. In Dover Furnace, New York, where he was spending the summer with the Group Theatre, working on various acting exercises, ideas about the play came to him. On July 8 he notes:

Here I am writing on the Beethoven play—when it's finished it may not be about Beethoven. What I should do is write that play about the Greenberg family, something I know better and is closer to me.[5]

The Greenberg play is *I Got the Blues,* later to become *Awake and Sing!*—the Greenbergs becoming the Bergers. (Even then Odets knew what his real subject was, but apparently he fought dealing with a theme he thought unworthy.) Later, he determines to pursue his ideal: on July 16, after listening to the "Eroica," he realizes "in a flash the whole blinding truth about Beethoven":

That is what Louis God Sweet Beethoven did; he sacrificed completely the man to his art, so greatly, so completely as no man before or since has done.[6]

On July 18 he records that he played Beethoven's Ninth Symphony on his 26th birthday.

Louis Brant, the protagonist of "Victory," is, in fact, modeled on Beethoven. Wild and uncouth, a brilliant pianist and composer, he flaunts convention and eventually goes deaf. Even the name "Louis Brant" echoes "Ludwig van Beethoven," although Odets, interestingly, adopted his father's first name for his protagonist. In his journal, Odets referred to Beethoven as "my friend Louis."

The play opens on a farm in rural New York, where Louis Brant and his family live. His mother having died long ago, Brant was raised by his drunken father. Also in the household are his brother Caspar and his girlfriend, who shares her sexual favors with Louis. A self-taught pianist, this prodigy is being taken to New York to begin what will be a brilliant career. His sponsors are Joyce, who will manage his career and exploit him, and Schindler, who will come to admire and love him.

Louis Brant himself is described in terms that forshadow aspects of later Odets heroes: "Arrogance and pride and aspiration are written all over him, particularly in the way he carries himself. The eyes are brilliant and show great vitality." He has a card (similar to one Odets had printed for himself in his father's shop) proclaiming, "Louis Brant, Pianist, Conductor, Composer, and Great Man. Dover, N.Y. U.S.A." And like Odets, he declares a double goal: "Two things I want from life—to be famous and to be loved." His fate, as developed here, is indeed, to prove eerily prophetic of his creator's own conflicted career. Brant wants to devote his time to composing, but is continuously induced by Joyce to perform; the conflict between art and commerce, which also plagued Odets through much of his life, thus becomes a major theme. Despite his grueling concert schedule, however, Brant does persist in composing, for he is dedicated to his art and convinced that the real value of his work will be understood by future generations: "My music is written for a future time. . . When future critics will throw out the windbag Brahms and say instead, Bach, Beethoven and Brant." In his 1940 Journal Odets would write:

Why is Brahms an inferior artist, all other things equal? Because his last period is given over to resignation and acceptance. He did not have the same passion of the HEART which was Beethoven's. That is why any last Brahm's work is child's play compared to any last Beethoven work.[7]

Brant meets and falls in love with a woman named Julia, but he decides that he cannot marry her and thereafter ignores her letters. He walls himself off from the world in order to concentrate on his composing, and his self-imposed isolation becomes even more pronounced when he learns that he is going deaf. Eventually Schindler, who has become Brant's closest friend, marries Julia though she still loves Brant. When they meet again after her marriage, Brant tells her:

I would not ask another to share my miserable state. For me it is my art and to live alone, always at war with myself. What would it be when we were together? You know what I would do? Take your life and break it in little pieces.[8]

Julia's response reflects the kind of love that at least one side of him felt the need for but, perversely, could not accept:

A woman wants to make a home for the man she loves. It's a woman's purpose to make his life easier, so he can work in peace. She wants to shut out the clamor from him.

This play also reflects Odet's evolving conviction that the artist must open himself up to the social world and respond to the history of his times. Turner, Brant's favorite student, and, along with Schindler, his chief advocate, knows that his teacher's art, like Beethoven's, is rooted in his times. When Julia remarks, "Put Brant in a cave and he'll write the same music," Turner responds, "Not at all. No artist can go beyond his culture." As if on cue, Brant then enters, wet, disheveled and bloodied, reporting that he has witnessed policemen clubbing political agitators and that he got involved. Now, he says, he will make music about this experience. Odets, too, is awakening to history, as his first performed play, *Waiting for Lefty*, will clearly demonstrate.

The action then enters a downward progression, as Brant's brother Caspar, who has also come to New York, embezzles funds from his employer, Brant's own financial adviser. When he asks his brother to bail him out, he is refused and soon commits suicide rather than face going to jail. Julia then leaves Schindler, thereby breaking his spirit, in order to marry Brant. When, later, she dies giving birth to Brant's stillborn child, Schindler accuses Brant of killing Julia by his silence and brutality. He then pronounces a final judgment on Brant:

His music and the arrogant faith of self will avail him nothing. Men need faith in some outside thing, a love outside themselves. . . .Mr. Brant hasn't got it.

In the next scene Brant, drunk and alone, is reviled by another drunk in a speakeasy and shown tenderness by a prostitute. In his notes for the scene Odets remarks that the drunk represents "people in a competitive system, brutal and heartless," and the prostitute "all those lost and yearning." The central decor of the bar includes two crossed American flags beneath which is a sign, "No Trust." At last recognizing his isolation ("So this is what life must be—to go on alone and suffer."), Brant decides to dedicate himself fully to his art. He fantasizes about going to Europe, where he is respected, but Joyce replies, "No country would suit you. . . . What you want is a paradise where you can sit and be God."

From this point on, the play remains sketchy. Scene eight introduces Brant's nephew Conrad, Caspar's son, whom he is supporting. Rebellious and insensitive, Conrad is a disappointment, but Brant, nevertheless, gives him a car for his eighteenth birthday. The boy's later injury in a crash anticipates the climax of *Golden Boy*, wherein Joe Bonaparte kills himself in a car crash; in the original draft of that play, Joe, too, is eighteen years old.

The final scene depicts Brant's death. Defiant, like Beethoven, he refuses to give in, and, again, there is an uncanny parallel to Odets's behavior on his own deathbed thirty-one years later, as recounted by Brenman-Gibson:

At times he extended an arm at full length, shook his fist, and shouted, "Clifford Odets, you have so much to do!" More than once he said, "I want to yell, can I yell?" And then he shouted, "Yell!"—prolonging the word interminably like a siren. Those who heard it forgave its theatricality because it was evident there was something penultimate in the howl.

Brant is dying of a stomach disorder, "water gushing from my belly," while Odets died of stomach cancer; at the end his belly was very swollen, and tubes carried wastes that his body could no longer eliminate from his side to a jar by his bed. Brant, however, unlike Odets, is able to take comfort from his art: "I have found nothing on earth to satisfy my desires but I have imagined for myself that loveliness I seek." Odets's notes indicate that he planned to have Brant reborn, though this scene is not written out. He is to find a new life back on the farm, surrounded by students as rough and uncouth as he was, representing "new growth and vision."

In this play, especially in his notes, the young Odets is imagining his own potential victory in the triumph of the artist over an uncomprehending and insensitive world. He is also grasping at his more realistic self, that part of him that succumbed to the lures of that world even as he foresaw his own destruction and death. Eight years later, in his journal, he would return to contemplation of Beethoven and the triumph of the true artist. By then America's most admired and successful playwright, he was confronting unaccustomed defeat, for his most recent play, *Night Music,* had just failed on Broadway, and he was doubting himself and his ability to create new works and new forms suitable for his time. He turned to Beethoven for inspiration:

A form which does not fit one's content is intolerable to the creative personality, whether in work or in daily life. You cannot live in old forms, or work in them, when your life has brought you ahead to a new point. . . . Otherwise the spirit dies a death and sterility is the only outcome. Beethoven is the only man or artist I can think of at the moment who never once faltered in this difficult task: he was a fanatic! He hacked and chopped, twisted and tortured, but he did not EXCLUDE a drop of his experience from his work; in each phase of his life he found the right form for an increasingly higher and deeper experience. That is Beethoven's final lesson. . . . Life is a series of rebirths, worked with, coped with, understood, used and used by, never going back, but always moving ahead and higher. . . .

Odets's own genius was to be certified in his ability to give voice, shape, and form to his time, in seven plays written between 1935 and 1940. His tragedy would lie in the dual recognition of his artistic mission and of his inability to move "ahead and higher" in the remaining years of his life.

3

The Chekhovian Vision
Awake and Sing! (1935)
Paradise Lost (1935)

Verily, verily, I tell you, life is a dream.

—Clifford Odets

I believe in the vast potentialities of mankind. But I see everywhere a wide disparity between what they can be and what they are.

—Clifford Odets 1935

Odets wrote the first two acts of *I Got the Blues*—subsequently retitled *Awake and Sing!*—in the winter of 1932–33. A first version of the play was ready by the summer of 1933, when the Group Theatre left for Green Mansions, an adult camp in Warrensburg, New York, to begin rehearsals for Sidney Kingsley's *Men in White*. In exchange for a place to live and work the Group performed for the camp, and one such "entertainment" was the second act of *I Got the Blues*. Harold Clurman noted that "The audience loved it."[1] However, the play, which Lee Strasberg disliked, was not produced until 1935, after the opening of *Waiting for Lefty* had made Odets a celebrity and champion of the left.

Odets was disturbed that the Group did nothing with *I Got the Blues* for so long a time. In *The Fervent Years* Harold Clurman admitted to having had serious reservations about the play: "The first act was cluttered with some rather gross Jewish humor and a kind of messy kitchen realism; the last act I thought almost masochistically pessimistic."[2] Clurman's objection was consistent with his philosophy as director of the Group, which was to encompass not political theater but a more objective reflection of the political and social realities of America. Theirs was to be primarily a theater of celebration, for, according to Clurman, they believed in "the perfectability of man, or at least the inevitability of the struggle against evil." The Group's first presentation, *The House of Connelly* by Paul Green, in 1931, dealt with the struggle between the old and new orders in the South. Finding the original ending too pessimistic, Clurman persuaded Green to change it to suit his affirmative, mystical ideal of theatrical purpose.

Odets's original play was hardly affirmative either, and Clurman, as he noted in *The Fervent Years*, was never happy with what he called Odets's "gloomy fatality." Odets, like Green, therefore revised his play to align it more closely with Clurman's mystical bent. It is possible that the revisions may have been more directly determined by Odets's own sudden celebrity. *Waiting for Lefty*, Odets's first produced play, was an unqualified success when it opened on January 5, 1935. It was a radical play that seemed to touch a responsive chord with audiences. In order to preserve his newfound reputation as a champion of the dispossessed and the popularity that now afforded him access to the Broadway theater, Odets may have decided to revise *I Got the Blues* to make it more in keeping with his progressive, forward-looking image. In addition, Odets's personal views were apparently changing as his new success eased the bitterness of his former failures as an actor and playwright.

Awake and Sing! opened at the Belasco Theater on February 19, 1935. Reviews were generally respectful, if not glowing. The more ecstatic critics proclaimed Odets better than O'Neill; some called him an American Chekhov; others compared him to O'Casey. The leftist press was harder on the play: Nathaniel Buchwald in the *Daily Worker* found it "politically muddled," and Michael Blankfort in *New Masses* wrote that the play was comprised of "well documented and well-observed puppets." *Awake and Sing!* was not a commercial success, playing until the summer and reopening briefly in the fall. In 1936 it toured Philadelphia, Baltimore, Chicago, Cleveland, and Newark, and it was revived by the Group in 1939, performed in repertory with *Rocket to the Moon*. The revival was met with added critical respect: Brooks Atkinson wrote, "When it was first produced, it seemed febrile as a whole and dogmatic in conclusion. It does not seem so now; it seems thoroughly normal, reasonable, true."[3]

The references to Chekhov were to plague Odets when *Paradise Lost* opened. *Paradise Lost*—like *Awake and Sing!*—was begun before *Waiting for Lefty;* Odets had written the first two acts by the end of 1933. That play opened at the Longacre Theater on December 9, 1935. The adverse critical response it received was in part due to Odets's mistaken attempt to shape the critics' expectations before the opening. Afraid that Lee Strasberg was right in charging that the play lacked a coherent plot line, Odets worked desperately on the third act. On the eve of the opening, still unsure of himself, he wrote to all the critics, trying to establish for them a frame of reference for the play. He stated that the hero is "the entire middle class of liberal tendency," and went on to say:

The characters are bewildered. . . . The best laid plans go wrong. The sweetest human impulses are frustrated. No one leads a normal life here, and every decent tendency finds its complement in sterility and futility. Our confused middle-class today, which dares little, is dangerously similar to Chekhov's people. Which is why the people in *Awake and Sing* and *Paradise Lost* (particularly the latter) have what is called a 'Chekhovian quality.' Which is why it is so sinful to violate their lives and aspirations with plot lines. Plots are primer stuff, easily learned.[4]

Odets's letter to the critics did not have the effect he hoped for, as many then harped on his reference to Chekhov, lambasting Odets for his audacity, in their largely negative reviews.

Despite the critical reaction and Odets's claim, the Chekhovian parallels in Odets's first two plays have never been fully explored. Even in 1958 in an article entitled "In Search of an American Cherry Orchard," N. B. Fagin dismissed *Paradise Lost* as a failed Chekhovian attempt without really exploring it in depth. Even Clurman, in *The Fervent Years,* minimizes the Chekhovian parallels, though he does go on to describe *Awake and Sing!* in Chekhovian terms: "There was in it a fervor that derived from the hope and expectation and the desire for it. But there was rarely any expression of political consciousness in it, no deep commitment to a coherent philosophy of life, no pleading for a panacea."[5] Clurman goes on to say that "it is his emotional experience, not his thought, that gives [Odets's] plays their special expressiveness and significance."[6]

These plays share too much with the Chekhovian model for the connection to be so casually dismissed. Like Chekhov's mature dramas, both Odets plays center on ordinary people living quite unremarkable lives. These are not complex characters, and Odets supplies few clues about influences that may have shaped their lives. As in Chekhov, the sense of the present seems all-pervasive: the past's capacity to unhinge the present does not figure in Odets's plays, while the future for his characters consists of a dream of escape, like going to Moscow for Chekhov's three sisters. And in Odets's world, the possibility of attaining such a bright future is no more realistic than the sisters' dream of Moscow. The dream may be as powerful a force in life as the reality of the present, and it may even serve to make the present endurable, but Odets is as careful as Chekhov to suggest that his characters' concept of the future is only a mirage.

Both playwrights are ultimately less interested in specific predicaments than in the emotional preoccupations of characters who are defined largely in terms of their personal aspirations. They hope for a better future (Ralph and Jacob in *Awake and Sing!* or Leo and Pike in *Paradise Lost*), or they are filled with regret and disappointment and long for the past (Myron in *Awake and Sing!* and Gus and Ben in *Paradise Lost*). Such emotions, however painful, remain essentially undramatic, unsuited to schematic development, and this accounts for the lack of traditional dramatic conflict and resolution in Odets and in Chekhov. Odets may resort to the occasional melodramatic device, such as Jacob's suicide in *Awake and Sing!* or Ben's death in *Paradise Lose,* but both events are reported, not depicted on stage. Each one timed to close an act, the announcements of these deaths are made so abruptly and amidst so much confusion as to minimize the emotional impact on the other characters and on the audience. A week elapses between the announcement of Jacob's death at the end of act 2 and the beginning of act 3, when any memory of the man is swiftly dispelled by the Bergers' dickering over his will. In *Paradise Lost* eighteen months pass between the end of act 2, wherein Ben's death is confusedly hinted at but never specifically mentioned, and the confirmation of it early in act 3, by which time both the shock and the presumable emotional effect on the family have faded with time. Clearly the dramatic value of such a scene is secondary to its emotional impact on the other characters, and since both deaths are presented as having little lasting effect on those characters, the audience's reaction must be minimal as well.

Harvey Pitcher, in isolating the major characteristics of the Chekhov play, cites Chekhov's ability to create an "emotional network" in which it is the interplay of emotions that grips the audience, not character development. He goes on to elaborate:

Emotional preoccupations in the Chekhov play do not remain private and submerged, but are brought to the surface as the characters intermingle and become emotionally involved with one another. This as it were activates the emotional network, and emotions may come to vibrate between particular individuals. At one extreme, these emotional vibrations may be full of tension and disharmony: as when one person is seeking from another an emotional response that is not forthcoming, or when a character feels that someone else is standing in the way of the fulfillment of his desires. At the other extreme, there are occasions when emotions vibrate with unusual sympathy and harmony: as when individuals come to share a common outlook, a common yearning or a common grief.[7]

This insight pertains as well to *Awake and Sing!* and *Paradise Lost,* for both plays present groups of closely intertwined characters whose emotions reverberate throughout the action because they share common aspirations and griefs. Odets places his families in situations where their emotional preoccupations will be most clearly exhibited, thereby challenging the audience to respond on an emotional level to tensions and sympathies these character groups generate and experience among themselves. We are not to judge Odets's characters so much as simply to respond to them.

The thematic modes common to both plays are frustration and estrangement, which negative energies commonly serve to ignite the emotional network not only in Odets's stage families but in Chekhov's as well. All of their characters are caught in the eternal comic contradiction between their dream of life—"Life is a *Chullim,* a dream" says Jacob in an early draft of *Awake and Sing!* entitled *I Got the Blues*—and its reality. The inability to bridge this gap, despite occasional attempts to do so, underlies the emotional conflict and whatever dramatic tension the plays contain.

These two Odets plays demonstrate, as well, certain structural similarities to the works of Chekhov. The characters are regularly confined to a single location, the house. *Paradise Lost* even follows a basic Chekhovian progression in the movement of the family from inside to outside the house when the family is dispossessed. The lives of the characters thus confined are already deeply interconnected when the action begins, for these plays focus on families and their immediate contacts. The nonfamily members are so often in the house that they come to be considered family members, interacting not as visitors but as integral members of the family. In *Awake and Sing!* Moe, a frequent visitor in act 1, moves into the Berger house by the beginning of act 2; Gus in *Paradise Lost* moves in with the Gordons after his daughter marries the Gordons' son. All the characters thus know each other so well that they often can anticipate what one another will say at a given moment: they have heard it all before. Sequences in the plays wherein this occurs, when characters speak to each other but do not seem to respond directly to each other's words, may be misinterpreted as evidence that the characters are preoccupied with their own worlds and alienated from others. This is not generally the case: these people don't have to listen to each other, for each knows exactly what the other will say. Sometimes this habitual inattention leads them to ignore even insulting or provocative remarks.

This preoccupation with family naturally influenced Odets to discard the traditional notion of the hero, and neither play features a single central character or protagonist. Like Chekhov, Odets was writing for a theater ensemble and therefore conceived his plays without a star player in mind. The Berger and Gordon families are thus the aggregate protagonists of their respective plays, as are the Prozorovs and the Ranevskayas of theirs. As in Chekhov, one character may emerge from the group at a certain point and briefly seem like a protagonist, but he or she eventually recedes as another character takes center stage. This shifting of focus is limited to three or four characters in each play, but no one of them alone bears the thematic weight of the play. The group remains paramount, and the interplay of the group yields the theme.

The plots of these plays, then, develop from the family's response to a disruptive element or series of disruptive elements. In Odets's early plays the prime force affecting the group is the collapse of the economy, the Depression. Other problems may exacerbate the central situation, but all reflect the basic economic catastrophe: Hennie's pregnancy in *Awake and Sing!,* Ben and Libby's marriage, and the Gordons' business dealings in *Paradise Lost.* These are the forces that, in Pitcher's phrase, "activate the emotional network" in Odets's plays, as did changes in the Russian economy and social structure in Chekhov's plays, where the aristocracy is being gradually replaced by the bourgeoisie. In Odets, too, there is a sense of displacement, but it is not a problem of class, for the Bergers are lower class, the Gordons middle class; there is, rather, a sense of pervasive displacement, in fact, disintegration. Nor is there any of the mitigating feeling of historical continuity evident in Chekhov. Chekhov's acquiescence in the historical inevitability of social change and his awareness of the wasted lives of his characters give his plays their essential comic thrust, for there is an implication that the change will better, at least the surface, of Russian life. This distancing perspective is absent from Odets's worldview, and therein lies his essential break with Chekhov. Writing at a time of economic collapse, about a society already firmly rooted in the industrial age, Odets could convey no sense of transition, no promise of progress. What keeps his plays from falling into a miasma of utter despair is his characters' refusal to accept this bleak finality. Like many Chekhov characters, they persist in the belief that the future will be better than the present, that if they must suffer, surely future generations will enjoy a better life.

In Odets's early plays economics has thus replaced the gods of classical drama as the central force in the lives of the people. Yet this is not a determinist force, for although powerfully hampered, individuals can extricate themselves from the grip of poverty. Odets, moreover, concentrates not on the broad economic disaster of his time but on human reactions to the conditions they live under. If Odets's characters fail, he makes it clear that they have no one but themselves to blame for their plight. A character's own weakness or inability to act may prevent him from escaping or rising above his circumstances, but he is not allowed to claim external opposition for his excuse.

Accordingly, Odets avoids presenting characters who are definably good or evil, although they may be identified as either sympathetic or unsympathetic. Even here Odets usually qualifies the response, withdrawing complete approval from a sympathetic character such as Jacob in *Awake and Sing!* by exposing his basic passivity, whereas Moe, a gangster and cynic, is clearly drawn as a man who is capable of purposeful action as well as generosity and sympathy. In *Paradise Lost* there are no unsympathetic characters except, perhaps, the minor figure of Foley, the neighborhood political leader, and whatever contempt may be directed at him remains secondary to the affection generated by the Gordon family as a whole. Even Katz, Leo's partner, apparently a type of the crass, unfeeling businessman, is eventually revealed to have been spiritually and emotionally defeated by his impotence. Odets does not ask his audience to take sides in his plays, and his skill at characterization is such that it is clear that all of these people share the same handicap and the same bitter fate.

Odets would vary the dramatic structure of his plays throughout his career. He experimented with different forms, and his refusal to isolate a protagonist yielded later in the cases of *Golden Boy* and *The Big Knife*. In closely following the Chekhovian model in his first two plays, however, he succeeded in capturing the emotional resonance of families struggling for survival in a voice unique in the American theater.

Awake and Sing! is a family play whose central characters share one abiding action or nonaction—they dream. The Berger family is caught in the grips of the Depression; money is scarce and there are five in the family. Every day is hard. In his notes at the beginning of the play, Odets writes that all the characters "share a fundamental activity; a struggle for life amidst petty conditions." Yet most of the characters do not really struggle, they dream. They have been defeated by the system and the inadequacy of their own natures. They are most vibrant and eloquent when speaking of the "dream of life," not in living life itself. Odets does present some characters who actively participate in life, but in the pursuit of their success they have become distorted, almost grotesque. There seems to be no middle ground in the world of this play, where the dreamers have lost their self-respect and the doers have lost their souls.

Many critics have erred in emphasizing economics—"the system"—as the villain of the play and its thematic center. It would be foolish to ignore them as important in Odets's work, but they are not central. Economic pressure is what ignites the play's emotional network, but it is the Berger family that Odets is most interested in, and his primary focus is on the revelation of their characters.

The older characters in the play are defeated before the action begins: they are not going anywhere, but look for their lives to be redeemed through their children and their grandchildren. Beyond this, their greatest emotional satisfaction comes from dreaming. The dream may be a regression to a past when life was seemingly better, or a vision of a glorious future when the structure of society will be different, or a romantic present perspective, full of Hollywood images of love and romance. For Odets the media serve as stimuli for the emotional life of his characters; Ralph says at one point, "I'm flying to Hollywood by plane—that's what I'm doing," and much of his dialogue is peppered with references to movie stars. Since these images are clearly out of reach, Odets uses the movies and the dreams they perpetuate to suggest that the new generation will progress no further than the old. The older generation also draws comfort from the movies: Myron, Ralph's father, also frequently refers to movie stars. For the old movies are a comfort, a way to make the hopeless present more bearable. Jacob, the grandfather, defines the lure of the movies when he says:

He [Ralph] dreams all night of fortunes. Why not? Don't it say in the movies he should have a personal steamship, pyjamas for fifty dollars a pair and a toilet like a monument? But in the morning he wakes up and for ten dollars he can't fix the teeth.[8]

His son Morty teases him for this, referring to him as a "real Boob McNutt" and "Charlie Chaplin." Morty, a successful man, tries to defuse his father's remarks by suggesting that life is essentially comic and ridiculous. In his character summary Odets writes that Morty "sees every Mickey Mouse cartoon that appears," obviously condemning Disney as a perpetuator of dangerous (because simplistic?)

popular myths. The image of Mickey Mouse recurs in *Paradise Lost,* when Ben, reduced to selling Mickey Mouse dolls on the street corner, ironically identifies with the toy. (Charlie Castle in *The Big Knife,* written years later, describes himself in a similar way.) As early as 1935 Odets thus demonstrates an awareness of the power of the movies to force the average citizen into creating a dream life more real than reality, a theme developed brilliantly by Daniel Fuchs in *Homage to Blenholt* in 1936 and by Nathanael West in *The Day of the Locust* in 1939. Odets returns to these images and ideas in later plays as well.

Awake and Sing! begins with Ralph Berger questioning the prospects for promotion in his job: "Where's advancement down the place? Work like crazy! Think they see it? You'd drop dead first" (p. 41). Even the possibility of thinking realistically about progress in the present is undercut immediately, as Myron, his father, answers him immediately with a platitude from the past, "Merit never goes unrewarded. Teddy Roosevelt used to say————." And Ralph's sister, Hennie, who already recognizes that few realistic possibilities exist for the Berger family, replies, "It rewarded you—Thirty years a haberdashery clerk!" Odets then structures his entire first act on the articulation and subtle deflation of the dreams by which his various characters live.

If the possibility of advancement is unlikely, the Berger family has certainly not accepted it. Myron long ago has been beaten down by the system and by Bessie, his wife. He is the first in a series of weak husbands in Odets's work, initially described as a "born follower." Having happily removed himself from the present, he relates most comfortably to Theodore Roosevelt and to an American past that was rich in possibilities. Yet, although Myron was once a part of that world, he never realized any of the possibilities, certainly never achieved any riches. Like other Odets dreamers, this man cannot claim to have been ruined by the Depression, for he was a failure before the Depression hit, and he still is. He is, however, neither bitter nor even much depressed about his failure, remaining a sweet, unassuming man who seems to enjoy his life in spite of all. He presents a clear contrast to the many Jewish literary characters of this period who express great bitterness about America's failure to redeem in their personal lives the promise of "streets paved with gold."

Myron also cannot claim to be the head of his family. Respected by neither his wife nor his children, he is treated as the baby in the family. At two crucial times in the play he is totally ineffectual when he needs to be assertive: when it is discovered that Hennie is pregnant by a man whose whereabouts are now unknown, he cries while his wife takes charge of the situation; and when Bessie breaks her father's records, Myron is stunned but cannot say anything to his wife. Instead, after she leaves the room, he characteristically talks about the past:

There are no more big snows like in the old days. I think the whole world is changing. . . . I was a little boy when it happened—the Great Blizzard. It snowed three days without a stop that time. . . . A silence of death was on the city and little baby's got no milk. . . . they say a lot of people died that year. (p. 86)

This is a moving point in the play, Myron's most poignant moment, crystallizing his entrapment in a world that is no more and in all likelihood never existed. It also makes clear that like the children he too "died" then, for he is emotionally a child, frozen in his own world. And, lastly, it presages Jacob's suicide, which closes the act when he jumps from the roof and falls onto the snow-covered street below.

When Myron is not dwelling in the past, he does contemplate a financially secure future to be ensured by a winning lottery ticket. In act 1 he even wins a few dollars in the lottery, but, as Moe says to Ralph at the end of act 2, "Your old man believes in Santy Claus. . . . It's a fake. There ain't no prizes. It's a fake" (p. 87).

Jacob, Bessie's father, is also a dreamer, but he dreams of a Marxist society, clearly another form of "Santy Claus." He, too, Odets makes clear, is an ineffectual man. He lives with his daughter's family and is not working. He used to be a barber, and he still gives haircuts to his son Morty, who occasionally visits. But even when he was young, Jacob was unable to hold a job. Never much of a provider for his children, he is, like his son-in-law, not much respected by them now: Bessie and Myron, both staunch materialists, find his politics a joke. As far as Bessie is concerned, his major function in the house is to take out the dog.

Jacob is clearly intended to be a foil to his daughter, a strong-minded woman who loves her family but knows what it takes for them to survive. She runs the house on an economic basis; her concern for money has overwhelmed her maternal nature. Jacob finds this family situation deplorable. When Hennie's pregnancy is revealed, Bessie decides immediately to marry her off to Sam Feinschrieber, clearly an unsuitable match, but one she considers socially respectable and economically sound. This pains Jacob, who, unlike Myron, is willing to argue with Bessie, crying out, "Marx said it—abolish such families." Bessie's reaction is, "Go in your room." Jacob reluctantly complies. This exchange echoes a more comic one early in the play when Jacob says, "If this life leads to a revolution it's a good life. Otherwise it's for nothing." Bessie's reaction is, "Pass the salt." This is a Chekhovian moment, as the attempt to say something important is undercut by more immediate and mundane matters. Jacob again keeps quiet.

As a foil to Bessie, Jacob is a sympathetic figure, for Bessie has denied much of her humanity in her effort to keep the family together. But Bessie at least is active, while all Jacob does is talk and theorize about a more perfect future. When he is not talking politics, Jacob's greatest pleasure is to retire to his room and listen to his records, his particular favorite being a recording of Caruso singing "O Paradiso" from the opera *L'Africaine*. He sets the scene for Moe:

Caruso stands on the ship and looks on a Utopia. You hear? "Oh paradise! Oh paradise on earth! Oh blue sky, oh fragrant air—" (p. 51)

The Marxist dream, at least as it is presented through Jacob, is thus equated with hiding in a room and listening to artistic projections of Utopia. Jacob was never any more active in politics than he was as a father. Odets suggests that Jacob's political visions of a more perfect society can exist only in the mind's eye, perhaps in the realm of art (the opera), but not in the real world. When the emissary of the real, Bessie, breaks Jacob's records, she symbolically puts an end to his dream. That scene is analogous to Chebutykin's smashing of the porcelain clock that the sisters treasure in Chekhov's *The Three Sisters*. As is usual with Chekhov and Odets, these incidents are at once simple and ambiguous. In both cases the action is presented as a deplorable destruction of others' lives, but there is also a shared implication that Chebutykin's and Bessie's lives were long ago smashed to bits, and so now they will smash other lives. The ambiguity of the impression is valid realistically and emotionally, for the characters (and audiences) of Odets and Chekhov must regularly contend with the sense of uncertainty coupled with sadness and anger at the actions of others.

Jacob is further undercut by Odets, when, after his death, Ralph, who Jacob hopes will put his ideas into action, enters his grandfather's room and finds that half his political books have their pages still uncut. In the original draft of the play Odets was even more emphatic: none of the books has been opened. This is reminiscent of the incident in Ibsen's *The Wild Duck* when Hialmar Ekdal, another ineffectual dreamer, decides to leave home and take his scientific books with him, whereupon his wife Gina, the practical one, asks if he is referring to the books whose pages are still uncut. Ibsen thus deflates Ekdal's dream of being a great inventor, and Odets echoes the effect in undercutting his own character's pretension.

If Jacob and Myron are hopelessly paralyzed, Ralph seems to be continuing the pattern into the third generation. Despite being able to confront his father and call him a fraud, he is really no more capable of handling his own affairs. When Jacob tells him that he will "graduate from my university," he is being more perceptive than he realizes. Ralph, too, dreams of a new life, but he is not motivated by political philosophy. He is in love, and he hopes that in marrying his girlfriend Blanche he can transcend the petty life-style of the Berger household. Jacob opposes this match, arguing that marriage will ruin Ralph's dream of escape, that women are "death to men's souls." Bessie is against it because Blanche is a poor orphan who will only add to the family's economic burden. Despite the opposition, Ralph is determined to marry. (It is interesting that in the early version of the play Blanche is a Catholic who spent time in a convent, which makes her seem even more remote from the hard necessities of the Bergers' existence. Odets eliminates this detail from the final version, for, like Chekhov, he is interested in paring down the potential melodrama of his plots.)

Odets accentuates Ralph's nature in two speeches he makes. In act 2, scene 2 he says to Jacob:

When I was a kid I lay awake at nights and heard the sounds of trains . . . far-away lonesome sounds . . . boats going up and down the river. I used to think of all kinds of things I wanted to do. What was it, Jake? Just a bunch of noise in my head? (p. 76)

Later in act 3, motivated by Jacob's suicide, he talks of changing his direction. When Bessie eggs him on to "go out and change the world," Ralph replies:

Life's different in my head. Gimme the earth in two hands. I'm strong. There . . . hear him? The air mail off to Boston. Day or night, he flies away, a job to do. That's us and it's no time to die. (p. 95)

Odets is undercutting Ralph here, for he cannot change the world because, like Jacob's, his dreams are in his head. They may reach beyond the horizon, like the airplane, but the dreamer remains earthbound. In the stage directions following this speech, the sound of the plane fades and Myron gives Bessie the alarm clock to wind, reasserting the concept of the real. Obviously Ralph will never be able to realize his dreams until he learns to cope with reality. In an earlier draft of the play that features a more dramatic and negative ending (to be discussed in more detail later), Odets concludes with stage directions again referring to the sound of the airplane, re-emphasizing that the characters' dreams are far away and will not be fulfilled.

Ralph's inability to deal with the reality principle represented by his mother is again revealed at the end of act 2, scene 1, when Blanche informs him that her family is sending her to Cleveland because they cannot afford to support her anymore. Ralph, who spends much of his time promising Blanche and himself that he will take some action to remedy the situation, never does. He can dream of a life with his love, but he cannot act to attain it. When she calls in act 2, scene 1, Bessie hangs up on her. Then, when Ralph calls her back and finds out that she is leaving, he can only cry on Jacob's shoulder. Before the two embrace in tears, Bessie enters the room and turns off the radio—another escape image, reinforcing the triumph of reality over dreams and passive dreamers. At the end of the play Blanche again calls Ralph but he is afraid to pick up the phone, and when he finally does, he doesn't know what to say, so she hangs up on him. At this point it is clear that Ralph, like his father, will forever remain trapped in the mundane life of his family.

Bessie, on one level, is the most realistic-minded character in the play. She is the decision maker and the force that holds the family together because the men around her are ineffectual. However, Odets does not propose Bessie as a model, for in her obsession with achieving respectability and success for her children she has become something of a grotesque. She displays little warmth or affection for her children, her father, or her husband. And in the recording-smashing scene at the end of act 2, she performs the play's most alienating act. This deliberate destruction of her father's dreamworld stands out, as such heartless gestures do in Chekhov's plays, which are similarly dominated by sympathetic, weak, and harmless people incapable of responding to this kind of emotional and physical violence. In spite of her strength, therefore, Bessie does not serve as the protagonist of the play; if anything, she is the chief antagonist. Odets clearly sympathizes with his *luftmenschen,* admiring the quality of their dreams and their generous impulses. And while Bessie's strength and forcefulness are necessary within the context of her family, the end result on her character makes these qualities seem suspect.

In earlier drafts of the play Bessie was made a more negative character. In act 3 when discussing Jacob's insurance policy, Myron reveals that Bessie has four thousand dollars in the bank; her response is to slap her husband. She also threatens to leave her family and live with her brother Morty and even threatens to send Jacob to a home. In act 1 when Bessie suggests that Hennie marry Feinschreiber, Jacob's angry explosion at his daughter suggests years of pent-up antagonism:

From you and your kind comes a smell to suffocate the world. I see it! So bad I never imagined you could be. Better I drowned you before—

Later he calls the house "a garbage dump, a place of evil, black like a forest at night."

Odets clearly saw the danger of making Bessie too much a villain, so the play's final version omits Jacob's speeches as well as the slap and her cruel taunting of her father. Her character is further softened by the insertion in act 1 of a scene with the building superintendent, Schlosser (a character apparently created specifically for this scene, for he doesn't exist in the earlier versions of the play), wherein she defends her father:

Please don't yell on an old man. He's got more brains in his finger than you got—I don't know where. Did you ever see—he should talk to you an old man? (p. 46)

This filial loyalty coupled with her momentary desire to buy a lottery ticket in act 1 (when she hears that Myron has won some money) makes Bessie more human—even Bessie seems susceptible to dreaming, if only for an instant.

Despite Odets's modification of the character, Bessie is still the force against whom all the other family members react. Jacob feels, and repeatedly declares, that the kind of family Bessie is trying to mold should be abolished. Ralph, by the end of the play, rejects her values, as does Hennie, who abandons her family and any notion of respectability to run off with Moe. Interestingly, Hennie's final actions serve as another antidote to Bessie's seeming callousness, for despite the sentimental appeal of the couple going off together, the audience must be distressed by Hennie's abandoning her baby. Bessie would never do such a thing, despite her threats of leaving her family of grown-up children, and her stature does grow as a result. Myron, of course, has withdrawn from the struggle long ago.

Bessie's brother Morty shares many of his sister's characteristics. He is the one family member who is successful, and he clearly enjoys his status as the rich uncle. Loud, boorish, and ignorant, he does not, despite his wealth, send the family much money to support his father. Nor does he treat his father with much respect; he is condescending to the old man, and, like his sister, scornful of his Marxist sentiments. When he sees that Hennie is upset and depressed, the most he can do is offer her some dresses from his shop. A man defined by his subservience to money, he exhibits no soul nor any real feelings. Obviously he is not a character who interests Odets very deeply. (In *I Got the Blues,* when Bessie threatens to move in with Morty, Odets is indicating that they belong together, not with the other, more sympathetic characters in the play.) It is interesting that in a play that deals with three generations, Bessie and Morty have rejected their father to pursue success, while those in the third generation, particularly Ralph, have rejected Bessie and Morty, not necessarily returning to the political idealism of the grandfather, but decisively rebelling against the stifling materialism that has replaced it.

Moe Axelrod is a figure who straddles both worlds of the play. A veteran who has lost a leg in the war, he has been hardened and made cynical by his war experience. Having rejected the ideal of America and the notion of rising in the business world, he makes his money in the rackets, which he considers no different from "legitimate" business and the politics of war: "It's all a racket from horse-racing down." Of the war itself he says:

That's why they had the big war—to make a new world, they said—safe for democracy. Sure every big general laying up in a Paris hotel with a half dozen broads pinned on his mustache. Democracy! I learned a lesson. (p. 50)

Between his government pension and the money he makes in the rackets, Moe is financially comfortable. But unlike Morty and Bessie, he is not obsessed with his success. Instead, he is searching, as ultimately most Odets characters are searching, for a sense of family—a home. He tells Hennie in act 3:

Was my life so happy? Chris', my old man was a bum. I supported the whole damn family—five kids and Mom. When they grew up they beat it the hell away like rabbits. Mom died. I went to the war; got clapped down like a bedbug; woke up in a room without a leg. What the hell do you think, anyone's got it better than you? I never had a home either. I'm lookin' too! (p. 98)

Moe feels a keen sense of displacement. His longing for a home is the reason he moves in with the Bergers in act 2, and he clearly has a great deal of sympathy and affection for Jacob, playing cards with him, and Ralph, urging him to act and be decisive. In act 1 Moe is disturbed that he can't get an orange in the Berger house. Fruit plays an important symbolic role in these early plays, where the lack of it indicates that neither family home is an Eden, a haven, that the family does not truly sustain its members. The association with paradise is established when he says to Jacob, "Ever see oranges grow? I know a certain place—One summer I laid under a tree and let them fall right in my mouth" (p. 50). Moe's complaint, "What the hell kind of house is this it ain't got an orange!" concludes act 1.

The incarnation of Moe's sense of family is Hennie: she is his "orange," and he even calls her "Paradise." When first introduced in the play, he has come to take her out, and during the course of the play he tries to woo her away from her husband with visions of romance:

Come away. A certain place where it's moonlight and roses. We'll lay down, count stars. Hear the big ocean making noise. You lay under the trees. Champagne flows like— (p. 98)

Moe's vision of paradise is right out of the movies, and, Odets implies, just as facile. The irony is that Moe's dream comes true. Hennie agrees to come with him, and as the play ends they are off to Havana. Hennie won't keep her date with him in act 1, but goes off with him in act 3. The play thus is given a certain symmetry, but its circular motion is also a sardonic commentary on Moe and Hennie's dream of romance.

The ending of *Awake and Sing!* has often been criticized. Even Odets's own opinion of it varied over the years. Many critics, including John Howard Lawson, found in its conclusion abrupt and unconvincing changes in the characters, particularly Ralph, suggesting that Odets forced a happy ending on the play that could not support it. Ralph is conceived as too weak and childish a figure to be capable of changing so quickly into a committed revolutionary:

Let Mom have the dough. I'm twenty-two and kickin'! I'll get along. Did Jake die for us to fight about nickels? No! "Awake and sing," he said. Right here he stood and said it. The night he died, I saw it like a thunderbolt! I saw he was dead and I was born! I swear to God, I'm one week old! I want the whole city to hear it—fresh blood, arms. We got 'em. We're glad we're living. (pp. 100–101)

The play's ending, with Hennie leaving her husband and child and

going off to fulfill her romantic dream with Moe Axelrod, is also
often judged excessively sentimental.

It should be noted that *I Got the Blues* is a much bleaker play and
the ending more overtly stark. In that play the final actions and
revelations reveal Odets's despair. As mentioned earlier, Myron reveals that Bessie has over four thousand dollars and she slaps him.
Ralph discovers that Jacob never opened even one of his books on
political philosophy. Hennie then agrees to run away with Moe, but
as they are making arrangements to leave, some police enter and
arrest Moe on a racketeering charge. Hennie is forced to go back to
Sam Feinschreiber, her hope for a new life destroyed before it even
begins. The final words of the play belong to Myron, not Ralph;
instead of an upbeat speech pointing to revolutionary action, Myron
meditates on the death of love:

When I see her layin' there that way it reminds me . . . I don't ever forget
how she sent me to the hospital with pnemmonia [sic] the second we were
married . . . just didn't want to nurse me I guess. But I don't forget a thing
like that. . . . How that ambulance came clanging up to the front . . . and
they came up for me. . . . Two of them and an officer of the law. . . . And I
just cried like a baby. No fruit in the house lately.

The play concludes on the failed paradise image, the failure emphasizing the collapse of human communication and communion.

Odets's revised ending is less devastating though hardly optimistic, and it must be considered as part of the pattern of failed
paradise images and Chekhovian motifs. All of the characters'
dreams are shown during the course of the play to be unreachable. In
the first act Moe's dream of an island paradise where oranges fall
from fruit trees is juxtaposed with Jacob's images of paradise in the
opera, demonstrating that Moe, though a man of action, shares
certain qualities with Jacob. He longs for something better outside
of himself, something that he will not achieve, which separates him
from Morty, who cannot see beyond his business. His orange, as was
pointed out earlier, is Hennie, and the sexual image of sucking on an
orange (Hennie) underscores Moe's need for a mother figure. It is
certainly part of his desire for a home; something he feels that he has
never had. But Hennie is clearly not the answer to his dream. Hennie
is very much like her mother, proud, energetic, and self-reliant; like
her mother, she clearly rules her household, her husband Sam, a

weak man like her father, remaining subservient to her. She, too, is dissatisfied with her life.

Odets makes clear that Bessie, in pursuit of success and respectability, has lost her claim to being a mother and wife. Hennie, like her mother, will most likely not succeed in this direction either, for in leaving Sam and her baby, she proves that the demands of motherhood are not as attractive as the claims of romance. Bessie has at least tried to keep her family together against tremendous odds, while Hennie deserts hers at a moment's notice. The play also never makes clear that Hennie is in love with Moe. She breaks a date with him in act 1, and while Moe is the first man she ever slept with, she never indicates that she loves him. To Hennie, Moe seems merely different, a diversion. When they argue in act 2 they demonstrate an understanding of each other's vulnerabilities: Moe knows that Hennie is trapped in her marriage, and Hennie sees that Moe is ensnared by his ideal of her and of family life:

MOE: I know you from the old days. How you like to spend it! What I mean! Lizard-skin shoes, perfume behind the ears. . . . You're in a mess, Paradise! Paradise—that's a hot one—yah, crazy to eat a knish at your own wedding.

HENNIE: I get it—you're jealous. You can't get me.

MOE: Don't make me laugh.

HENNIE: Kid Jailbird's been trying to make me for years. You'd give your other leg. I'm hooked? Maybe, but you're in the same boat. Only it's worse for you. I don't give a damn no more, but you gotta yen makes you—

MOE: Don't make me laugh. (p. 69)

Moe is entrapped not only by his dream of family, but also by his despair. A creature of contradictory impulses and some confusion, he is cynical about the promise of America and a better world but seems to hold on to that promise for himself. His experiences in war seem to have soured him on life but he still believes in love. But will Moe be able to give Hennie more of a life than Sam? What happens after the trip to Havana? What happens after the romantic dream fades and Hennie wakes up to her real life with an amputee and a racketeer? The image of Havana, as Gerald Weales points out, is itself a deliberate image of a failed paradise:

The advertisement that Moe tempts Hennie with in II, 1 is tepid compared to the promise of "Havana in *fiesta* mood" that could be found in one of the great number of ads that filled the travel pages of the Sunday New York *Times* (November 25, 1934): "Visit Havana when her year-round play-time season reaches its merriest climax . . ." False paradises are the business of travel advertising, but that fakery is not the point here. At this time Cuba was ruled by the Mendieta-Batista dictatorship and, although the tourist business was not seriously hurt, there were sour notes in the *fiesta* music. The president of the Cuban Tourist Commission had to assure travel agents that tourists would be safe in Cuba and, just as Havana was reaching that "merriest climax," the Chief of National Police announced that an English-speaking policeman would accompany each automobile of sightseers, presumably to protect them from beggars, pickpockets and peddlers.9

Ralph's conversion is also suspect. All through the play he has been depicted as a weak and whining character, continually complaining about what he didn't have as a boy (dance lessons, black-and-white shoes). He clearly cannot handle the problems he is having with Blanche and cannot act decisively in any way to resolve those problems; when things get difficult he cries on his grandfather's shoulder. If Hennie is Bessie's daughter, Ralph is his father's son, weak and incapable of action. At the end of the play, just before his big speech, he gets a final call from Blanche, but he can only complain to Moe that he doesn't know what to say to her. He can't act, but she does: she finally hangs up on him. In this light Ralph's speech takes on comic overtones, undercutting his stirring call to action. What Odets sympathizes with, and what an audience might find satisfying, is Ralph's determination to persevere, to continue to aspire. That is consistent with his character. Like many Chekhov characters (Vershinin, Trofimov, Sonya) he will maintain a belief in the future or even in his ability to effect that future in spite of all evidence to the contrary. This resilient strain of aspiration is what Odets finds ennobling in his characters, even if he does not, apparently, trust in their ability to achieve those dreams. This ambivalence is what maintains the play's tension and may be considered the heart of its technique. When Odets discussed the ending of *Awake and Sing!* with Michael Mendelsohn, he was referring to possibilities, not probabilities:

No, not so much *Awake and Sing!*, because I believe in the possibilities expressed in the last scene. I do believe that young people can go through an experience and have their eyes opened, and determine from it to live in a different way. I do believe that older and more crushed human beings can pass on some lifting values to the younger generation. I do believe that, as the daughter in that family does, she can make a break with the groundling lies of her life, and try to find happiness by walking off with a man who is not her husband. I believed it then, and I believe it now. I think I believed it more *simply* then. I did not express roundly or fully the picture, but I don't think that ending is a lie.[10]

The ending is not a lie, thus, in the same way that Vershinin's hopes in *The Three Sisters* that life will be better in two hundred years is not a lie. The human persistence in believing in human progress despite hardship and disappointment is what Odets and Chekhov project in these characters. Ralph's final speech, then, is fully consistent with his established tendency to dream and to talk, and Odets clearly does not mean it to be taken seriously as an indication that Ralph has changed.

In the context of *Awake and Sing!* Ralph's final speech serves, rather, as a confirmation of the destructive cyclical pattern of the entire play. The unfailing aspiration expressed there recalls, inevitably, the Marxist ideology that prompted Ralph's grandfather to buy books he never read, as well as the romantic vision that inspired Moe to go off to war and later to elope with Hennie. Coming soon after his inability to speak to his girlfriend Blanche, Ralph's speech is also undercut by the implication that he has merely replaced one romantic aspiration with another. In the face of opposition Ralph is willing to abandon Blanche to her relatives in Cleveland, just as, in the face of difficulty, Hennie has abandoned her own child. Odets thus brings his dramatic portrait of dreamers defeated and the power of dreaming revived to a close on an ecstatic note, at the same time conditioning his audience to suspect that Ralph's sudden rhetorical inspiration will not prove substantial enough to prevail against the accumulated weight of compromise and loss that are the true lot of mankind. This "new" generation, like those before them, will awake and sing, and then grow old in the gradual fading of the song's refrain.

Like the earlier play, *Paradise Lost* is clearly Chekhovian in form, projecting no central action and no single protagonist. Again the drama is created by the interaction of varying strains, particularly the conflict between desire and will. More than *Awake and Sing!* this play is dominated by an elegiac tone, its sad lyrical mood ending in a delusory ode to the future, one that will clearly not affect the characters, but which, critical wisdom to the contrary, is thematically consistent with Odets's design.

Whereas *Awake and Sing!* revolves around the thematic pattern of dreams fragmenting when confronted by reality, *Paradise Lost* displays a less schematic structure, offering rather a confluence of voices, of individuals exposing their personal points of view and their characteristic reactions to the harsh circumstances of their lives. The rhythmic interplay of these voices moves the plot along. As in *Awake and Sing!* there are dramatic incidents that propel the story forward, but, again, the revelation of character is Odets's primary concern.

This play, too, concentrates on a family group that Odets composes of character types similar to the Berger family. The Gordons consist of Leo and Clara, their sons Ben and Julie, and their daughter Pearl. The extended family includes Gus, who becomes a family member when his daughter Libby marries Ben; Mr. Pike, the furnace man; San Katz, Leo's partner, and his wife Bertha. Kewpie, a friend of Ben and Libby, also figures prominently in the action.

Unlike the Bergers, this is a middle-class family, but their fortunes are declining during the course of the play. Odets reaches for a more symbolic, generalized reference in drawing these figures, in part by making the family less-recognizably Jewish—he changed the family name from Greenberg to Gordon during revision. Still, their speech inflections and mannerisms link them to the Bergers, and the Gordons are clearly a Jewish family.

If the Gordons are representative of their class, it is a class in a state of decay; *Paradise Lost* reads like Odets's version of *The Waste Land.* The play is permeated by images of death, desolation, and sterility: early on it is revealed that Julie is dying of encephalitis and by act 3, he is merely a figure in a wheelchair with his back to the audience. Ben is killed at the end of act 2, his marriage to Libby already a shambles. The Katzes are childless, and in act 2 Sam is declared to be

impotent. Pearl and her boyfriend Felix cannot afford to marry, and
he eventually leaves for Chicago. Mr. Pike has lost his two sons
during World War I. Thus it seems that the future generation is
decimated, and at the end of the play the older generation is left
onstage having lost their home as well. The present is barren; there is
no future.

Unlike Myron Berger, Leo is clearly the head of his household,
and he is successful in business. However, he, too, lives largely in
dreams, another Odets *luftmensch* who is simply not comfortable in
the real world. It is his partner Sam Katz who handles the financial
dealings of their women's handbag business while Leo designs the
products. In act 1 when a shop delegation comes to protest working
conditions, Leo is clearly shocked, for he is quite ignorant of their
salaries, hours, and other labor conditions. He is likewise unaware
that his partner has been cheating him. What he does enjoy is talking
politics and philosophy with his friend Pike and listening to his
daughter play the piano. He is Odets's most deliberately modeled
Chekhovian character. His query "What is to be done?" is repeated
in various contexts throughout the play, as he remains puzzled by
the collapse of the economy, moral values, and human commitment.
He cannot understand why "Never in my forty-seven years have I
met a happy man." Yet despite the economic and moral collapse
around him, he displays a Chekhovian faith, firm in his commitment
to life. At the end of act 2 when Clara poses his rhetorical question
to him, "What will we do now?" he answers, "We'll go on living."

Clara is a spunky, realistic woman, like Bessie, but without the
hard edges. She has achieved the respectability that Bessie longs for
and has the leisure to socialize and play cards. She can be abusive;
unlike her husband she has little fondness for Katz and tells him so.
If her husband is always wondering "What is to be done?" her
response to most crises is "Take a piece of fruit"—her insistence on
providing fruit in her failed paradise is a measure of her desperate
but eroding grip on home and family.

The Gordons find themselves caught up in the general economic
collapse and are confused by the political situation in Europe. Their
greatest personal tragedy, however, is their children. Odets's weakest
creations in the play, Ben and Julie, are, unfortunately, overtly
symbolic, unlifelike characters. Julie is a bank clerk who plays the

stock market in his head, where he achieves great financial success. However, he is dying of sleeping sickness, and whatever success he achieves is purely imaginary. Despite his dream of success and his growing lethargy, he senses that there is no longer any sense of family or warmth in his home; Julie's refrain line is that "the house feels empty."

His brother Ben, too, lives primarily in an imaginary world. He is a former running champion, and a godlike statue of him dominates the stage. Once the embodiment of youth, beauty, and physical prowess, now he is a man frozen in the past, unable to function in the present. He seems incapable of making a living (he is always borrowing money) or even satisfying his new wife. He is suspended between a glorious past and visions of the future:

The doctor says I'm through! But I saw Alfred Bond yesterday—the big A.A.U. official—he says not to worry, a swell berth waiting for me in Wall Street. Will we make money! All the books you can read, Leo. A concert career for Pearlie—that—dope! And Gus can have a better stamp collection than the King of England! Just be patient.[11]

The present, however, is empty: heart problems force him to end his athletic career; he has "magnetism" but no real skills, and he remains dependent on his gangster friend Kewpie for money and help.

Ben's frustration over his inability to make anything of himself is compounded when he discovers tht Kewpie has been sleeping with his wife and giving her money. (Kewpie's relationship with Libby is similar to Moe and Hennie's.) When Ben confronts him, significant images are crystallized:

Are we the same kids who used to go up to Whitey Aimer's roof and watch the pigeons fly? You and me and Danny? There's one old pal we know what happened to, where he is. The three of us under the ice with our skates on and not being able to get him out. Then sticking him dead in the box.

. . . .

Last night I couldn't sleep. All the way over to the new bridge, I walked. Stood there for a long time looking in the water. Then I began to run, down the street. I used to like to be out in front. When I fell in that rhythm and knew my reserve—the steady driving forward—I sang inside when I ran.

Yeah, sang like an airplane, powerful motors humming in oil. I wanted to run till my heart exploded . . . a funny way to die. (pp. 202–3)

Ben thus identifies with images of flight and water, symbolic modes of escape from earthly reality. Their import emerges in the coalescence of images, of the friend frozen in the ice and Ben's statue: ultimately Ben will realize his dream of flight only in death. When, at the end of act 2, he leaves with Kewpie on a job that will kill him, he gives his medals to Julie. In handing over his essential self to his dying brother, he is acknowledging their kinship and symbolically prefiguring the death/suicide that will occur at the end of the act.

Pearl, his sister, is linked thematically to her brothers. She is a gifted pianist; her playing opens and closes the play, providing an idealized frame that ironically counterpoints the various characters' dilemmas. She spends much of the play alone in her room playing the piano, the music forming her haunting leitmotif, like Ben's statue. In her central scene, she is forced to acknowledge that she and her boyfriend Felix, another musician, will never marry because they have no money. Art collides with the reality of economics, and romantic dreams are smashed. As Felix remarks, "What lies we believe." He decides to leave New York for some other city, other possibilities. Acknowledging the necessity of his departure, Pearl can only urge him "not to smoke in bed."

At the end of the play Leo tells her that he will be forced to sell her piano, a particularly poignant loss, for the family is now outside; their home lost, the furniture is on the street. During the final act, Pearl remains upstairs playing the piano. A counterpoint to the reality outside, like the chopping of Chekhov's cherry orchard, the music produces an aural reminder of a way of life, or a dream of life, which has no place in the bleak economic world of America.

The two spokesmen for alternatives in the play are Kewpie, a clear descendant of Moe, and Pike, who resembles Jacob. Kewpie, a cab driver, says early in the play that he is "sore on his whole damn life." Unlike Moe's, this man's discontent arises not from any specific loss, though he, too, appears to long for a place to belong. He is in love with Libby, but she has married Ben. Also strongly suggested is a painfully constricted attraction between the two men, which may, in

turn, have prompted Kewpie's affair with Libby. Even after involving Ben in the scheme that kills him, Kewpie returns to the Gordon
house in act 3, but is rejected, not only because of his implication in
Ben's death, but because of what he stands for.

Like Moe, Kewpie is a survivor because he has no real ideals or
poetic temperament. His is the type of personality clearly fit to
function in a fallen paradise:

You gimme worms, the whole bunch! A pack of tramps making believe they
own the world because they read a book! I don't read, see! But I saw the
handwriting on the wall. . . . Well, take a lesson from little Kewpie—if you
don't like the Constitution, make it over! Christ, then it's my falt 'cause Ben
killed himself. That's what he did. He dug his own grave. He was a little kid
in a man's world . . . you make him like that. He couldn't earn a living, and
he was ashamed. (p. 223)

On the surface Kewpie seems harder than Moe, but he is not
villainous. Odets hints at his vulnerability, his capacity for affection
and love. In a fallen world, Kewpie may be a survivor, but he is
clearly also a victim; he is more a part of the Gordon family than he
realizes.

Pike is the play's socialist reformer. He works on the furnaces
underground and occasionally emerges to talk with the Gordon
family, usually Leo. His first action is to show the Gordons a sketch
he has made of a dead man, someone who starved to death, thus
reinforcing the specter of death first introduced in the play by the
appearance of Julie. Pike clearly sees that the promise of America is
dying. Although claiming American ancestry dating back to the
seventeenth century, he is clearly dissatisfied with a system that
allows men to starve to death and makes wars that kill young boys.
When a local politician accuses him of being a "Red," he eloquently
defends his commitment to America:

For one generation of Irish you're talking pretty big. I'm what they call one
hundred per cent American. My ancestors didn't come over on the May-
flower. They missed that one, but came over on the next ferry. I come stock,
lock and barrel out of the Parson family. We fought all your wars, from 1776
up to 1918. Two of my boys . . . my only two . . . you call me a Red and I'll
break your goddam neck! (pp. 168–69)

Later, however, he denounces American idealism:

There's for idealism! For those blue-gutted Yankee Doodle bastards are
making other wars while we sleep. And if we remain silent while they make
this war, we are the guilty ones. For we are the people, and the people is the
government, and tear them down from their high places if they dast do what
they did in 1914 to '18. (p. 191)

Nevertheless, shortly after making that speech, when Leo asks,
"What is to be done?" Pike answers, "I don't know . . . I mean I
don't know." Pike is a stronger, more articulate man than Jacob.
Clearly disgusted by the capitalistic system, he looks forward to
change but does nothing to put his theories into action, nor does he
seem entirely sure that the system should be changed. It is never
quite clear whether Pike is truly politically motivated or whether his
is a personal disgust caused rather by the loss of his sons in a
senseless war.

Odets, however, was clearly interested in Pike as a character, for in
the early version of *Paradise Lost* he played a much larger role. He
spoke more often, perhaps too often, the speeches more hard-edged
and didactic. One speech, about the cemetery in France where his
sons are buried, is very moving, concluding with the observation
that it took "ten years for the trees to grow—there will be another
war in ten years." In revision Odets may have felt that Pike's
character was overwhelming the play and that his lengthy harangues
shifted the play's emphasis from the character study he intended to a
political statement with which Odets was evidently uncomfortable.
Another exchange in act 2 is telling: Julie and Pike are discussing
changing conditions in society when Pearl interrupts by saying,
"Systems will come and systems will go, but spiritual values will
remain." Pike angrily snaps back, "Don't you know it ain't coming,
that land of your dreams, unless you work for it." This is a deeply
Chekhovian concept, the need to extract oneself from mere speculation and work for one's dreams. This activist spirit removed, the Pike
of the final version of the play is weaker, and when confronted with
Leo's "What is to be done?" he can only reply, "I don't know."
Clearly Odets resisted putting too much emphasis on the radical
voice in *Paradise Lost*.

Gus, like the play's other central male characters, is humane and
ineffectual. Like Myron in *Awake and Sing!* he is preoccupied with
the past, nostalgically reverting to a better time:

I can't explain it to you, Mr. G., how I'm forever hungerin' for the past. It's
like a disease in me, eatin' away . . . some nights I have cried myself to
sleep—for the old Asbury Park days; the shore dinners at old Sheepshead
Bay. (p. 207)

After making that speech he puts on an aviator's helmet, recalling the
flight images associated with Ralph in *Awake and Sing!* Gus's dreams
of the past balance Pike's dreams of the future, all of them amount-
ing to very little. In reality Gus cannot get a job and receives little
respect from his daughter Libby.

His one significant act comes at the end of the play, when he sells
his beloved stamp collection to help the Gordons, who are now
bankrupt. It is a gesture at once futile and touching, for the money
he raises is not nearly enough to help the Gordons. However, as an
example of this rather helpless man's refusal to surrender and despair, it logically prefigures Leo's speech that closes the play.

The ending of this play also has drawn much critical fire. Here,
even more dramatically than in *Awake and Sing!* there is a pattern of
decline: in act 1 the characters' problems are introduced and the
shop delegation hints that Leo and Sam's business is in trouble; in
act 2 Sam Katz is revealed to be impotent and an embezzler, and Ben
is shot and killed; in act 3 the family has lost its home and is out on
the street. And yet the play's final speech is one of hope, as Leo
reveals in his hope for man and future:

Yes, I want to see that new world. I want to kiss all those future men and
women. What is this talk of bankrupts, failures, hatred . . . they won't know
what that means. Oh, yes, I tell you the whole world is for men to possess.
Heartbreak and terror are not the heritage of mankind! The world is
beautiful. No fruit tree wears a lock and key. Men will sing at their work,
men will love. Ohhh, darling, the world is in its morning . . . and *no man
fights alone!* (p. 230)

Again the critics have questioned Odets's ending in light of the
preceding action, and, again, on the surface the critics seem justified.

Odets, as evidenced by the early drafts, had trouble deciding on an ending. In the ms. dated 1934–35, Leo's speech about the future comes at the end of act 2. Leo has turned down a suggestion, favored by his partner and his wife, that he have his business burned down for the insurance money. Sam has already confessed that he has embezzled funds. When Clara claims that "We don't live in paradise, we live in hell," Leo delivers his paean to the future. The play later concludes very melodramatically: when the police come to force the Gordons to put their furniture back in the house, a policeman breaks Ben's statue. Leo, in anger, raises an ax to threaten the policeman and is shot dead. Pike then lifts the ax and taunts the police with a vision of the future, where "fruit trees will grow where our ashes are." In a ms. dated 1935 Odets moved Leo's speech about the future into act 3, but concluded the play with Gus getting shot by the police and Pike threatening that "we are witnesses" to the policeman's brutality.

Both endings are obviously excessive and unsuited to the mood and method of the play, although they do serve to maintain the downward movement. *Paradise Lost* is a play in which Odets attempts, falteringly, to sustain a balance between realism and symbolism. It is dramatically consistent that Ben should die, because he is created primarily through a network of symbolic images, incarnating the vitality and promise of a dream that has lost its value. As such, like Julie, who represents the failure of business, he has to die to maintain the play's allegorical thrust. In keeping with the dramatic method that Odets developed in the first plays, however, Ben's death takes place offstage, like Jacob's suicide in *Awake and Sing!* The action on stage is primarily devoted to episodic representation of the comic and painful moments of this troubled family's existence. Leo, Clara, Gus, and Pike demonstrate Odets's concern with revelation of character, set against the symbolic weight of the children, and this nucleus of characters must remain central if the play is to retain its poignancy and thrust. In act 3 they dominate the action, for the children are gone: Julie no longer speaks, Ben is dead, and Pearl is offstage playing the piano.

Leo's speech is consistent with his character as developed throughout the play. A man of the spirit, not of action, he does make decisions, but on an emotional, not a rational, basis. The play opens with his wish to get rid of his German canary because of the situation in Germany. It is a humorous moment, and it defines Leo's notion of decisive political action. Later he does not even want to look at Pike's drawing of a dead man on the garbage dump. His other acts are to give a wage increase to his workers and to reject May's proposal to burn his business for the insurance, both virtuous rather than practical choices, those of an idealist, not a Sam Katz or a Kewpie. Leo can live and function happily only in the utopian world of his imagination. Prior to his final speech he remarks, "So in the end nothing is real. Nothing is left but our memory of life. Not as it is . . . as it *might* have been." Shortly thereafter he asks Clara, "Tell me what to do." The rhapsody that concludes the play, then, is no call to political action, but an ode to a more glorious future, one not drawn from any specific dogma or philosophy, but a New Jerusalem that Leo sees in his mind's eye.

The end of *Paradise Lost,* like the end of *Awake and Sing!* demonstrates Odets's hope, rather than his belief, in human possibilities, and his perception that people continue to believe and persevere in the face of extreme adversity. Leo, after all, has lost his business, his home, one son, and will soon lose another. But it is inherent in this man's character to seek refuge in visions of transcendence, as consistent as Ralph's predilection for dreaming. If these two plays are read as mirrors of the human condition rather than political tracts or thesis plays, Odets's characters may be seen to speak and behave with perfect consistency, and each play's ending provides an emotional, and yet quite logical, capstone to the dramatic design.

The principal features of the Chekhovian mode distinguish Odets's first two full-length plays, setting them apart not only from the works to follow, but from the main body of American popular drama. As Chekhov does in his mature plays, Odets provides groups of character-types—businessmen and gangsters, strong-willed women and ineffectual fathers, idealistic dreamers and leftist spokesmen—whose counterpointed affections and animosities constitute representative family units that reflect the social context of the playwright's world. Odets's characters, like Chekhov's, deal in emotions, which remain essentially nondramatic and unresolved. They face no climactic moral tests; none of them changes or grows. They appear on stage at a certain moment in the present, go through the prosaic process of living, and are finally left fixed in a moment of characteristic emotional fervor. *Paradise Lost,* with its symbolic substructure, is more ambitious, but even its central characters do not evolve: they have lost their home, but, like the Ranevskaya family in *The Cherry Orchard,* remain largely unaffected by it.

Such is Odets's thematic strategy. Portraying the frustration shared by sleepwalkers and dreamers alike in an imperfect world, he projects not decisive conflict nor dramatic change, but the plaintive chorus of human longing for a better life. The unanswerable question "What is to be done?" runs like a leitmotif through *Paradise Lost,* echoing in Leo's query to his wife, "What is happening here? Once we were all together and life was good." The promise of America is enormous—Ben's symbolic value in *Paradise Lost*—but it remains unrealized; indeed, it seems to have disintegrated. Odets's paradise images, art references, and preoccupation with fruit, are evocations of loss, of elusive possibilities, like Chekhov's Moscow and cherry orchard, but all remain unresolved and unrealized, beyond scope of these weak and limited people.

It would be a mistake to dismiss entirely the political implications of these early works of Odets. One of the central images of the plays is entrapment, for the families are trapped not only in the physical sense, but a mental one as well. The impoverished urban setting forms a real physical trap, enforced by the impression that there is nothing outside the tenement but a terrifying reality shaped by years of exploitation. And yet most members of Odets's families accept as dogma the economic laws that they have been taught, investing them with almost metaphysical significance, although the acceptance of this metaphysic limits and cheapens their lives. And so Odets's world presents a double trap imposed from without as well as from within. Economic necessity deforms and demeans the individual by leading him to worship at the altar of material success, thus opening a chasm between aspiration and reality. For the Bergers and the Gordons to deny the validity of the American dream would be to deprive themselves of what is most real to them. As a result, in these plays images of escape and flight vie with overwhelming sensations of claustrophobia and constriction.

The force and immediacy of these political/social implications give Odets's plays a harder edge than Chekhov's, for the sense of entrapment is more insistent. Still, Odets remained more deeply concerned about his characters than about the fallen world they inhabit. His plays are not really indictments of capitalism, for, like Chekhov's, they more specifically focus on the potential for moral and spiritual revolution for people waking up and recognizing their own spiritual failures and coming to grips with them. But Odets's characters are too weak to change the world or even to progress in themselves. The gap between aspiration and reality is never bridged. As in Chekhov's work, the tension and energy of the plays derives from the dramatic confrontation between the hopeful spirit of the characters and the playwright's sad presentiment that these hopes will not find fulfillment, that the dream of life, however powerful a force, is not as strong as life itself.

Few American plays manage so thoroughly to embody the way certain people lived at a certain moment in time. The plays, however, are not defined by their Depression setting, for the longings, dreams, and hopes of such individuals are timeless. The plays capture real people dealing with mundane dilemmas, but Odets dramatizes not only their despair and frustration, but also their vitality, their humor, and their strength. The dreams may not be realized, but neither Odets nor his characters will abandon hope. This ability to "sing" even in the dust gives these plays an enduring power that qualifies them as landmarks in the history of the American theater.

4

The Tragic Vision
Golden Boy (1937)
The Big Knife (1949)

Essentially it *[The Big Knife]* dealt with the tragedy of lost integrity everywhere.

—Clifford Odets

It was his duty to keep the Kingdom of the Movies free from the ancient enemy of the people—Art.

—Ben Hecht on Louis B. Mayer

"So many artists today stand in relation to Hollywood as our hero in relation to his double career." So wrote Harold Clurman in his introduction to *Golden Boy,* which he called Odets's "most subjective play." Odets, indeed, made his first trip to Hollywood before writing *Golden Boy:* in 1936 he signed a four-week contract to write *The General Died at Dawn* for producer/director Lewis Milestone, and he was paid $27,500 for his work on that film. Odets had been courted by Hollywood before; he was offered a number of deals after *Waiting for Lefty* opened, and Harold Clurman noted that MGM, which financed part of *Paradise Lost,* went as high as three thousand dollars per week.

Odets's attitude toward Hollywood was, however, always ambivalent. He was attracted by the money, the technical expertise of films, the audience they attracted, and the potential for saying something important to that audience. At the same time, he disliked the Hollywood product and the negative influence it had on people, and he made his reservations clear as early as Jacob's speeches in *Awake and Sing!* In 1936 he told the *New York Times* "I won't be party to the fraud the screen has been perpetuating on the public for years. Boy gets girl. Life is swell."

The General Died at Dawn, the one film that bears Odets's name from this period, is a dull adventure-romance concerning an American named O'Hara (Gary Cooper), who helps the Chinese peasant revolt against the wicked General Yang (Akim Tamiroff), and in the process wins the heart of Judy (Madeleine Carroll). The dialogue makes some allusion to the plight of the worker—"You ask me why I'm for oppresed people? Because I got a background of oppression myself, and O'Haras and elephants don't forget. What's better work for an American than helping fight for democracy?"—but this motif was eclipsed by the film's most famous lines: "Judy darling, we could have made wonderful music together—a circle of light and warmth," and "Someday, maybe there'll be a law to abolish the blues. Maybe a constitutional amendment, for all of us." The release of the film prompted Frank S. Nugent to ask, "Odets, Where Is Thy Sting?"

While working on the film Odets was taken to a boxing match by Lewis Milestone:

I had two tickets to the Canzoneri-Ambers championship fight, and knowing Clifford had never seen a prizefight, I invited him to come along. During the prelims he paled and pulled out his notebook. When it seemed to me he was too busy writing to see the main event, I complained that I had bought two very expensive seats and that he could write at home. His reply was "You have just given me a very fine play, and what's more it will make money for the Group." He appeared to be very happy.[1]

Odets later told Elia Kazan that he would soon have a hit show for the Group that he was then calling "The Manly Art" or "Golden Gloves." The play *Golden Boy* did turn out to be the Group Theatre's greatest hit despite mixed reviews. And it came at a critical time, for the Group had dispersed, most of them to Hollywood, after the failure of their previous play *Johnny Johnson* by Paul Green, so *Golden Boy* served as the vehicle that brought the Group back together and allowed them to function for another three years. The play ran on

Broadway for 250 performances; there was a West Coast production, and even engagements in London and Paris.

It was also the first Odets play sold to the movies. Directed by
Rouben Mamoulian, with a script credited to four screenwriters,
Columbia Pictures' *Golden Boy* opened in 1939, and it even featured
one member of the Group in the cast, Lee J. Cobb, playing Mr.
Bonaparte. The play was then revived in 1952, with Odets directing
and John Garfield starring. (Odets had wanted Garfield to star in the
original production, but was overruled by Clurman, who chose
Luther Adler.) At the time of his death Odets was even working on a
musical version about a black boxer who falls in love with a white
woman; the play was completed by William Gibson and it opened in
1964 with Sammy Davis, Jr., starring as Joe.

John Garfield starred in the Broadway opening of *The Big Knife* as
well. When Odets wrote the play, he had been living in Hollywood
on and off for almost thirteen years (the same length of time Charlie
Castle has been in Hollywood in the play), though he did move back
to New York in 1948 where he wrote the play. The reviews were
generally unkind, most critics unaccountably coming to the defense
of Hollywood at Odets's expense; *Variety* called Odets "the champ
sorehead of show business." The play did manage to run for 108
performances, primarily because of the box-office appeal of John
Garfield.

In *The Fervent Years* Harold Clurman wrote that "for Odets . . .
Hollywood was a sin." To a large extent this was true, for until the
end of his life, Odets had difficulty reconciling his attraction to
Hollywood with his need to produce significant art for the theater. It
is certainly easy to read *Golden Boy* as a metaphor for that division in
Odets and *The Big Knife* as a highly subjective apologia as well. But
this is merely to skim the surface, for in both these plays Odets
managed to transform his personal conflicts into explorations of
broader issues related to his constant themes: the soul's difficult
journey on earth, and its need to find a haven, a home. As Charlie
Castle says in *The Big Knife*, "We're homesick all our lives," and this
human dilemma is ultimately more important than the discovery of
personal reference in the writer's work. In both plays Odets was able
to project aspects of contemporary American experience into the

realm of tragedy, exploring the dividedness of the spirit in two distinctive protagonists living in different times and in very different worlds.

Golden Boy is a different kind of play than *Awake and Sing!* and *Paradise Lost,* for in writing it Odets was experimenting with new techniques, baffling the critics, who apparently expected him to continue in the same vein as his earlier work. His desire to break away from the realistic/naturalistic mode of *Awake and Sing!* was evident in *Paradise Lost,* where he imposed a symbolic framework within the play, involving the characters of the Gordon children and, to a certain extent, Sam Katz. This device, unfortunately, weakened the play's thematic unity, and while *Paradise Lost* is among Odets's richest works, its awkward structural duality ultimately defeats the characters' emotional interplay.

Golden Boy, on the other hand, works best as a symbolic play. Odets clearly intended it as an allegory; indeed, he subtitled an early draft *An American Allegory.* Yet it is Odets's particular accomplishment in *Golden Boy* that his characters are so vividly presented as to transcend their allegorical functions and propel their personal conflict into the realm of tragedy. In order to stimulate a tragic apprehension, dramatic characters must engage an audience's sympathy and passion more fully than can be done either in simple allegory or in the realistic, slice-of-life antidramas of Odets's early career. *Golden Boy* thus represents a departure from his previous practice, for, instead of attempting to minimize theatrical involvement and impact, here Odets exploits the conventions of theater to heighten the formal eloquence of his story.

This play's most obvious conventional feature is the introduction of broad theatrical types; suddenly Odets peoples his stage with readily identifiable heroes and villains. At the center of the play stands Joe Bonaparte, a larger-than-life, emotionally engaging protagonist whose aspiration to be *somebody* in America at length leads to his death. Joe's is a story of thwarted potential, unfolding within an overriding mood of doom. It follows the classic tragic formula of an individual's rise to power and subsequent fall, precipitated by the recognition of irreparable error committed in the use of that power; for this he suffers and dies, having exhausted all the possibilities of his life. Odets moves his hero toward an action that causes great suffering, and then by exposing the consequences of the deed reveals to him the true nature of his ambition. The actions of other characters are related closely to various stages of this hero's passage. Joe's story, however, is more than a tragic study of the danger of courting success in America, for Odets is again exploring herein his favorite theme, the soul's yearning for a secure haven in this world. At this level *Golden Boy* reaches beyond the quintessential American dilemma that supplies its plot, attaining a dimension of universal significance in its symbolic progress.

This play also departs from Odets's past practice in its utilization of space. In the first two plays the characters are confined to the living area of the home, as Odets demonstrates their spiritual and emotional entrapment by contriving a sense of physical constraint. This closed setting also conveys Odets's suspicion of the family itself as a kind of trap that the individual must escape if he is to achieve personal fulfillment. The impulse to escape, however, remains an ambivalent one, since the family home represents also the striver's ultimate goal, as the source of emotional support and place of belonging that is the soul's prime object.

In *Golden Boy* Odets opens up the stage to encompass various settings: Moody's office, the Bonaparte home, the park, and the dressing room. Joe, who is Odets's first major protagonist, cannot be confined to the living room; he needs to go out into the world and see what is there. Accordingly, the audience's sense of possibility expands as Joe moves about the stage, extending its space until it becomes its own world, rich in imaginative potential. The proscenium, emphasized in the earlier plays, seems to disappear here, along with any suggestion of permanent walls, thereby transporting character and action beyond real space into metaphysical space, and this liberation of setting heightens the audience's sense of exhilaration in Joe's journey of discovery.

Joe himself is initially introduced in a deliberately theatrical manner: rather than entering prosaically, he seems to materialize on stage at a significant moment, as if summoned by dramatic necessity. The play has opened upon Moody, a fight manager, arguing with his girlfriend Lorna about her decision to leave him. Tired of waiting for Moody's wife to divorce him and evidently determined to force the issue of their relationship, Lorna feels trapped but is afraid to leave Moody. Like *Awake and Sing!*, *Golden Boy* thus begins on a characteristic Odetsian note of movement and stasis, involving a character's need to break out and frustrating inability to do so. Moody, too, is trapped, not only by his wife's demand for five thousand dollars as the price of a divorce, but also by his failure to find a boxer who can revive his managerial career. As for any hope that his current mediocre fighter, Kaplan, might win him some money, Lorna remarks, "It's the twentieth century . . . no more miracles." Regretting this lack of miraculous potential in the present, Moody, like many Odets characters, reverts to the past, the twenties, when he was successful and there was plenty of money. Lorna undercuts his reverie by mentioning that her mother died in 1928, and this exchange provides the first of many instances of the linkage of success and death, a dominant thematic concept in this play. Then, when Moody kisses Lorna, promising to give her anything she wants, Joe appears. Odets's stage direction is significant: "Suddenly a youth is standing at the office door. Lorna sees him and breaks away." Moody's reaction is, "Don't you knock when you come in an office?"

Joe's entrance is reminiscent of Hilda Wangel's in Ibsen's *The Master Builder*. The protagonist of that play, Halvard Solness, is introduced as a man preoccupied with youth, lamenting his own waning creative powers and a marriage that has trapped him. His longing for youth and love is answered just as he is thinking of it, when, in a marvelous theatrical coincidence, Hilda (youth) comes knocking at his door and changes his life. Moody's line, thus, is Odets's acknowledgment of a debt to Ibsen. On a literal level, Joe functions in the same way as Hilda. Moody longs for a miracle, a winning boxer who will reverse his professional decline and personal fortunes, while Lorna wants love and the sense of family lost at her mother's death, and Joe will answer both their longings. Lorna instantly recognizes this, for when she sees him, she moves away from Moody.

Joe's mode of theatrical entrance becomes a motif in the play, a stylistic device that confirms his story's symbolic thrust. In act 1, scene 2, which takes place in the Bonaparte home, Joe's brother Frank and his father are discussing him, and again he appears unnoticed, this time "in the shadows." Odets's use of lighting here underscores visually Joe's estrangement from the home image, for he has committed himself to Moody's world in scene 1. In act 2 scene 3, he once more appears as Moody and Lorna are kissing, after Lorna has again threatened to leave, this time because of Joe. When Joe enters he is followed by Eddie Fuseli, a gangster who serves as the embodiment of the shadow from the earlier scene; Eddie is the epitome of Joe's worst self. Joe's final "appearance" is in act 3, scene 2, when Fuseli is threatening Lorna with a gun, and once again his sudden entrance is timed to break up another man's confrontation with Lorna. The repetition is significant, for it is Joe's movement toward Lorna that comprises the symbolic progress of the play.

Odets's treatment of the hero typifies his adherence to the Nietzschean tragic system, whereby the playwright designates action and character to function as metaphysical complements to the physical world. Nietzsche's theory, in *The Birth of Tragedy* appropriately, draws upon Schopenhauer's definition of music as a universal language, the "immediate language of the will." Nietzsche explains that music, which he associates with the Dionysian strain, stimulates the imagination to embody the immaterial world:

Image and concept . . . gain a heightened significance under the influence of truly appropriate music . . . music incites us to a symbolic intuition of the Dionysiac universality; [and] it endows that symbolic image with supreme significance.

Music, then, is Odets's metaphor for the soul, the immaterial, that mode of exaltation that Joe strives after but cannot attain. The energy of this creative inspiration, represented in his violin playing and his love for Lorna, supplies the play's Dionysian dimension.

The Apollonian element, in Nietzsche's words "the transcendent genius of the *principium individuationis*," inheres in Joe's desire for more material success, his will toward individuation, which is metaphorically embodied in his determination to become a boxer. The need to break free of the spiritual anonymity and poverty arising from his immigrant status and to revenge himself on those who have excluded him—his family name and his cockeye are emblematic of past pain—makes Joe a readily sympathetic figure. However, if the Nietzschean tragic pattern is to be realized, the hero must "deliver us from our avid thirst for earthly satisfaction and remind us of another existence and higher delight." Ultimately Joe, too, must comprehend the error of his pursuit of success and revenge and then willingly embrace his own death; thus, in Nietzsche's words, he realizes himself "not through his victories but through his undoing."

Odets, moreover, seeks to superimpose this tragic model of a contemporary story in order to articulate the distinctive American experience. In an essay entitled "Democratic Vistas in Drama," published in the *New York Times* after *Golden Boy* opened, Odets quoted Whitman's complaint about the lack of an authentic American drama:

In his essay "Democratic Vistas" written in 1871, Walt Whitman wrote: "Of what is called the drama or dramatic presentation, in the United States, as now put forth at the theatres, I should say it deserves to be treated with the same gravity, and on a par with the questions of ornamental confectionery at public dinners, or the arrangement of curtains and hangings in a ballroom. . . .

"I feel with dejection and amazement that among writers and talented speakers, few or none have yet really spoken to this people, created a single image-making work for them, or absorbed the central spirit and the idiosyncrasies which are theirs—and which, thus, in the highest ranges, so far remain entirely uncelebrated and unexpressed."[2]

Agreeing with Whitman that the modern theater had failed to express the American spirit, Odets then advanced a rather bold claim for the time, that the movies had, at least partially, supplied the lack:

Let us, for once, give the movies some credit. They have spoken to this people. The movies have explored the common man in all of his manifestations—out of the Kentucky mountains, out of the Montana ranch house, out of the machine shop, from the docks and alleys of the great cities, from the farm, out of the hospitals, airplanes, and taxicabs.

The movies are now the folk theatre of America. But they are still not what Whitman asked for in 1871. . . . Hollywood producers will tell you gladly that they are not interested in presenting their themes "significantly." They are not interested in interpretation or criticism of their material. Their chief problem, they contend, is the one of keeping the level of human experience in their pictures as low as possible. They keep to primary colors with the expected result: The good will be rewarded, the wicked punished; success lurks around every corner; love is only a matter of the right man looking the right girl in the eyes; and so on and so on and so on.[3]

The movies' treatment of theme therefore remaining "puerile in every respect," Odets concluded with the suggestion that the theater adopt the movies' themes but "tell the truth where the film told a lie." The playwright committed to this high cultural calling could thus become in Whitman's term a "celebrator and expressor" of the American experience.

In pursuit of this calling, Odets utilizes in *Golden Boy* a cinematic scenic format that, as mentioned earlier, diverges sharply from the tightly knit structure of the earlier plays. The later play's succession of brief scenes and multiple settings was undoubtedly influenced by Odets's recent Hollywood screenwriting experience. This important technical innovation also represents a probably deliberate imitation of the basic form of the gangster film, which became, in the early thirties, a significant expression of the popular culture, uniquely suited to dealing with the traumatic societal upheaval of the Depression years.

Like *Golden Boy* the gangster film typically features an aggressive, violent protagonist of immigrant descent, whose obsessive rise to prominence in the mob is played against scenes of (usually idealized) family life. Odets echoes this pattern, only substituting a devoted father for the widowed mother more common to the family model of the movies, and the change more likely reflects Odets's own troubled relationship with his father than any conscious variation on the film genre. In the play as well as in the movie versions, the nurturing family functions as a counterpoint to the characteristically violent success story. Consequently, the destruction of the family, and often, the substitution of a false family for the real one become recurrent themes in these films; likewise, in *Golden Boy* Joe rejects his family/father for successive surrogate fathers in the fight game, and this betrayal of the values of home eventually leads to his undoing.

The most meaningful affinity between the ganster film and Odets's play is to be found in their makers' corresponding rejection of the demands and essential rewards of modern life: Robert Warshaw claims that the gangster film rejects "Americanism itself."[4] In making this rejection the film genre offers no alternative, either political, social, or economic, to the bleak picture of corruption and degradation conveyed in its narrative. Neither does Odets, and this is consistent with his attitude in the previous plays, where criticism of the system is implied, but no blueprint for the future is offered. Here, however, Odets provides a central character who, unlike Ralph, Jacob, or Leo, recognizes the moral emptiness of his society, and this rejection moves *Golden Boy* into the realm of authentic tragedy.

Like tragedy, the gangster film insists that man is a being capable of success or failure. The gangster fiercely pursues his finite goal and succeeds, in Warshaw's words, in "emerging from the crowd," defying the anonymity of the city. Nevertheless, like any "tragic" hero, he must be defeated at last, often dying alone in the street. The gangster figure has asserted himself as an individual, but he must die because of it. The genre thus echoes the conventions of tragedy but finally falls short of it: whereas tragedy chronicles a protagonist's doomed struggle with necessity and forces him (and the audience that views his story) to acknowledge the inevitability of his fate, it also celebrates man's need to give meaning to his fate. The gangster film, on the other hand, ultimately offers no real meaning, no sense of nobility to account for the ambition and the downfall of its protagonist. If the Apollonian sense of individuation is celebrated, the Dionysian, musically symbolic connection with the infinite, that which "breaks the spell of individuation and opens a path to the maternal womb of being" is missing. In the character of Joe Bonaparte, however, Odets not only gives expression to the human condition in the American city of the 1930s, but also celebrates a broader human experience as well. For if this fighter and Apollonian individualist pursues the finite goal of success and fails, his complementary aspiration toward the infinite imparts nobility and meaning to his struggle and his fate.

The first act reveals the three major settings of the play: Moody's office, the Bonaparte home, and the park—each locale representing an alternative in Joe's struggle to come to grips with himself and the conflicting possibilities offered to him. The Bonaparte home is a kind of haven, a nourishing paradise where—unlike the Berger house of *Awake and Sing!*—it is possible to grow and produce "fruit." In the second draft of *Golden Boy,* Odets gave Mr. Bonaparte this speech, which was eliminated from the final version:

I think sometimes in terms of a citrus grove. I like to think to raise such trees and distribute to a world of children the fresh, natural juices of the fruit.[5]

In this impulse Mr. Bonaparte is related to Jacob in *Awake and Sing!* and Leo Gordon in *Paradise Lost,* all kindly, moral men who "love to slice philosophical salami," though unlike them, he seems unconcerned with the economic situation or even his own poverty. He is in love with life and his children and external troubles seem unimportant in comparison. Joe's ambition for material success does not impress him, for he feels "a good life 'sa possible," achievable in an attitude of self-acceptance and contentment with the simple pleasures of living:

You say life'sa bad . . . well, is pleasure for you to say so. No? The streets, winter a' summer—trees, cats—I love a them all. The gooda boys and girls, they who sing and whistle—very good! The eating and sleeping, drinking wine—very good! I gone around on my wagon and talk to many people—nice![6]

Even Mr. Carp, his best friend, cannot convince this amiable man that his philosophy has no place in modern-day America.

Carp is the serpent in the Edenic garden of the Bonaparte home, countering Mr. Bonaparte's native optimism and his hopes for Joe's career in music with gloomy cynicism:

In the end, as Schopenhauer says, what's the use to try something? For every wish we get, ten remains unsatisfied. Death is playing with us as a cat and her mouse! (p. 249)

The reference to Schopenhauer is important, for Carp proves to be prophetic in his assessment of Joe's pursuit of the American dream. Briefly, Schopenhauer posited that conflict between individual wills is the cause of continuous pain and frustration, and the world is thus a place of unsatisfied wants and unhappiness. Man's intellect and consciousness are mere instruments of the will, while music, the ultimate expression of the soul, provides a means of momentarily transcending the conflict, investing human life with higher significance. Odets's reference to Schopenhauer through Carp confirms the Nietzschean tragic model in the play, for Carp's discussions with Mr. Bonaparte provide in themselves harmless instances of the clash of opposites that causes conflict.[7]

The fateful significance underlying the two friends' contrasting outlooks is emphasized most powerfully in scene 2, when Mr. Bonaparte shows Carp the violin that he has bought for Joe's twenty-first birthday; Carp comments that "it looks like a coffin for a baby." (The coffin image recurs in scene 3, when Moody, disgusted with his ex-wife's constant demands for money, declares, "If I had fifty bucks I'd buy myself a big juicy coffin.") Carp's remark, then, not only prefigures Joe's death but also taints the redemptive music motif with a suggestion of abortive effort. Again, the transcendent impulse seems linked, in Odets's world, with a movement toward renunciation and death.

Joe, unlike Ralph Berger or any of the Gordon children, is a strong, decisive character capable of achieving success; in so doing he rejects his father's home, where he learned music and was encouraged to develop his talent. For Joe, a boy growing up in America, the old-world values of Europe, represented by his father, are not enough—one of many thematic motifs in *Golden Boy* is the generational conflict between the European immigrant and his son. In this context music represents an extension of the European sensibility that cannot survive on the streets of America. Joe, like many first-generation Americans, must reject the ways of the father completely, although in embracing the values of the new land and its ethic of "making it," he risks losing his soul. Joe's rejection of his home suggests that Odets felt the temptations and pressures of the American economic condition were undermining the nurturing influence of the family; certainly his immigrant families, torn between the conflicting demands of two cultures, find little peace or sustenance in the new world.

Joe replaces his father with two successive surrogate fathers who seek to advance his career as a fighter: Tom Moody, his manager and chief rival for Lorna, and Eddie Fuseli, the gangster who eventually comes to dominate Joe's career. Moody serves as a kind of transitional figure here, his values falling somewhere between those of Mr. Bonaparte and his antithesis, Fuseli. Odets even demonstrates a certain affection for Moody, a man down on his luck and in need of a good fighter to revitalize his career as a manager. Joe appears, as discussed earlier, as if in answer to this need, and his declared allegiance works to rejuvenate the older man's spirits. Moody is also in need of a divorce from his wife so that he can marry Lorna, a much younger woman, and so he sees Joe not only as his economic salvation, but a "spiritual one as well." In act 1 Moody longs for the twenties, when the economy was booming and he was successful; he is like the country itself, decimated by the Depression, nostalgic for a former glory and hoping for some miraculous, youthful talisman to revive him. But Moody does not know what to do with the two young people who seem ready to perform this miracle for him: he wants only to exploit Joe's talent, regardless of his best interests or of the spiritual dilemma that troubles Joe, and, when the need arises, he exploits Lorna as well. When Joe seems doubtful as to whether to continue fighting, Moody uses Lorna, along with the promises of fame and fortune, to seduce him back to the ring. In consequence, he eventually loses both Joe and Lorna.

Jealous of Moody's hold on Lorna and increasingly impatient for greater success, Joe gravitates toward Eddie Fuseli, Odets's first truly loathsome character. Basically an outgrowth of the gangsterlike Moe Axelrod and Kewpie, but without any redeeming characteristics, Fuseli is clearly the villain of the play, and when Joe adopts him as his manager, his fall is complete.

A strong link between the two is established in the manner of his first entrance: he comes onstage unnoticed, interrupting a conversation betwen Moody, Tokio, and Lorna. Shortly after saying hello, he "drifts out of the scene on his cat's feet." A few minutes later, when Joe joins the conversation, he appears "unseen by others" and listens. Thus Odets is emphasizing that Fuseli, like Joe, is a figure of the theatrical world, a poetic double who will figure prominently in the drama of the soul that will unfold.

A significant element in Fuseli's resemblance to Kewpie involves the homosexual overtones with which Odets characterizes the two gangsters' relationship to the young men they befriend. There is in *Paradise Lost* some suggestion of such an attachment between Kewpie and Ben, and in *Golden Boy* Odets provides similar hints about Fuseli's attraction to Joe. When they first meet, the stage directions read, "curiously Eddie is almost embarrassed before Joe"; later Moody calls him a "queen." In addition, Odets associates Fuseli with a cluster of phallic images. After his initial appearance, Lorna comments, "What exhaust pipe did he crawl out of?" Later in the play he threatens her with a gun until Joe appears to stop him. The exhaust pipe image, further, links Fuseli to the Dusenberg that Joe buys and that eventually becomes his "coffin," as he rides it to his death. The gun and the car are two of the central iconographic images of the gangster film, and their prominent use here indicates that Joe's embracing of Fuseli constitutes another Odetsian indictment of the success ethic of America.

Other image patterns are equally suggestive. Just before Fuseli's entrance Moody is complaining to Lorna about getting Joe away from the influence of his home; he employs a vivid simile to express his concern: "We can't afford no more possible bad showings at this stage of the game. No more apparitions, like suddenly a fiddle flies across the room on wings!" (p. 274). After Fuseli appears, Moody once again waxes poetic: "Every once in a while he shoots across my quiet existence like a roman candle!" The images are similar but with widely differing connotations: Joe is described in transcendent terms, Eddie in phallic, violent ones. Once more, in the reiterated flight image, the linkage of music with death is reinforced.

These two image patterns become fused in the final scene of act 2 that takes place in a dressing room before a fight. Here the disparate elements of Joe's world converge, as Mr. Bonaparte, Lorna, Moody, and Fuseli all appear in the scene. Mr. Bonaparte's dissociation from this setting is emphasized in Lorna's greeting to him "What brings you to this part of the world?" and when Joe confronts his father he irrevocably breaks with his true father:

I have to fight, no matter what you say or think: This is my profession! I'm out for fame and fortune, not to be different or artistic! I don't intend to be ashamed of my life! (p. 298)

Shortly before this, he has remarked to Moody, "Eddie's the only one who understands me." Having thus rejected both his father and

Moody, he tells Tokio, his trainer, "Now I'm alone. . . . When a bullet sings through the air it has no past—only a future—like me." The image pattern thus echoes Moody's twin similes and confirms Joe's new spiritual allegiance to Fuseli. The act ends when Joe has knocked out his opponent. Returning to the dressing room, his "eyes glitter" and his hands are broken; this changed Joe exults, "Hallelujah! It is the beginning of the world!" Odets's stage directions are significant: "Joe begins to laugh loudly, victoriously, exultantly." He seems almost demonic, and Fuseli, Odets writes, "watches with inner excitement and pleasure."

However, Joe's most important relationship in the play is with Lorna Moon. Her name has overt symbolic overtones, but she functions effectively as a realistic character as well. On one level she feels that she is a "tramp from Newark," survivor of a rough childhood, and she looks to Moody, a man old enough to be her father, to make her respectable. She is impatient for Moody to get a divorce from his wife and marry her because, like Kewpie and Moe, she is anxious for a home. In Moody she is looking for a combination father and husband; Lorna wants what Joe seeks to escape.

When she meets Joe, however, her values are overturned, as she responds to the young man's tenderness and artistic aspiration. She is that familiar movie type, the cynical city girl who was really waiting for true love to rescue her from herself. In her two scenes in the park with Joe, her symbolic function is established, and they are the most expressionistic scenes in the play. Odets emphasizes carousel music and the changing colors of the traffic lights, seemingly projecting his characters into a world apart, where their true inner selves can be revealed. In act 1, scene 4 Lorna compares herself to a butterfly, a traditional symbol of the soul, and Joe literalizes the image when he asks her, "What does your soul do in its perfumed vanity case?" In the next scene, which takes place in the Bonaparte home, she reveals that she was once an airplane hostess, and Odets repeats the airplane image from *Awake and Sing!* again conjuring up the dream of leaving the earth behind in aspiration for a better life. Here Lorna seems to become a personified spirit of the music with which Joe needs to identify himself; he even explains this spiritual need to her in personal terms:

With music I'm never alone when I'm alone—Playing music . . . that's like saying, I am a man. I belong here. How do you do world—good evening!" When I play music nothing is closed to me. I'm not afraid of people and what they say. There's no war in music. (p. 263)

In this scene, however, Lorna is trying to persuade Joe to pursue his boxing career, though she will intuit the error of her ways by the end of the scene. Joe, too, despite his obvious attraction to Lorna, leans toward the other world, and he moves from this discussion of music and the soul to his desire to buy a car, which is "poison" in his blood.

Lorna's name supplies the most obvious symbolic undercurrent in Joe's attraction to her. The moon was a popular symbol among the Romantic poets, particularly Wordsworth and Coleridge, as the ultimate inspiration of poetic reverie and heightened imaginative consciousness. An effective example is found in Wordsworth's short poem, "A Night-Piece," where a glimpse of the moon affords the poet, "whose eyes are bent to earth," a glimpse of the infinite:

> He looks up—the clouds are split
> Asunder—and above his head he sees
> The clear Moon, and the glory of the heavens.
> There in a black-blue vault she sails along,
> Followed by multitudes of stars.

The moon again appears in a climactic scene in *The Prelude*, where viewing it, Wordsworth has a glimpse of "the soul, the imagination of the whole." Clearly, then, Joe must move toward this moon figure in the play, toward a reconciliation with the Dionysian spirit of the eternal. Lorna's name is not, as Margaret Brenman-Gibson writes, a symbol of the "cool, inhospitable, unattainable woman" for Joe has the ability to attain her if only he could resist the Apollonian ambition and understand his true nature.

Lorna, too, will be worthy of Joe when she recognizes her salvation in him and not in Moody, and she does so in act 2, scene 2, the second and last park scene. She is no longer trying to keep Joe away from music; Joe even compares her to his music: "You're real for me the way music was real." He wants her to teach him love and to be his family, his new life. The music in this scene is provided not by a carousel, but by a whistling duet that Joe and Lorna perform. After trying to resist him, even struggling with herself, Lorna admits to Joe that she wants him: "I've been under sea a long time! . . . Take me home with you."

Joe finally unites himself with Lorna after killing the Chocolate Drop in the fight ring. Now he understands how he has violated his own nature:

What will my father say when he hears I murdered a man? Lorna, I see what I did. I murdered myself, too! I've been running around in circles. Now I'm smashed! That's the truth. . . . But now I'm hung up by my finger tips—I'm no good—my feet are off the earth! (p. 315)

Lorna then declares her love for Joe and consoles him:

We have each other! Somewhere there must be happy boys and girls who can teach us the way of life! We'll find some city where poverty's no shame— where music is no crime!—where there's no war in the streets—where a man is glad to be himself, to live and make his woman herself! (p. 316)

Obviously she is referring to death, for no such place can exist in the real world. Joe understands this, realizing that in order to salvage his soul he must separate it from his body, and the language of his declaration strangely echoes Wordsworth's "A Night-Piece":

We'll drive through the night. . . . You're on top of the world then. . . . That's it—speed! We're off the earth—unconnected! (p. 316)

After the poet has been inspired by the moon, as noted before, Wordsworth likewise emphasizes speed:

> There in a black-blue vault she sails along,
> Followed by multitudes of stars, that, small,
> And sharp, and bright, along the dark abyss
> Drive as she drives: how fast they wheel away.

The play concludes in the Bonaparte home where Frank announces the deaths of Joe and Lorna to Mr. Bonaparte, Moody, and

Fuseli. The play's final words, "Joe . . . come, we bring-a him home
. . . where he belong," are spoken by Mr. Bonaparte, and they recall
Joe's description of music to Lorna in act 1, scene 4 as well as the
ending of O'Neill's *The Hairy Ape*. Odets labored over the ending,
changing the final speech a number of times before settling on this
rather elegant coda. In one draft Mr. Bonaparte flatly says, "Let us
go there . . . and bring the bodies home." In another draft the
conclusion is even less satisfying, as Frank cries, "What waste, what
waste . . . what ugly [foul] waste." The final version, in contrast,
conveys an acknowledgment that the true closure of the soul's longing comes only in death—perhaps it is the only true paradise. Or
possibly, as Odets demonstrates here in his compelling tragic vision,
paradise must rather be sought in the transcendent power of art to
unify and pacify the conflict of wills that undermines the human
condition.

Odets began writing *The Big Knife* in 1948, copyrighting it as "A
Winter Journey." He changed the title, it seems, late in 1948, having
extensively revised the play a number of times. In explanation, Odets
said that the earlier title implied "a difficult passage in one's life,"
whereas the new one alluded to "a force that moves against people."
This comment, in fact, illuminates an unresolved problem in the
play, for one title emphasizes character, the other exterior forces
operating on character. Much of the criticism of the finished play
would focus on the protagonist, Charlie Castle, as an insufficiently
developed character who was seemingly swallowed up in Odets's
vitriol against Hollywood. The early drafts confirm that Odets was
struggling to balance the exploration of character with the representation of forces operating from outside it.

When *The Big Knife* opened on Broadway in 1949, it was Odets's
first play there in eight years. The critics were not kind, as was
generally the case for the plays after *Golden Boy;* even Harold Clurman and Joseph Wood Krutch, always supporters, dismissed *The Big
Knife*. The play has fared no better with more recent critics of Odets,
and it has rarely been revived.

Much of the disparagement centers on the play's biographical
parallel, the critics complaining that Odets, who worked in Hollywood for many years after the collapse of the Group Theatre, was
protesting too much. Having made a great deal of money there,

now, it seemed, he was suddenly offering an extended bombastic apology for having abandoned his art and the "serious" work of the theater. Clurman criticized the play as defeatist and suggested that Odets was attempting to project his own sense of guilt onto society. More recently, Gerald Rabkin, in his study *The Drama of Commitment,* questioned the protagonist's climactic "act of faith," and unfavorably comparing the play to *Golden Boy,* wrote that *The Big Knife* presents no social alternative as does the earlier play.[8] Some of this criticism, particularly the biographical issue, is beside the point. Readings such as Rabkin's are more disturbing and need to be answered, for *The Big Knife* remains one of Odets's most widely misinterpreted and yet most compelling plays. (Only Edward Murray has attempted to deal with it in detail.)

Both Clurman and Rabkin imply that in this play Odets tried to write a serious tragedy, in a sense, to duplicate the strengths of *Golden Boy,* and simply failed. However, despite its many similarities to that earlier success, *The Big Knife* is sufficiently different in structure and technique to indicate that Odets was attempting here to convey his tragic vision in a very different mode. *The Big Knife* is, in fact, closer in form to *Awake and Sing!* and *Paradise Lost* than to *Golden Boy,* its action confined to a single set, "the playroom" of Charlie Castle's house in Beverly Hills. The sense of entrapment is made even stronger, for if the stage space of the two early plays was shared by family and friends, now it is a lone protagonist's space. Charlie remains at the center of the play, onstage continually until he goes upstairs to kill himself at the end. Other characters enter and leave this space, but no one stays for very long; it is as if everyone has access to the world outside the stage except Charlie, who is confined to the Hollywood castle that his own name betokens.

This intensive, and thematically significant, use of setting provides a strong resemblance to Ibsen's *A Doll's House,* a play that shares various motifs with *The Big Knife,* among them the exposure of a fatal secret from the past. Like Charlie Castle, Ibsen's Nora is confined to the drawing room of her home, and during the course of the play various characters, including her husband and children, become part of her world and then leave. She is the devoted wife and mother, nothing more, and while the others have access to the world outside the drawing room, Nora does not. Ibsen's point is that Nora, as a woman, is trapped in her society, just as she is trapped in her room, without scope for realizing any wider potential. Until she takes her life into her own hands and decides to transform herself, she remains a doll in a doll's house, neither a woman nor a human being. Her walking out at the play's end provides not only a spiritual release but a physical one as well, for by that time the audience has begun to feel as confined as Nora.

While the structures of the two plays are thus alike, the circumstances of their protagonists' captivity are quite different. Plainly, Nora is victimized by her society, locked into a box by the social dictates of her world; her conflict, then, is between herself and her husband and the larger world that her husband represents. Nora is a person who is acted upon, and until the end of the play she does not react to oppose or escape the restraining conventions of her situation. Charlie Castle, on the other hand, is trapped in a predicament primarily of his own making. Formerly a man of deep political conviction, a talented actor, and a loving husband, he is now a wealthy studio star playing endless variations of the same superficial role, estranged from his wife and son, and extremely dissatisfied with himself. The central issue of this play, as in *Golden Boy*, involves the protagonist's conflict of identity, here polarized in Charlie Castle's sense of his true self, represented by his real name Charlie Cass, and the corrupt self represented by his stage name Charlie Castle. Again, life has posed contrasting opportunities, entailing self-defining choices, and again the terms of choice require a dedication either to idealism or to materialism. The Hollywood environment exerts pressure on Charlie to surrender to his worst impulses, but Odets makes clear that this society, however flawed, is not the primary culprit, and that his protagonist, unlike Ibsen's, is and always was free to make his own choices. Charlie Castle's sense of detainment in the playroom that is Hollywood results from his belated recognition of the falsity of the values he has chosen to act upon in life.

Nevertheless, the Hollywood setting is important to the play's thematic design. In an interview before the Boston opening of the play, Odets declared:

The big knife is that force in modern life which is against people and their aspirations, which seeks to cut people off in their best flower. The play may be about the struggle of a gifted actor to retain his integrity against the combination of inner and outer corruptions which assail him, but this struggle can be found in the lives of countless people who are not on the wealthy level of a movie star. I have nothing against Hollywood per se. I do have something against a large set-up which destroys people and eats them up. I chose Hollywood for the setting for *The Big Knife* because I know it. I don't know any other company town. But this is an objective play about thousands of people, I don't care what industry they're in.[9]

This, of course, is rather disingenuous, for Hollywood is, as Odets was aware, more than a conveniently familiar "company town"; the very name of the place serves as perhaps the primary symbol of those cultural forces that endanger the "integrity" of the idealist in America. Edmund Wilson wrote, "Everything that is wrong with the U.S. is to be found there in rare purity." Certainly that is the basic premise of most literary representations of the Southern California scene; and the aspect of Hollywood most pervasively emphasized in the literature is its artificiality, as in Nathanael West's memorable image of a rubber horse at the bottom of a swimming pool in *The Day of the Locust*. For writers this falsity of environment underscores the betrayal of the promise of America: those who succeed in Hollywood learn that such material success is empty, while those who fail only see the chasm between dreams and reality all the more clearly.

Two prominent thematic motifs in *The Big Knife* are the abuse of sexuality and the meaninglessness of work, both problems commonly attributed to the hedonistic life-style of the moviemakers' society.[10] Sexual freedom was a prime component of the Hollywood image, at least until the lurid sex scandals of the twenties; by the midthirties Hollywood literature had replaced the orgiastic tone with one of either sexual revulsion or indifference, suggesting that the revelry of the past had given way to disillusionment and exhaustion. Similarly, the wild energy that had fueled the growth of the film industry had given way, in its heyday, to a complementary attitude toward the work itself. The work ethic, always a basic component of the American experience, was somehow betrayed in Hollywood, where the rewards were excessive, and the stories of people, especially writers, paid enormous sums for not working became legendary. The work, moreover, has always been seen as trivial, nonfulfilling, and debilitating.

Odets's characters and dialogue build upon these connotations of the Hollywood setting. The atmosphere of unreality is pervasive: Charlie's "playroom," where all of the action takes place, is itself a false front for the man he is not, for the piano and the paintings by Maurice Utrillo, Georges Rouault, and Amedeo Modigliani embody an artistic pretension that is belied by the movie industry and Charlie's films themselves. Even Charlie's professional name, Castle, is a glibly regal substitute for the more mundane Cass. In one of the play's most vivid exchanges, Charlie sums up Hollywood's affectation for his neighbor, Dr. Frary, explaining that "we all wear these beautiful expensive ties in Hollywood. . . . It's a military tactic—we hope you won't notice our faces."[11]

Another such façade of success and respectability is discredited in the portrayal of the various marriages in the play. The destructiveness of sexuality in its divorce from love and commitment has concerned Odets in earlier plays; here it becomes obsessive. Charlie Castle and his wife are separated when the play begins. As Charlie says, "The place is hell on married life!" Charlie hopes for a reconciliation with her, but the depth of their estrangement is revealed when, in act 2, Marion tells him what Hollywood has done to him and their relationship:

You've taken the cheap way out—your passion of the heart has become a passion of the appetites! Despite your best intentions, you're a horror . . . and every day you make me less a woman and more the rug under your feet! (pp. 62–63)

Meanwhile Charlie is indulging in an affair with the wife of a close friend, Buddy Bliss, who is likewise struggling to save his marriage. Charlie also has had an affair with Dixie Evans, who was with him in the car on the night of the accident in which a child was killed, and the concealment of this incident has fused the implications of sexual infidelity with the betrayal of friendship (Buddy Bliss was blamed for the accident) and the reckless, hit-and-run destruction of life. Near the end of the play when the studio fears that Dixie will talk about the incident, it is suggested that Charlie marry her to prevent her testifying against him in court. The dispassionate calculation of this proposal only reinforces the emptiness of the marriage bond in this Hollywood society.

The prime exemplar of Hollywood values in the play is the studio head, Marcus Hoff. In a lengthy speech in which he tries to persuade Charlie not to listen to Marion's plea that Charlie leave Hollywood and not sign a fourteen-year contract with the studio, Hoff delivers the industry's basic business pitch, based on the priority of moviemaking over the personal commitments of love and family. Feigning emotion for effect, he complains of his own wife's suicidal neurosis as an unpardonable interference in his business life:

One day, in my office—Smiley was there—Frank Lubner, a pioneer in the industry—I drank a light scotch and soda and I began to cry. I don't think I wept like that since I was a boy. Because I saw, by a revelation of pain, that my wife had determined, in her innermost mind, to destroy me and my career out of wilful malicious jealousy! You ask me why? I ask you why! But from that day on I realized an essential fact of life: the woman must stay out of her husband's work when he's making her bread and butter! The wife of a man in your position should have the regard and respect to advance his career! . . . Because sometimes it becomes necessary to separate ourselves . . . from a wife who puts her petty interests before the multiplicity of a great career! (p. 41)

Charlie's own dissipated life-style is in part a by-product of his disgust with his work, which he considers trivial and beneath contempt. In his films he plays a variation of the same role again and again from a series of properties that the studio buys for him. Charlie has, in effect, become a studio property himself, and by the time the play opens, this mechanization of his life and his art has become intolerable, although he continues to enjoy the money and the luxury of star status. Unlike Joe Bonaparte, or any other Odets protagonist, Charlie Castle is not aspiring toward material success when introduced; he has already achieved it and accepted it, and now he must deal with the implications of that acceptance. Charlie has seemingly realized the American dream, but the painfully divided consciousness resulting from his recognition of the various betrayals involved in the achievement make Charlie a tragic protagonist comparable to Joe Bonaparte in the exploration of the corruptibility of the American ideal.

Odets makes occasional oblique references to *Golden Boy,* both to emphasize the connection and to separate this new play from it. While talking to his best friend, a writer, Hank Teagle, Charlie observes:

CHARLIE: When I came home from Germany . . . I saw most of the war
  dead were here, not in Africa and Italy. And Roosevelt was dead . . . and
  the war was only last week's snowball fight . . . and we plunged ourselves,
  all of us, into the noble work of making the buck reproduce itself! Oh,
  those luscious salmon eggs of life!
HANK: If you feel that deeply . . .
CHARLIE: Get out of here? Does the man in your book get out of here?
  Where does he go? What, pray tell, does he do? Become a union organizer? Well, what does he do?
HANK: Charlie . . . I can't invent last-act curtains for a world that doesn't
  have one. You're still an artist, Charlie. (p. 111)

The Big Knife, then, represents a world that differs from Joe Bonaparte's more deeply than in its wealthy setting. *Golden Boy* was set
in a period when the seeds of World War II were being planted; now
the war is over, leaving behind it the postmodern world, wherein
people's hopes for the future have been drastically reduced. Charlie's
reference to becoming a union organizer is a direct reference to Joe's
brother Frank in *Golden Boy,* where Frank represented an alternative
to the success world of boxing. But the implication here is that
Frank's idealism and activism are now out of place and only another
pipe dream.

The loss of a kind of innocence is this fallen world is indirectly
evoked in the beginning of the play as well, when the gossip columnist Patty Benedict speaks of Charlie's killing "that child in your car."
In the context of the *Golden Boy* parallel, Odets is referring symbolically to Joe's essential youth and idealism—he, too, was killed in
a car—and possibly to Ralph and the Gordon children as well,
inhabitants of another time and another place. Charlie seems to be
related to these characters and yet somewhat beyond them. There is
an aura of hopelessness about him that did not figure in the earlier
plays, although Odets, again, does not allow the implication that this
man's life holds no possibilities. Hank's protest, "You're still an

artist," implies that the artist still possesses some power in society and may still act on his principles.

Charlie Castle is thus carefully differentiated from Joe, and he is also a more complex character. *Golden Boy* ends with Joe's realization that materialism will not make him happy and that the pursuit of it has tainted his soul. But Charlie is partly in love with his success, and he has been capable of sacrificing most of his integrity to it. Joe kills himself after he murders the Chocolate Drop, but Charlie manages not only to live with a killing, but even to let his friend go to jail in his place and then to sleep with that friend's wife. He does, however, stop short of deliberate murder: when the studio boss hints that Dixie Evans may be killed in order to ensure her silence about the accident, Charlie at last rebels against the cold-blooded evil of the business and his own implication in it.

Like other Odets drafts, the early version of *The Big Knife* is overly long and very preachy; in final form, its action is more compact and suggestive, and the forward movement more direct. The basic story outline remains the same, but Odets eliminates certain characters and cuts the parts of others in order to focus more narrowly on his central figure. Charlie's business manager, Harold Waterman, has an extended scene in the first draft but is only an offscreen presence contacted by telephone in the final version, while the character of a publicity agent named Jerry White is simply incorporated into Buddy Bliss. In the early drafts Buddy is an actor who knew Charlie when they were young men struggling to find work in New York. Still struggling, he has become Charlie's stand-in. In the final version the youthful association is retained, but Buddy's function changes.[12]

Odets's most revealing cuts and changes, however, relate to the character of Charlie Castle himself. In the early drafts Charlie is an incessant whiner and complainer, constantly moaning about what a terrible place Hollywood is while at the same time enjoying all of its rewards. Most unfortunately, he seems to blame the place and not himself for the moral surrender he has committed there. By the end of act 2, as a result, his suicide comes as rather a relief, which is clearly not what Odets had in mind. This early Charlie is also endowed with a more detailed past than the final version, but the detail only serves to simplify him, turning him into a typical agit-prop character from the thirties, an effect Odets wanted to move away from by 1948. The overt politicization of his character is apparent early in the play when Charlie speaks to the gossip columnist Patty Benedict about the death of his parents:

They were both killed in the Ludlow Massacre in 1912. That's one of the great scandals of what they call "the History of the American Working Class." Federal troops wiped out a whole tent colony of miners and their families who were striking for a better wage.

Meanwhile, Charlie's abandonment of his past is emphasized by his wife's identification of the symbol of what he has become:

You're debased. . . . Like the currency. In fact you're currency itself—every gesture and word modulated. Every real human impulse made negotiable.

Odets also introduces the subject of anti-Semitism in the early versions, which is interesting in itself, for although he was Jewish, this subject is rarely addressed elsewhere in his work. Charlie mentions that he was raised by his aunt and uncle after his parents' death. His aunt was not Jewish and, although married to his uncle, she was not, according to Charlie, fond of Jews. Later, when Charlie quotes his uncle, Patty remarks, "That's a very Jewified remark." Charlie replies, "I have nothing against Jewified remarks." Odets apparently seeks not only to allude to anti-Semitism in Hollywood, but also to associate Jewishness with the more moral aspects of Charlie's nature, from which he has distanced himself. This association extends also to the studio head, Marcus Hoff, a man of no moral fiber, whom Charlie calls an "apocalyptic beast" (a remark that was removed in the final draft), and Nat Danziger, Charlie's agent, who, despite a sweet nature, tends to look the other way for the sake of business. At one point utterly repelled by Hoff, Nat cries, "That a man like you is now a Jew to shame and harm my race!" This and all other references to Jewishness were also cut, as distractions from Odets's focus.

The Charlie of the early versions is obviously too completely an idealist, his change too simplistic. The final version exhibits little of this background, retaining only the information that Charlie was raised by an aunt and uncle and was once a stage actor in the East. This pared-down portrait is more suggestive than the original, not reducing Charlie or society to convenient stereotypes, but implying that the main flaw resides in Charlie, as Charlie himself is to some extent aware. He is an exceptionally imaginative man, and his qualities as an artist are attested by those around him. Odets emphasizes both that Charlie is (or at least was) an artist and not just another pretty face, and that Hollywood is fatal to Charlie because there is something within him that responds too readily to its lure. At the same time Hollywood represents the larger world, and when he surrenders to it, he becomes entangled in a web of fate. The play, indeed, unfolds as a series of circumstances that work to enmesh this protagonist in a horrific nightmare of his own making. Perceptive about his own ambition and the stimulation he receives from power and success, Charlie is also disgusted by his capitulation and remorseful about ignoring the dictates of his better self. At last his conscience overwhelms him as his imagination confronts him with the image of a damnable man. In an early draft he remarks, "To myself I am not an institution—I'm a weak, self-disgusted, very human man, very ordinary, guilty, . . . lonely . . . trapped."

Near the end of the finished play Charlie remarks to Nat Danziger, "It's too late, from *my* point of view. I can't go on, covering one crime with another. That's Macbeth. . . . Macbeth is an allegory, too: one by one, he kills his better selves" (p. 135). Clearly, Odets had *Macbeth* in his mind when he wrote *The Big Knife*; in an interview he referred to Dixie Evans as "Banquo's ghost." Like Macbeth, Charlie Castle is an extremely tormented character, perhaps the most suffering character in Odets's canon. In Edward Murray's words he is a character, "sickened by compromise and driven to self-destruction in an effort to expiate his sins." *The Big Knife*, therefore, is more than a simple attack on Hollywood, because Charlie's dilemma results as much from the divided nature of his own soul, torn between conflicting values and unable to reconcile them, as from the moral emptiness of his environment.

The early versions, in fact, display a number of references to *Macbeth* that were cut from the final. Near the play's end, for example, Charlie says to Marion, "Macbeth doth murder sleep." He then alludes to a web of deceit and hints at his suicide: "Burnham wood is moving up. I hope you know Shakespeare." There are also a number of references to blood, images of which permeate Shakespeare's play. In a scene later cut from the early portion of the play, Patty says to Charlie, "Blood's more saleable than water, sweetie. A thimbleful of blood is relished now and then by the best of readers." After Charlie's suicide, his butler comments, "All that blood, all that blood and water. . . . Ain't no blood left in him." Most important is Charlie's description of Hollywood:

I'm afraid of Hollywood because it's a tough, desperate world. They play for keeps here. It's as deadly as anything you read in Shakespeare, plots, intrigues, revenge, and cynicism—it's here, including corruption, intimidation, suicide and murder for succession.

In the tragic career of Odets's Macbeth figure, Hollywood, epitomized in the character of the producer Marcus Hoff, plays the role of Shakespeare's witches, tempting Charlie with wealth and fame undreamed of when he was a poor boy growing up in Philadelphia. There he read the authors in his uncle's library—Jack London, Upton Sinclair, Henrik Ibsen, and Victor Hugo:

Hugo's the one who helped me nibble my way through billions of polly seeds. Sounds grandiose, but Hugo said to me: "Be a good boy, Charlie. Love people, do good, help the lost and fallen, make the world happy, if you can!" (p. 9)

Having elected, instead, to pursue the promise of riches and power conveyed in Hoff's visions of moviemaking glory, Charlie now feels imprisoned by compromise and a life that violates his better nature. The burden of guilt generated by the fatal accident and its tangled consequences only objectifies the deeper sense of self-ruination that plagues him in the recognition that his success is hollow, that he has subverted his idealism and wasted his art for an ignoble goal. Marion voices this sense of spiritual loss in her complaint about the man Charlie has become:

Charlie, you're half asleep right now! I haven't seen you sparkle since the day Billy was born! You used to take sides. Golly, the zest with which you fought. You used to grab your theatre parts and eat 'em like a tiger. Now you act with droopy eyes—they have to call you away from a card game. Charlie, I don't want you to sign that contract—you've given the studio their pound of flesh—you don't owe them anything. We arrived here in a pumpkin coach and we can damn well leave the same way! (p. 22)

Charlie, however, knows that in his case no such fairy-tale exit is possible, for he has become too far embroiled in the ugly business of faked glamour and casual destruction. Throughout act 1 he agonizes over whether or not to sign the new fourteen-year contract with Hoff's studio; his compliance is at last extorted when Hoff threatens to expose Charlie's part in the hit-and-run accident. Critics have argued that this early capitulation robs the play of its dramatic tension, when its effect, rather, is to deflate the melodrama of Charlie's predicament, focusing the remaining action instead upon the emotional disintegration caused by his entanglement. Charlie's own sense of fatal incrimination is reflected in Smiley Coy's remark, "Just keep in mind that the day you first scheme . . . you marry the scheme and the scheme's children," which supplies a clear analogy to Macbeth's lament, "I am in blood stepp'd in so far that, should I wade no more, returning were as tedious as go o'er" (act 3, scene 4).

Odets's central thrust in the play is to bring Charlie to a final awareness of what he has become. Already in act 1 he seems to be aware of the falseness of his position, but he is not yet ready to accept fully his personal implication in the corruption he sees around him. Macbeth, too, knows his crimes, but only at the banquet scene does he reach his breaking point, when the true horror of his own nature is exposed to him. Charlie, likewise, proceeds toward his breaking point, remarking his progress of enlightenment in act 3, scene 1: "Murder is indivisible, Smiley. I'm finding that out. Like chastity, there's no such thing as a small amount of it. I'm finding that out" (p. 62). Finally, in act 3, scene 2, when he says to Marcus Hoff, "Now . . . I realize what I am," his understanding echoes Lady Macbeth's in a prior scene:

> Nought's had, all's spent,
> Where our desire is got without content:
> 'Tis safer to be that which we destroy
> Than by destruction dwell in doubtful joy. (act 3, scene 2)

At last he recognizes that in subverting his better self he has destroyed his family as well, that the comfort and joy he enjoys is very "doubtful" indeed.

Charlie's internal conflict is revealed primarily through his conversations with Hank Teagle, a close friend and a writer who has decided to renounce the Hollywood life-style and return East to work on a novel. Teagle is Marcus Hoff's opposite number, a kind of Banquo figure, reminding Charlie of what he once was and what he could do if only he could regain his youthful idealism. Teagle has even proposed to Marion, vowing to take her back to New York, to a more normal and fulfilling life; like Banquo, he will have the "heirs," whereas the wasted potential of Charlie/Macbeth will ultimately yield him nothing.

During a central conversation between the two friends Teagle tells Charlie about the book he is writing, "I still try to write out of Pascal's remark: 'I admire most those writers who tell, with tears in their eyes, what men do to other men.' This book is about a man like you" (p. 109). Explaining why he wants to take Marion away from the Hollywood environment, Hank expands the Hollywood metaphor to encompass an entire contemporary state of mind:

Marion's future interests me deeply. No. I don't think she'll be happy here with you! I don't want Marion joining the lonely junked people of our world—millions of them, wasted by the dreams of the life they were promised and the swill they received! They are why the whole world, including us, sits bang in the middle of a revolution! Here, of course, that platitude carries with it the breath of treason. I think lots of us are in for a big shot of Vitamin D: defeat, decay, depression, and despair. (p. 109–10)

Finally, he charges that Charlie is destroying himself trying to choose between moral values and success, sarcastically recommending that he simply yield to the Hollywood ethic: "Your wild, native idealism is a fatal flaw in the context of your life out here. Half-idealism is the peritonitis of the soul—America is full of it! Give up and really march to Hoff's bugle call!" (p. 110). When Hank leaves, Charlie is still torn, unable to act. Only when the studio pushes him to acquiesce in the murder of Dixie Evans does Charlie decide to take his fate into his own hands.

The conclusion of *The Big Knife* is in certain respects similar to

Golden Boy, as Charlie breaks with Marcus Hoff and so makes himself a Hollywood outcast. When he tells his agent Nat and then Marion that he now recognizes his own culpability and the degradation of his life, Odets employs an Ibsenian stage device to reinforce the suggestion of clearing sight, of startling enlightenment. As in *A Doll's House,* Charlie twice turns on a lamp in act 3, scene 2, once as he says, "Now I realize what I am" (p. 134). The second time, when he says good-bye to Marion, he observes, "Keep meaning to put larger bulbs in these lamps" (p. 139). In his farewell Charlie also remarks, "Aren't the times beyond us, cold and lonely? Far away as the stars." The image echoes Odets's use of the moon in *Golden Boy,* at once a death image and a romantic symbol of aspiration that moves the lovers beyond the bounds of the physical world. Embracing Marion, he pledges to her a better future, then goes up to the bath to slash his wrists. For Charlie, as for Joe Bonaparte, death represents the only way out of a spiritual dilemma.

Charlie's suicide is discovered by Smiley Coy and Marion when they notice a water spot behind the stairs, ominously recalling Lady Macbeth's inability to remove the blood spots from her hands during her mad scene. Charlie's suicide here precipitates Marion's madness, for after viewing the body, she begins screaming "help," the word that concludes the play. Odets's final stage directions read: "Hank has his arms around her, but the word does not stop and will never stop in this life" (p. 147). It is Odets's most devastating ending, indicating a tragic loss so profound that Marion, unlike Lorna, is unable to comprehend it.

The loss of Charlie Castle attains the dimension of tragedy because the man has come to recognize the futility of his worldly success as well as his own implication in the sordid business of maintaining it. Like Macbeth, he is guilty of a series of crimes committed in the pursuit of an ephemeral glory and in defiance of his own higher nature. Yet, like Shakespeare's overreacher, he is consistently portrayed as a man of stature, clearly superior to the Hollywood types who surround him, and commanding the love and loyalty of Marion and Hank Teagle, the two most sympathetic characters in the play. Just as Macbeth's preeminence as a soldier is established by the wounded soldier at the play's beginning, and his personal virtues attested by his wife and by Duncan, Charlie Castle's integrity and potential are indicated by the deference and affection of his friends and confirmed in the extraordinary perceptiveness he displays in judging his own actions. The weighty catalog of his sins is thus matched by the nobility of his spirit. Ensnared at the last in a mounting calamity of his own making, he destroys himself as "a final act of faith," a victim, like Macbeth, of the dagger of his own ambition.

5

Visions of Romance
Rocket to the Moon (1938)
Night Music (1940)

Conformity is basically a psychotic state. That is the frontier that has
to be opened. To hell with astronauts. To hell with the moon. There's
a whole sky in your chest that's waiting to be explored.
—Clifford Odets, 1962

When he started outlining *Rocket to the Moon,* which he called his
"dentist play," Odets had just come off his greatest hit, *Golden Boy,*
and was inundated with lucrative offers from Hollywood. The *New
Yorker* published a profile of Odets, "Revolution's Number One
Boy," in which John McCarten provided a very unflattering portrait,
presenting Odets as a hypocritical Communist party-liner now grab-
bing at all that Hollywood money. Deeply offended by the piece,
Odets sent McCarten a note saying, "Next time you need a couple of
hundred bucks, you don't have to cut anybody's heart for it. Come
to me and I'll be glad to give it to you."[1] He refused the Hollywood
offers, deciding to stay in New York and work on two current
projects, his labor play "The Silent Partner," and a play about Cuban
revolutionaries, "Law of Flight."

In 1938 the world was in turmoil, on the brink of a second world
war. Odets was torn between the desire to write about the so-
ciopolitical situation and the increasing pressure of his personal
troubles. The problems of maintaining dual careers on different
coasts were destroying Odets's marriage to the actress Luise Rainer.

94

She was working constantly, at one point making seven movies in three years, and she was at the height of her career. (She won Academy Awards in two succesive years, 1936 and 1937, for *The Great Ziegfeld* and *The Good Earth*.) Odets, meanwhile, was struggling with a series of plays that he could not effectively develop or complete. He and his estranged wife exchanged numerous letters and telegrams, trying to assert their love for each other while recognizing that career pressures were undermining their marriage. They had discussed having children, but both seemed hesitant. When in May 1938, Luise telegraphed that she was pregnant, Odets's reply was cold and indifferent. She decided then to have an abortion and file for divorce.

His marriage dissolving, Odets left for London on the *Queen Mary* with the Group to begin rehearsals for the English production of *Golden Boy*. He remained sullen during the trip, refusing to mention his marriage problems. During the voyage, however, a newspaper reported the breakup, the headlines proclaiming, "Luise Rainer Sues Odets for Divorce as a Sulker"; Sylvia Sydney cabled the news to Harold Clurman on the *Queen Mary*.

Golden Boy turned out to be an enormous success in London, the English press hailing Odets as the "white hope of English dramatic letters." Interviewed at the Mayfair Hotel, Odets expressed surprise that he had been compared with Shakespeare and George Bernard Shaw, adding, "I could have been a first-class composer but will always be a second-class playwright."[2]

As the months dragged on, Odets found himself increasingly preoccupied with his "dentist play." In the original outline, begun only a few weeks after his wedding to Luise Rainer, the secretary, Cleo, succeeds in winning the dentist from his wife. As he started to work on the play in a more concentrated way, he found that Cleo was taking over the play, replacing Ben Stark, the dentist, as the center of interest. Odets told Clurman that the new play would be about "love and marriage in America." By October 1938 he had copyrighted three acts of *Rocket to the Moon*, but, as was usually the case, he was still having trouble with the resolution. Luise had earlier told him that she thought it a mistake for Cleo to reject all the men, that she should accept one of them, probably Prince.

Odets continued to revise the play, even acting out a new third act for the Group during a Boston tryout, and during this time he reconciled with his wife. Still unsure of how to end the play, he inserted a coda (later eliminated) in which he added a traveling salesman who "found love and can't wait to get home to his wife." This character, Odets said, was to demonstrate that "love is possible," serving as an antidote to the more cynical Prince. He enters shouting, "War is declared!" which turns out to be a joke, for the man is declaring his own war on unsafe tires, claiming that he is selling safe ones. His cry, nevertheless, briefly evokes the political climate of the time, as the Spanish Civil War was ending with the victory of Franco.

Rocket to the Moon opened on November 24; Odets, expecting the play to fail, stood in the bathroom of the Belasco Theater, vomiting. The reviews, however, were mostly good, although the critical consensus held that the play was too long and the third act indecisive. Brooks Atkinson wrote in the *New York Times* that *Rocket to the Moon* was "a play torn out of the quivering fabric of life . . . written with the hard brilliance of his past work," and then added that "although Mr. Odets' rocket leaves the stage in the first act with a shower of sparks and a roar of glory, it bursts before it touches the moon." Richard Watts, Jr., of the *Herald Tribune* wrote:

Mr. Odets continues to be the most exciting and the most exasperating of the younger American dramatists . . . a writer of really brilliant first acts, fine and moving dialogue, true and breathing characters, of brooding power and of plays that end by being curiously disappointing.

Some critics were pleased that Odets had finally abandoned his economic focus and pronounced the play his most mature in its examination of human psychology. The play, however, did not do well at the box office. The Group tried alternating it with *Awake and Sing!*, but it closed after 131 performances.

Shortly after the opening of *Rocket to the Moon*, Odets appeared on the cover of *Time* magazine, the caption under his picture reading, "Down with the general fraud!" The piece was very complimentary to Odets:

The reason that Odets has gained and held a public that, by and large, does not share his Leftish ideas is obviously not the ideas themselves but his rich, compassionate, angry feeling for people, his tremendous dramatic punch, his dialogue, bracing as ozone. In every Odets play, regardless of its theme or its worth, at least once or twice during the evening every spectator feels that a firehose has been turned on his body, that a fist has connected with his chin.[3]

In 1938 the Group went to Lake Grove, a Christian Science children's school near Smithtown, New York, to prepare for what would be its final season. The outbreak of World War II affected the mood of the Group, introducing a feeling of desperation and gloom. It was announced that the Group would present Odets's adaptation of Chekhov's *The Three Sisters,* which was later abandoned, and his new play, *Night Music.*

During that summer, also, Odets began an affair with the actress Francis Farmer, who had joined the Group to play Lorna Moon in *Golden Boy.* She was at the time married to the actor Leif Ericson; Luise Rainer, at the same time, was having an affair in Switzerland. Odets eventually tried, unsuccessfully, to win Luise back and broke off his relationship with Francis Farmer. Meanwhile, he was working on *Night Music,* trying to write a more experimental play, what he called "a song cycle on a given theme." He would give voice not only to his own sense of homelessness, but to that of an entire generation as well.

At this time one of Odets's oldest friends, Albert Lewin, a film executive, asked Odets to join him in creating a new film company. Odets would later turn down this offer, but the association with Lewin would prove fruitful, for Odets eventually made a deal with Lewin to finance *Night Music,* contributing twenty thousand dollars toward the production. In turn, Odets agreed to write the screenplay for *Night Music* for Lewin's new company, Loew-Lewin (this project was never completed). Even so, Odets still had to provide twenty-one thousand dollars of his own money toward the production of his play.

Early in 1940 Odets was visited in his hotel room by a lovely teenage girl. She told him that she was sent by Harold Clurman, who thought that Odets might use her in the play. Within an hour he promised her that she could understudy the female lead and was making love to her. The girl was Bette Grayson, who would later become Odets's second wife and the mother of his two children.

The production of *Night Music* was complicated. Hans Eisler composed a musical score for the play, necessitating an orchestra at performances, and it required numerous large and detailed sets, which created technical problems. Odets, moreover, was concerned about what he considered as Clurman's "heavy-handed" direction. He was especially unhappy with Elia Kazan's performance as Steve Takis, which he thought uneven and too "boisterous and uncouth."

Night Music opened in Boston to very poor reviews. Odets discounted them as "provincial" and awaited the New York opening. The reviews in New York, however, were no better: the play was attacked by critics of the right and left. Devastated, Odets wrote in his journal:

> My feelings were and are very simple. I felt as if a lovely delicate child, tender and humourous, had been knocked down by a truck and lay dying. For this show has all the freshness of a child.[4]

Odets invested fifteen thousand dollars more in the show to keep it running, but soon decided that this was foolish; the play closed after twenty-two performances. Many years later, recalling this event, he told Peter Bogdanovich, "I went to the men's room and I cried. I cried for five minutes. And that was the end of the Group Theatre."

Rocket to the Moon and *Night Music* are both quest romances, linked thematically in that both concern a central character's need to find a home. The two plays differ, however, in structure, *Rocket to the Moon* recalling the single setting, "closed" structure of *Awake and Sing!* and *Paradise Lost*, while *Night Music* more closely resembles *Golden Boy*, its action more wide-ranging, more cinematic in conception.

A further linkage arises in Odets's use in each of these plays of a character who seems an emissary from another world. Clearly not intended to be realistic or consistent with the other characters, these figures function as poetic spirits or guides summoned from a world of romance to give the central character(s) glimpses of possibilities beyond their own experience. They become spokesmen for the liberating potential of romance as an alternative to the drab and

difficult world of social, economic, and political hardship that the
protagonists inhabit. In his earliest works, Odets had attempted to
deepen the resonance of the slice-of-life, realistic play, but had seen
no way out for characters trapped both within and without. Next
adopting the tragic mode, he found, especially in *Golden Boy,* more
freedom to explore the creative possibilities of the American experience. In these final two plays written for the Group Theatre, Odets
seems to want, instead, to impose some magical element on the
stage, as if to insert idealized images of his own sense of potential
into the lives of his characters.

Neither play is a romance in the strictest sense, but both exploit
romance conventions to important effect. Closer than any other
literary form to "the wish-fulfillment dream,"[5] the romance is characterized by the search for an imaginative ideal in time and space, and
it celebrates "fecundity, freedom, and survival."[6] Henry James wrote
that one of the central characteristics of romance was "experience
liberated." In some romances, particularly the more modern manifestations, the sought-after ideal is sharply contrasted with a sterile
world of mundane reality, where disease, poverty, and struggle
persist. Northrop Frye writes that romance is antithetical to "winter,
darkness, confusion, sterility, moribund life, and old age."[7] In
Freudian terms, the romance genre represents the impulse of the id
or libido toward a fulfillment of desires, toward freedom from the
difficult, ambiguous, and stark world of reason and necessity. In the
union of male and female, fertility and youth triumph over sterility
and age.

For Odets, romance is indeed the mythos of youth, which in these
plays is associated with the creative imagination. His romance figures inhabit a world beyond the Depression-decimated experience of
the other characters. The contrast is strongly felt between the youth,
innocence, flowers, and sunshine of the romantic spirit and that
other world of loneliness, pain, separation, and exile. In *Rocket to the
Moon* the Depression serves as a time frame and as a kind of emotional backdrop, but its economic effects do not pose a direct influence on the lives of the characters as in the earlier plays. Odets's focus
here is on the personal dilemmas of a varied group of troubled souls,
and his emphasis is heavily psychological. Of the plays he wrote for

the Group Theatre this work is most unusual in its scant reference to
the social situation of the outside world.

This play reproduces the formal closure of *Awake and Sing!* and
Paradise Lost, featuring a single set that remains unchanged
throughout the play. Again Odets emphasizes the characters' entrapment within that space (though here there are exceptions). Missing, however, are the lively family exchanges and the variety of
character types that charged the atmosphere of the earlier plays.
Now most of the characters are depressed, spiritually dead, and so
the set seems even more confining (and the play's title ever more
ironic). If the spirited dialogue of *Awake and Sing!* and *Paradise Lost*
sometimes "expanded" the stage space, here the characters' lethargic
interplay only echoes its constriction.

Rocket to the Moon locates this lifeless world in Ben Stark's dental
office, where the action takes place during a sultry June, July, and
August. Odets emphasizes the heat throughout the play as an at-
mospheric metaphor for the aridity of his characters' lives as well as a
physical force that deepens their discomfort and exposes them even
more sharply to the spiritual despair reflected in their barren environment. The single most important prop is a water fountain that
the characters continually turn to for refreshment, as if driven by an
unslakable spiritual thirst as well as the physical. Thus the symbolic
landscape of *Rocket to the Moon* anticipates *The Flowering Peach,* a
retelling of the Noah story, wherein a flood literally washes the
world clean. The need for water to revitalize a sterile society is
pervasive here as well, but in the modern world there is no god and
no miraculous salvation; man must confront the wasteland himself.
And, as usual, Odets's characters remain incapable of redeeming
themselves.

Even if no flood is provided to wash this world clean, Odets does
offer a vision of possible renewal in the character of Cleo Singer.
Much critical misunderstanding about the play has resulted from the
attempt to deal with Cleo as a realistic figure: Gerald Weales considers her a "weak character"[8]; John Gassner and Edmund Gagey
disliked her; even Clurman found her "rattlebrained and silly."[9]
Other critics judged her awakening at the end of the play unconvincing. Only Margret Brenman-Gibson sees her as the symbolic
character that Odets surely intended her to be.

Cleo functions as an emanation of the world of romance: by becoming one with her, one might take "a rocket to the moon." The titular link to the Lorna Moon of *Golden Boy* is significant, and Odets confirms it by giving the two women similar speeches:

LORNA: Somewhere there must be happy boys and girls who can teach us the way of life! We'll find some city where poverty's no shame—where music is no crime—where there's no war in the streets—where a man is glad to be himself, to live and make his woman herself![10]

CLEO: Don't you think there's a world of joyful men and women? Must all men live afraid to laugh and sing? Can't we sing at work and love our work? It's getting late to play at life; I want to *live* it. . . . You see? I don't ask for much.[11]

Apparently each of these women represents a spiritual ideal that the male protagonists must aspire to.

The romantic symbol of the moon represents both the imagination and sexual fulfillment. Lorna, in keeping with the plaintive vowel sound in her name, embodied also the death wish implicit in *Golden Boy's* tragic mood; the aspiration Lorna represented could be satisfied only in death, in a union delivered from earthly restraint. Cleo, on the other hand, is a figure free of death associations, which are inimical to her romance world. Her influence, indeed, seems strong enough to neutralize the pervasive gloom of her surroundings, for *Rocket to the Moon* is Odets's first play in which no character dies. Cleo's promise, it seems, is within the grasp of the other characters, if only they were capable of recognizing and responding faithfully to the vitality of her spirit.

Cleo, then, incorporates Lorna, but she offers much more: she *is* youth, romance, and love. She is, as Brenman-Gibson calls her, a "symbol of creativity,"[12] but it is a creativity not only artistic but spiritual and emotional as well. Her name suggests both Cleopatra, the girl-queen for whom men would sacrifice empires, and Clio, the muse of history and lyre playing (the Greek word *kleos* signifies glory and reputation, which includes immortality in heroic poetry). "Cleo" also, as Brenman-Gibson points out, combined CL (Clifford) and O (Odets), so that Odets seems to be presenting in Cleo his own personal muse.[13] The surname Singer carries obvious, collateral connotations.

Although he conceded to Cleo certain recognizable human traits, Odets clearly intended her to function as a symbolic character, and she possesses as well some attributes of the typical romantic heroine. Frye discusses the romance genre's emphasis on virginity, pointing out that within the social conditions of the form, a woman's virginity corresponds to a man's honor, as "the symbol of the fact that she is not a slave."[14] Another convention he examines is this virginal heroine's need to resort frequently to craft and fraud in pursuit of the man she loves. At times disguise is a necessary tactic, an example being the charade carried out by Shakespeare's Rosalind, who must renew her inventions throughout the play. The orthodoxy of her conduct is acknowledged in her line: "I shall devise something; but I pray you, commend my counterfeiting to him."

In his play Odets, likewise, emphasizes his heroine's youthful innocence as well as her habit of imposture. Cleo's naive manner further distinguishes her from Lorna, "the tramp from Newark," who was introduced as the mistress and figurative "slave" of Moody, later to be set free by the love of Joe Bonaparte. Cleo evinces no such entrapment; at the end of the play she admits to having led a "difficult" life, but her involvements seem to have had little effect on her spirit. Like Rosalind, she readily invents stories about herself in order to attract the admiration of Ben Stark, the man she loves. She poses as a wealthy woman, declaring that she does not need her job as a dental assistant, masquerades later as a dancer and then a socialite, and claims to have visited California several times. Of course, none of this is true, but it serves a psychic purpose as part of her ruse, her romantic guise. On a purely realistic level, she is using these stories to make life more glamorous, and thus more "real" for herself.

The play opens on a very hot June afternoon in Ben Stark's office, where he and his wife Belle are involved in an argument. Ben wants to move to a new office in a nicer neighborhood and to specialize his practice; Belle wants him to stay put, afraid that the expense of such a move could ruin them. Again Odets begins a play on a note of tension between movement and stasis; within the image framework of this play, the conflict is between rejuvenation (transplantation) and gradual, wilting death. Odets makes an immediate visual parallel between Ben and a window box of drooping petunias that he gets up to water while speaking with Belle. He has trouble managing both his pipe and two cups of water, and so Belle has to help him—the element of sexual and re-creative innuendo in this simple stage business enables Odets succinctly to establish his dramatic themes of spiritual thirst and sterility and to define the nature of the Stark marriage.

Belle, like many women in Odets's work, dominates her husband. A determined realist, she argues from an economic standpoint while he dreams. Her comment, "Any day now I'm expecting to have to powder and diaper you," indicates that she is not only the boss but also a parent figure under whose dominance Ben has abdicated his potential for growth. Ben himself laments this lost potential:

I was a pioneer with Gladstone in orthodontia, once. Now I'm a dentist, good for sixty dollars a week, while men with half my brains and talents are making their twenty and thirty thousand a year! (p. 330)

When the couple's conversation turns to the other two central characters in the play, Mr. Prince, Belle's father, and Cleo Singer, the deep roots of Belle's own repressive personality are exposed. Estranged from her father, she blames him for her mother's evident misery: "If you'd seen the life of hell he gave my mother, you'd understand." Mr. Prince, a widower, would like to live with his daughter, but Belle refuses, and during the course of the play they resolutely try to avoid each other. For his part, Prince disparages Belle's mother, at one point implying that she was an unsatisfactory sex partner and accusing her of sapping his ambition:

In spite of her! I shouldn't be ambitious. Go work for somebody else for twenty dollars a week—a man with my brains! Play safe! A housewife's conception of life! (p. 347)

Clearly the troubled home life of Belle's childhood continues to distort her capacity for love. Because of her father she mistrusts men; she clings desperately to her husband—"I have to know my husband's there, loving me, needing me"—but because she is her mother's daughter, she has trouble expressing affection. The trauma of the past is further compounded by her present inability to have children. Now, on the third anniversary of the death of the Stark's baby,[15] Belle is brooding about her loss, and Ben's feeble reminder that "it's not as if we had him . . . he died at birth" cannot assuage her frustration and deep sadness. Like many Odets characters, Belle is looking for a psychological "home," but her wounded personality makes it impossible for her to find one.

Ben, too, is a frustrated, emotionally paralyzed individual, and like his wife's, his unhappiness seems to predate their marriage. Revealing in act 1 that he was an orphan raised in an orphanage in Philadelphia, Ben announces himself another lonely individual looking for a home. (The word "lonely" is repeated often in the play.) Apparently, Ben and Belle came to each other in a mutual quest for a stable family life, but the desperation of their emotional needs camouflaged the incompatibility of their natures. Ben displays a pensive, aesthetic bent that jars against his wife's hardheaded practicality. He loves to read Shakespeare and twice quotes from his work to Cleo. Belle, on the other hand, does not appreciate her husband's interest in Shakespeare and even resents the relationship he had with Dr. Gladstone, his teacher. Ben also demonstrates a love for flowers and speaks of his interest in botany. The implication is made that Ben may have violated his better self in choosing his prosaic career, perhaps motivated by the desire to please Belle. But Ben is not simply the victim of his wife's bitterness, for his wistful idealism seems just as stagnant as her pragmatism.

The opening sequence of the play thus establishes its primary thematic focus on a blighted emotional climate that finds objective reflection in the oppressive summer heat. Odets emphasizes the need for water, real and symbolic, for revitalization, and also introduces, in the unhappy couple's conversation, the concepts of loneliness and death. During the scene Ben is smoking a pipe, which Belle tells him repeatedly to "move away" from her; the reiteration of this obvious phallic image typifies the sexual frustration of the couple and suggests their inability to confront it openly.

During this verbal dissection of the Stark's future and their past, Cleo arrives—significantly, she enters just as Belle proclaims to Ben, "You know as much about women as the man in the moon." The first impression Cleo creates is that she is unsuited to her job as a dental assistant; she is late and she has forgotten to put an ad in the paper for Ben. More important, however, as Odets's emphasis indicates, are her symbolic qualities: her dress is made of "angel-skin satin" and she wears her hair "up in the air." Belle immediately attacks her for inefficiency and for the inappropriateness of her dress. Although Ben has backed down from his desire for a new office and a specialized practice, Belle clearly perceives in Cleo a threat to her renewed dominance and the grim security of her marriage.

Stressing the young woman's beauty and her pretensions to wealth and self-sufficiency, Odets, too, connects Cleo with the suppressed aspirations of Ben. Psychologically, she represents, as Brenman-Gibson points out, "the central identity element of the play, not yet the central character in its formal structure."[16]

Belle's confrontation with Cleo is interrupted by the arrival of Dr. Cooper, another dentist who rents office space from Ben and is now three months behind in his rent. Cooper is an utterly defeated man: his practice is a failure; he has no patients. His wife has died, and his son has just broken his arm—he jokingly says, "That's the only break I've had in years." He goes immediately to the watercooler, and he uses it continually throughout the play. He, too, incurs Belle's wrath, for not paying the rent and for his drinking. She threatens to throw him out of the office but backs down when she learns of his wife's death, mainly because she identifies with Cooper's motherless children.

Cooper functions as a warning figure for Ben, his disillusion and despair—"In my younger days, I was inclined to poetry. In my older days I'm inclined to poverty"—prefiguring Ben's eventual state if he does not take the chance to ally himself again with the "poetry" that Cleo represents. In juxtaposing scenes of Belle with Cleo and with Cooper (whose name carries both a connotation of confinement, in the sense of "cooped up," and a possible death reference, in its specific reference to a maker of casks or tubs), Odets enumerates Ben's possibilities: one offering rejuvenation and growth, the other emphasizing defeat. In Cooper, Ben and the audience may glimpse the painful consequences of forsaken idealism in the life of a man overwhelmed by the pressure of the mundane.

Belle's exit, soon after that of Cooper, clears the way for the arrival of Mr. Prince who has waited to avoid his daughter. Buoyant, vital, and successful, Prince is the most dynamic character in the play. Odets's description dwells upon these qualities:

There is about him the dignity and elegant portliness of a Jewish actor, a sort of aristocratic air. He is an extremely self-confident man with a strong sense of humor which, however, is often veiled. He is very alive in the eyes and mouth, the rest of him relaxed and heavy. (p. 339)

The first person Prince meets is Cleo, and he is immediately attracted to her, speculating that she needs someone to support her. When she tells him that she aspires to be a dancer, Prince replies that he, too, had great plans once but that his life has been ruined by his wife and daughter. Allied with Ben in his love of art, Prince remains bitter that his success has come in business, that his talent has found no aesthetic use, and for this, as usual, he blames his wife. The implication of this play, as of *Awake and Sing!* and *Paradise Lost,* is that such oversimplified self-pity is always suspect and of little use in confronting any more immediate problems. Prince, however, revels in the impression of his victimization, even reiterating his reasons for not realizing himself, as expressed to Ben earlier in the scene, and accusing his wife of "insulting his soul."

In the scene with his son-in-law, however, Odets subtly reveals the depth of Prince's despair. Ben's insinuation that Prince had affairs produces a break for the first time in the older man's air of self-confidence. He yells back at Ben: "Never! But NEVER! Not once did I make a sexual deviation!" but the exaggerated emphasis on the second "never" suggests that Ben has hit a nerve. Prince protests further that his wife "had more respectability under the blankets than you have on Fifth Avenue." Then Odets again indicates a shift in his composure; the stage directions read, "Now masking his feelings again," as Prince goes on to say:

Drip, drip, the matrimonial waters go, and a man wears away. My wife is dead, I'm an old man who missed his boat. Ida Prince had her revenge . . . her husband has disappeared in the corner, with the dust, under the rug. (p. 347)

When Ben disputes this, saying that Prince has not disappeared, his father-in-law again becomes passionate: "Without marriage I would have been one of the greatest actors in the world! . . . You don't believe it?" (p. 347). This sequence of exchanges reveals how vulnerable Prince is to the twin suspicions that he must have been as responsible for his wife's unhappiness as she was for his and that his dream of becoming a great actor was only an illusion, betrayed by his own failure of nerve. It seems that his memories have become confused by the habit of self-pity, and the resulting sense of uncertainty leaves him with ambivalent emotions about his present situation. His attempt to encourage Ben to have an affair with Cleo suggests that he still harbors strong resentment, for it is really a means to revenge himself on his wife through the daughter who is her present embodiment, and to hurt his daughter at the same time. However, his own loneliness prompts a sincere desire to move in with the Starks; to save face he insists it is because he likes Ben. Prince realizes that such an arrangement would force him to confront Belle, the exponent of her mother's suffering and chief accuser of her father's hypocrisy. Apparently, Prince feels the need to face this reckoning, but as an old man he is desperately afraid to deal with its implications.

Odets's characters are psychologically compelling, but his dramatic method, as in *Awake and Sing!* and *Paradise Lost,* remains indirect, challenging the audience to penetrate the oblique dialogue in order to discover motive and meaning. Ben, Belle, and Prince, though agonizingly conscious of their personal predicaments, are unable to articulate them, and their tactics of circumlocution add poignancy to the dialogue. This method, again, is Chekhovian; in terms of its "action" *Rocket to the Moon* may be the most Chekhovian of Odets's plays, because no perceptible change occurs in the basic situation. The characters talk a great deal about themselves, about the weather, and about love, but nothing actually happens. (Odets even eliminates such melodramatic devices as Jacob's suicide and Ben's death; as mentioned earlier, there are no deaths in this play.) In the process, much is revealed about the emotional state of this troubled family, but the characters are no different at the end than at the beginning. Only the causes and conditions of their mutual frustration have acquired sympathetic depth and significance.

Odets, however, has introduced Cleo into this stagnated world, and her sensuous charm provokes these sleepwalkers to a new awareness of their failures and of the inadequacy of the lives they lead. After the emotional confrontation between the two men Prince looks longingly at the Hotel Algiers, which can be seen from Ben's office window. Evocative in name and comparatively vital in aspect (the flashing red light that issues from its neon sign promises both energetic commerce and sexual adventure), the hotel functions in the play as a symbol of freedom and, in Brenman-Gibson's view, of "sexual vitality."[17]

Gradually it becomes a symbolic alternative to the constricted and suffocating world of the Starks; it is associated with Cleo, and with the romantic possibilities she represents. Urging Ben to change a life "where every day is Monday," Prince elaborates:

Why don't you suddenly ride away, an airplane, a boat! Take a rocket to the moon! Explode!

Laugh. . . . But make a motto for yourself: "Out of the coffin by Labor Day!" Have an affair with—with—with this girl . . . this Miss Cleo. She'll make you a living man again. (p. 350)

The coffin image, echoing *Golden Boy,* offers another death image: Ben is pictured as spiritually dead and in need of what Cleo offers, sexual rejuvenation—the image of an exploding rocket is obvious— and liberation of the spirit. Again Prince blames Belle for Ben's troubles, but Ben twice rejoins, as he himself senses, "It's not Belle's fault."

However, when Prince leaves, Ben becomes visibly upset, the placid composure he maintained before Belle and Prince now giving way to nervous abstraction. When Frenchy, a chiropodist who also has an office nearby, enters, Ben tells him that his father-in-law is "gloomy" and that "he disturbs me." Then he goes on to describe the malaise that has come over him:

A man falls asleep in marriage. And after a time he wants to keep on sleeping, undisturbed. I'm surprised how little I've thought about it. Gee!— What I don't know would fill a book. (p. 351)

Ben will repeat these words, to overwhelming effect, at the play's end.

Frenchy is described by Odets as an "amateur student of human nature in all its aspects." He occupies a midpoint among the characters in the play, neither totally defeated like Cooper (who announces, "I'm dead," as he enters) nor yet susceptible to the dreams of romantic renewal that will inspire Ben and Prince. Frenchy, indeed, proclaims the fallibility of such dreams:

Who can do that today? Who's got time and place for "love and the grace to use it?" Is it something apart, love? A good book you go to in a spare hour? An entertainment? Christ, no! It's a synthesis of good and bad, economics, work, play, all contacts . . . You have to bring a whole balanced normal life to love if you want it to go! (p. 404)

Insofar as the play's conclusion bears him out, Frenchy must be seen as the play's thematic spokesman.

Ben, nevertheless, is now ready to pursue his attraction to Cleo. When she enters at the end of act 1, Odets writes that he "looks at her as if he had never seen her before." When they are alone together and Cleo complains about Belle's scolding, Ben for the first time asserts his independence: "Mrs. Stark runs my home. I run the office." Unsure of himself and unable yet to express his emotions, Ben, again, speaks indirectly, instructing Cleo about the cleaning of dental instruments. Odets, however, makes clear the unspoken undercurrent of feeling when at the end of the scene, Ben moves to the window, and looking at the Hotel Algiers, fills and lights his pipe, that same symbolic prop that Belle protested about so insistently at the beginning of the act.

The remainder of the play concentrates on moving Ben closer to Cleo, allowing him a taste of the sensual experience that is so contrary to the aridity of his marriage. Act 2 opens upon him reading a volume of Shakespeare and smoking his pipe—another visual linkage of art and the imagination with sexual fulfillment. Cleo, significantly, sits by the watercooler. When Ben's pipe goes out, she gives him matches, directly counteracting Belle's stifling efforts, and then she brings him a cup of water. Thus associated with water and fire, Cleo clearly represents fertility as opposed to Belle's sterility, and her sexual aura is enhanced further in its affinity for the "creative fire" of Shakespeare. Ben then tells her of his attachment to Dr. Gladstone, who gave him the copy of Shakespeare, and it is implied that this mentor was an inspiring influence in Ben's life. But, like the stillborn baby and Belle's mother and Cooper's wife, Gladstone has died before the action of the play, reinforcing the pervasive sense of loss. Ben remarks, also, that Belle didn't like Dr. Gladstone, another indication of her chronic opposition to Ben's aspirations. Next, he reads a part of Shakespeare's Sonnet 70 to Cleo:

> For slander's mark was ever yet the fair;
> The ornament of beauty is suspect,
> A crow that flies in heaven's sweetest air.
> So thou be good, slander doth but approve
> Thy worth the greater. (p. 361)

Alluding to Frenchy's (and Belle's) hostility to Cleo, he is assuring her that this only increases her worth in his eyes.

Cleo, whom Odets portrays as a nymphet figure—she later vacuously informs Ben that underneath her flimsy dress she is naked—announces that she can't read Shakespeare because "the type is too small." Plainly, hers is not a developed consciousness; she lacks education and her reactions are childlike: she tells Ben that "happiness is everything" and speaks of her love of parties and dances. She also tells him that she loves to go on cruises and that traveling "by air back and forth" must be sublime.

The images of flight hark back to *Awake and Sing!* wherein Ralph regularly associated flying with escape to a world beyond the real. Unlike Ralph, however, Cleo is not bound by the mundane world, for she herself embodies the dream of escape. Her physical presence carries so potent a charge in this barren environment that experiencing her is like taking a cruise or an airplane flight.

Ben's intoxicated response to Cleo's naive zeal is, "I believe everything you want me to believe, Cleo." His reaction recalls Ibsen's *The Master Builder*, wherein a very young girl reawakens the aging protagonist's awareness of his capacity for artistic and sexual fulfillment, inspiring him to climb the tower and achieve his tragic destiny. Ben Stark, however, is no Solness, and *Rocket to the Moon* no tragedy; Odets's protagonist seems incapable of acting upon the romantic stimulation offered by his muse. The oddly spiritual dimension of her sexuality becomes more emphatic when Cleo remarks, "I don't care to think. Sometimes I wish I didn't have a head" (p. 372), and then adds, "Everybody forgets how to dream." Later she tells Ben that the purpose of life "is to live all you can and experience everything" (p. 374). Cleo functions here rather boldly as an id figure, advocating a hedonistic freedom from the restraint of reason. When she suddenly asks Ben to come to her and hold her, he does so and the scene concludes with their "fierce embrace."

This desperate caress is interrupted by Prince, who, as the ensuing scene will demonstrate, presents a vivid opposite to his son-in-law. Impetuously deciding to seduce Cleo himself, he is not hesitant, but emphatic and self-assured in action. Despite his age, he compares himself to her, declaring that he has "a body like silk" and "a voice of velvet." Crudely aggressive, he calls her "a honeydew melon—a delicious girl," and the image echoes Moe's bold pursuit of Hennie, whom he likened to an orange, in *Awake and Sing!* Unlike Hennie (and unlike *Golden Boy's* Joe with Fuseli), Cleo resists the worldly, successful man; she is neither desperate nor ambitious enough to accept his swaggering courtship. She will, however, respond to honest need and love, and since Ben is the man most obviously in need of her romantic redemption, Cleo can approach him in a spirit of love. Their renewed embrace at the end of act 2, scene 1 confirms her choice.

Scene 2 takes place a month later, and it repeats certain patterns of the previous scene. Like scene 1, this one opens upon Cleo and Ben, but there is a new element of tension between them, for Cleo is upset about Ben's continuing deference to his wife. Cleo receives a telephone call from Prince, who invites her to a concert, but she turns him down. Then she is confronted by Frenchy, who is concerned about Ben and warns her not to "take him over the coals. Unless you're serious, unless you love him." When he "smacks an imaginary moth between his palms," saying, "That was you, in effigy and promise!" Frenchy clearly indicates that he does not share Ben's idealistic view of Cleo, and warns her not to hurt his friend. The opening moments of scene 2 thus undercut the ecstatic climax of scene 1, and Odets enforces the mood of disillusion by introducing Willy Wax, a theatrical producer and patient of Ben's. A vulgar variation on Prince, he, too, is a successful and confident man who immediately fixes his leering attention on Cleo and offers her the patronage that could foster her dream of becoming a dancer. She is attracted by this prospect, and agrees to have lunch with him. Characteristically for Odets, Wax's offer to share with her his lunch of "stewed fruit" serves as an indication that he will not be able to offer Cleo what she wants. The climate of discontent then reaches its oppressive extreme as Belle returns, upset that Ben has been ignoring her, and proceeds to vent her anger at his behavior. For the first time in the play Ben speaks back to his wife:

Will you stop that stuff for a change! It's about time you began to realize there are two ends to a rope. I have needs, too! This one-way street has to end! I'm not going to stay under water like an iceberg the rest of my life. You've got me licked—I must admit it. All right, I'm sleeping, I don't love you enough. But what do *you* give? What do you know about *my* needs? (p. 393)

When, a few minutes later, the scene concludes with Ben looking at the Hotel Algiers and then kissing and embracing Cleo, Odets teases the audience with the possibility that the two come together and somehow manage to escape the stagnation of everyday reality.

Scene 2 has been criticized as a carbon copy of scene 1, hence lacking in dramatic impact. This assessment, however, ignores the effect of Odets's subtle variation of tempo in the second scene. Whereas, in scene 1, Ben is shown as tempted but still tentative and the climactic embrace as a promise of rebirth, scene 2 is more confrontational, with Prince, his surrogate Willy Wax, and Belle all seeming to band together to defy that prospect of escape. Frenchy, the chorus of the play, even implies that the union of Ben and Cleo is impossible. Thus the lovers' embrace at the end of scene 2 is more dramatic, especially after Ben's bitter confrontation with Belle. Rather than another version of Ralph, who backs away from his chance for love, Ben here displays the potential at least to take his future into his own hands, like Joe Bonaparte. This sense of real possibility will render his defeat in act 3 all the more poignant.

As was the case with earlier Odets plays, the third act of *Rocket to the Moon* was disparaged by critics as vague and indecisive. Again, this judgment demonstrates a limited appreciation of Odets's method, for in fact the action is powerful and exceptionally well structured. Here Odets has Ben confront his three central antagonists—Belle, Prince, and Willy Wax—meanwhile discussing his dilemma with Frenchy, who voices caution and concern for his friend's growing anxiety. By keeping Ben at the center of the action in this final act, Odets emphasizes that he is the play's protagonist; the chaotic rhythm of this final act reflects his indecisiveness and confusion.

The act opens like the first, with Belle and Ben, "each one revolving in his own tight little world." She is desperate and willing to forgive his affair with Cleo, but Belle's mounting emotion frightens Ben and he is unable to respond clearly to her agitation. When she demands, "It was only a thing of the moment, wasn't it? Wasn't it? Do you hear me—wasn't it?" Ben replies, "Yes! Yes!" but then adds that he has a responsibility, ostensibly, to Cleo. However, as Brenman-Gibson points out, Ben is not really referring to Cleo as much as to himself;[18] it is his responsibility to liberate himself from the "tight little world he is in." Unappeased, Belle leaves in anger, whereupon Ben turns out the light and sits in the dark. Symbolically this image prefigures his position at the end of the play.

At this point Fenchy enters. Ben remarks that he will soon be forty but "feels like a boy," and this feeling prompts him to ask, "Don't you want to get married?" Frenchy's reply in part reflects Odets's thematic judgment that love is not possible in the depressed modern world:

In this day of stresses I don't see much normal life, myself included. The woman's not a wife. She's the dependent of a salesman who can't make sales and is ashamed to tell her so, of a federal project worker . . . or a Cooper, a dentist . . . the free exercise of love, I figure, gets harder every day. (p. 404)

Frenchy's melancholy philosophizing, however, is soon interrupted by Prince, who comes in announcing that rain is expected, promising some relief for Odets's hot, parched wasteland. Prince is anticipating the refreshment of his own arid life as well, for he announces that he intends to propose to Cleo. He tells Ben, "Last night I fell asleep and dreamed the secret of the world. It is not good for man to live alone." Thus goaded into admitting that he loves Cleo, Ben becomes wild with jealousy and orders Prince to leave the office. He accuses his father-in-law of wanting to "buy" Cleo and calls him a villain. Prince's reply is among the most passionate in Odets's work:

Remember, Dr. Benny, I want what I want! There are seven fundamental words in life, and one of these is love, and I didn't have it! And another one is love, and I don't have it! *And the third of these is love, and I shall have it!* De corpso you think! I'm dead and buried you think! I'll sit in the long winter night with a shawl on my shoulders? Now you see my face, Dr. Benny. Now you know your father-in-law, that damned smiling villain! I'll fight you to the last ditch—you'll get mowed down like a train. I want that girl. (p. 408)

At last articulating his sense of frustration and loneliness and his need for the rejuvenation that Cleo represents, Prince is in turn interrupted by his less-attractive double, Willy Wax, who, because he has failed to seduce Cleo, consigns her to "the last century where she belongs," explaining disgustedly, "she's old-fashioned, romantic— she believes in love!" Ben reacts to Wax in the same way he reacted to Prince, commanding him to leave Cleo alone. Cleo then enters to second that ultimatum, declaring that Wax makes "love very small and dirty."

At this point Ben is exhausted; his confrontations with Prince and with Wax have made him feel soiled, and he leaves to "wash his hands." But neither the rain, which Cleo also announces, nor his own immersion in water will revive him. Prince then confronts Cleo with his declaration of love and challenges Ben to take a position. Now passive and unable to respond any longer to Cleo's love, Ben can say nothing except, "Help me." He tries to explain his sense of defeat and impotence:

Listen, Cleo . . . think. What can I give you? All I can offer you is a second-hand life, dedicated to trifles and troubles . . . and they go on forever. This isn't self-justification . . . but facts are stubborn things, Cleo; I've wrestled with myself for weeks. This is how it must end. Try to understand . . . I can't say more. (p. 415)

Prince, then, makes a last effort to win Cleo's companionship:

Miss Cleo, believe me, life is lonely, life is empty. Love isn't everything. A
dear true friend is more than love—the serge outlasts the silk. Give me a
chance. I know your needs. I *love* your needs. . . . What do you have to lose?
(p. 416)

When Cleo rejects him as well, Prince suddenly defines both the
charm and the elusive naïveté of Cleo's youthful idealism:

By what you don't know, you can't live! You'll never get what you're looking
for! You want a life like Heifetz's music—up from the roots, perfect, clean,
every note in place. But that, my girl, is music! (p. 416)

Cleo, who has functioned as the embodiment of this aesthetic wholeness, will go off alone to seek her own destiny in a world of joyful
men and women, where we "sing at work and love our work."
    Prince and Ben are, at last, left alone in the office, as Prince
pronounces their mutual doom, "But now, my iceberg boy, we both
have disappeared." This line is full of pain and sorrow, acknowledging that both men have lost their last hope for self-realization
through romantic love. Ben, like Odets's other *luftmensch* dreamers,
denies this and in an outburst reminiscent of Ralph, who was also
unable to take a chance on love, says:

Poppa, wait a minute. . . . For years I sat here, taking things for granted, my
wife, everything. Then just for an hour my life was in a spotlight. . . . I saw
myself clearly, realized who and what I was. Isn't that a beginning? Isn't it?
(p. 418)

But Ben will not make a new beginning any more than Ralph, for
they are both "as mixed up as the twentieth century." Both men
leaving, the play then concludes upon a deserted room, unlit "except
for the red neon lights of the Hotel Algiers and a spill of light from
the hall."
    The subdued ending has a distancing effect. The series of charac-
ters, who during the course of the play have been exposing the
emotional bankruptcy of their lives, make their separate exits: first
Belle, then Frenchy, then Cleo; finally only Prince and Ben, the two

men who have been given a taste of romance, are left empty and alone. As they, too, quit the stage, the closure effect of act 3 is complete, leaving only the hotel lights to recall the unfulfilled longings of the departed characters. This final image provides a transition out of the enclosed world of the play, into a transcendent realm beyond—the world of romance, of dreams and possibilities. It also provides a gesture of balance to the play's pessimism, testifying to the playwright's faith in the existence of beauty. Cleo and the Hotel Algiers remain Odets's muses; his next play, *Night Music,* will take us into the Hotel Algiers and show us that Cleo's world of romance can become a reality.

Night Music is an expressionistic play, taking place, as Odets put it, in the "nighttime of civilization." Despite its dark undertones, however, it is his most optimistic play, its mood celebratory rather than gloomy. The settings of the play are varied as Odets shifts his characters between the Hotel Algiers, Central Park, an airport, the theater district, and the New York World's Fair. Its constant milieu, however, is the magical world of romance wherein almost anything can happen. This world is presided over by a dying police detective, Abraham Lincoln Rosenberger, who appears to manipulate the action of the play, keeping a pair of young lovers together until they are ready to declare their love for each other. The play thus recalls both *The Tempest* and *A Midsummer Night's Dream* (though *Night Music* takes place in winter over the course of three—again the number is significant—days), placing the destinies of its protagonist-lovers in the hands of a powerful, all-knowing figure in a mythic setting. Music, a prime symbol in Odets's work, is again made significant, but instead of representing an idealized world, unattainable in the real one, Odets here merges his lovers into the world of music. The ideals of love and harmony are thus represented as realistic possibilities, and in this sense *Night Music* is a true romance, a wish-fulfillment dream celebrating fertility, freedom, and survival.

To some extent this optimistic spirit is clouded by the imminence of World War II, which functions as an insistent specter of the real world. As late as 1939, Odets shared the isolationist sentiment common among Americans. But the Nazis' invasion of Russia and their doctrine of a "final solution" for the Jews deeply affected him, and any reading of *Night Music* must take these historical events into account. For the first time Odets creates a world apart from the real and pushes it into the foreground of the play. When, toward the end of the play, Fay speaks about the music that crickets make, she encapsulates Odets's feeling in the play:

The last cricket, the very last. . . . Crickets are my favorite animals in all the world. They're never down in the mouth. All night they make their music. . . .
   Night music. . . . If they can sing, I can sing. I'm more than them. *We're* more than them. . . . We can sing through any night![19]

Once again Odets issues the charge to "awake and sing," but here he projects the characters who can actually do so—with a little help from a stage magician—rather than just talking about it.

The theme of this play is Odets's familiar one, the quest for a home, and here it is developed openly. All the characters are homeless, and the two central characters' gradual discovery of their need for each other and for belonging together provides the play's principal action. The protagonist Steve Takis, nicknamed "Suitcase," is literally bereft of home, for he has no family and he himself, like many Americans during the Depression, has spent a good portion of his life going from temporary job to temporary job; currently he is an errand boy for a movie studio. Like Lorna Moon, Steve seems defensive, brash, and arrogant, but underneath the flashy exterior is an insecure and vulnerable person, who is equally liable to retreat into a nostalgic past associated with memories of his mother or to fabricate, as Cleo Singer does, a fantasy life in which he figures as an important Hollywood executive. However, Steve is not very good at maintaining his tough-guy pose: when he asserts himself to a stage-hand at the beginning of the play, he is knocked down, and both Fay and Rosenberger are able to see through him. He is consistently loud and pushy, but Rosenberger remarks, "With all his noise, he makes a good impression." And Odets clearly wanted him to be seen as sympathetic; although many critics judged him an extremely unattractive hero, and a serious weakness in the play, Steve remains a complex and dynamic enough figure to command recognition and understanding.

The play opens on a Friday evening in a New York City police station. Steve has been picked up for scaring Fay Tucker on Broadway when one of the trained monkeys he has in charge for a movie company reached out and grabbed her locket. During the ensuing uproar and his subsequent arrest, Steve has lost his wallet and his plane ticket, leaving him without identification or money. The police decide to hold the monkeys until Monday, when they can confirm Steve's claim that he is employed to deliver the monkeys to the West Coast for Federal Pictures. Steve is thus left on his own for a weekend in New York City with only the possessions in his suitcase, launched upon an adventure by a freak accident. In accordance with romantic tradition, the hero has shed his old identity in order to rediscover a truer sense of self by meeting the challenges he is to encounter in a magical landscape.

Almost a composite Odets character, Steve is associated with several images reminiscent of the protagonists of previous plays. Most prominent among these is music; Steve's clarinet is the most treasured possession in his suitcase. Like the prized violin that links Joe Bonaparte to the artistic sensibility of his father, the clarinet was a present from Steve's mother, who died of cancer when he was a child, and it triggers memories of an idealized past when he had a true home. Steve identifies his mother with flowers: "Every window in our house had geraniums—since my mother died I can't stand Brockton" (pp. 89–90). Later, remembering his parents, he rhapsodizes about their marriage, "What a sweet girl she was! My father musta loved her like a sonofabitch" (p. 119) These images of a lost happiness persist in memory, idealized in his mind despite the intervening years of struggle and the intrusion of death and the violence of war—like Pike's sons in *Paradise Lost,* Steve's father was killed in World War I. Once again, Odets fuses the motifs of home, music, and death, sounding a muted note of sadness in an otherwise comic play.

Steve's music figures prominently in the action at two key moments in the play. When Fay takes him to the Hotel Algiers where she has a room, Steve plays his clarinet to soothe the tension between them. He performs a song of his own composition, entitled "I Got Those Nobody-Nothing Blues"; Odets writes that it is the music of a "lost boy, gloomy, apprehensive, lonely." Later in the play, it is Steve's playing that draws them together—Odets's stage directions specify that "his music is soft and gentle, lonely, filled with yearning," and Fay's reaction, which conveys her feelings without words, is detailed carefully: "She understands Steve's music: she comes to the door and stands there, listening and reaching out to him by her concentrated silence" (p. 198). During these scenes Steve and Fay are in adjoining rooms separated by a wall and a door; their situation echoes that of the figures of "Beauty" and "Truth" in Emily Dickinson's poem "I Died for Beauty," who are also in "adjoining rooms" and can merge only in death. Here, however, Steve's music provides the magic to break down the wall between the lovers and unite them in a moment of harmony.

Fay Tucker, unlike Steve, is doing her best to escape her home. From a comfortable home in Philadelphia (Odets's own birthplace), where "nothing, nothing, I tell you happens," she has broken her engagement to Eddie Bellows, a refrigerator salesman, who represents the lifeless, predictable life-style that awaits her there—Steve's reaction upon meeting Eddie is, "Your whole manner's anti-cupid!" (p. 153). Fay, like Cleo Singer, wants to "better herself in every honest way possible," and she has come to New York to be an actress. However, her career has reached a dead end, for the show she has been appearing in has closed on the night of her encounter with Steve, and she is left with no job and little money; she is already behind in paying her room rent. When she meets Steve in act 1, scene 2, both are penniless. Significantly, Odets stages their first extended encounter outside a theater, a place of unreality, of occasional "magic," implying that the forces of art (theater, music) can create the harmony and unity that seem impossible in life. In this, his most openly theatrical play, Odets strives to reconcile the disparate energies of his protagonists, turning the city itself into a kind of romantic stage from which the threat of war may be banished for a while.

One important setting in the play is the Hotel Algiers, which figures as a central symbol in *Rocket to the Moon*. Here the hotel is a gathering place for homeless, lost souls, its exotic name clashing with its appearance—"a kangaroo wouldn't live here"—and the nature of its clientele. The first scene in the hotel opens as a sailor on leave is being denied a room. He appeals to the management's patriotism, arguing that he is protecting them from "foreign menaces," but he is still turned away. The man of war has no place in this urban Forest of Arden, although his strident intrusion reinforces the sense of reality impending beyond the world of the play. Also occupying the lobby are prostitutes, a man in a phone booth trying to speak with someone but unable to make a connection, a girl waiting for a call from her boyfriend, and a "sleeping man" who is worried about his folks in Poland. All these characters are thus divorced from the comfort of home, in part, again, because of the disruptive force of the war situation, and they gather together, like the denizens of Harry Hope's saloon in O'Neill, hoping for some warmth, some sense of belonging. In the midst of this crowd of refugees and outcasts, Odets's lovers come together, drawn to each other by the spirits of music and romance, and set apart by the enchantment of their attraction.

As in *Golden Boy*, Odets sets two scenes in Central Park, but whereas Joe and Lorna seem to occupy their own space, virtually having the place to themselves, here the park is populated with potential intruders upon the courtship drama of Steve and Fay. Again the parade of lonely, homeless people emphasizes the hopeful magnetism of the protagonists. The park itself does not appear as romantic as in the earlier play; here it is characterized by "several thin denuded trees." Once again the specter of war makes its presence felt in the person of Roy, who tells Steve that he is joining the army so that at least he will have a place to eat and sleep. This prospect affects Steve, and he, too, will later resolve to join the army. Several nameless men pass through, including a "little man" who calls himself "the man nobody knows, another who designs bridges and cathedrals although they don't build them," and a blind man. During their night together, Steve and Fay sit on a bench and talk about their lives, Steve telling about leaving Brockton after his parents' death, while Fay describes her parents' life: "Living in a pot of lye and they don't know it." Despite the pressure of the outside world, Steve and Fay are able to form a world of their own, and the park thus functions, as in *Golden Boy*, as a place where the lovers can reveal themselves to each other and so cement the bond between them.

Overseeing the action of the play is Abraham Lincoln Rosenberger, a magical figure and a theatrically outrageous character as well. He appears whenever Steve and Fay need him, as if from nowhere, out of romantic necessity. Rosenberger is the officer who brings Steve to the station at the beginning of the play; he believes his story, despite Steve's erractic behavior, and shows compassion. When Steve's suitcase is stolen near the theater in act 1, scene 2, Rosenberger is there to retrieve it. He does so again in the last scene when Steve is prevented from boarding his plane to Los Angeles—it seems that Rosenberger is the protector of Steve's identity, represented in the suitcase and the clarinet inside it. He also arrives at the Hotel Algiers when Steve is denied a room, brings the couple sandwiches, oversees a breakfast during which he attempts to reconcile Fay with her father, and accompanies the lovers to the World's Fair.

The comical name of this guardian angel is significant within the play's symbolic context. In the spirit of the president whose name he bears, Rosenberger's guidance delivers Steve from the bondage of bitter loneliness, freeing him to realize his potential as a human being and a lover, and this transformation, in turn, liberates Fay from enslavement in the lifeless society of Philadelphia. And, in the manner of the first Jewish patriarch, Odets's Abraham becomes a strong father-surrogate who can soothe the longing of the orphaned Steve and provide the paternal direction that Fay needs. In German, Rosenberger means flowering hills, and this association with flowers recalls Steve's mother and her geraniums; Rosenberger, too, is dying of cancer, which makes the link more emphatic. At the end of the play, when Fay and Steve's love has been openly declared, Steve says to her, "You are a thing of beauty . . . Flowers on the hill"—a linguistic echo confirming the policeman's role as a spirit of the lost past that intervenes in the present on behalf of the love that will provide a home in the future.

Rosenberger believes in the future, perceiving in Steve and Fay a nucleus for building a better world out of the wreckage of the Depression and the threatening war. Unlike most of Odets's dreamers, however, he is an active optimist who refuses to sentimentalize the past:

I am a relic of the old days. . . . it was not good. We look at the past through rosy-color glasses, but it was bad days. Take the word of an expert.

Ignorance, poverty, very unsanitary conditions. . . . Today is better, in my humble opinion. I am like you, Miss Tucker. (p. 104)

In one central speech he summarizes an important aspect of Odets's artistic consciousness:

> I am in love with the possibilities, the human possibilities. Mind you, not for myself. . . . I'm an old dog and it's not my intention to live forever. But the younger generation is a very interesting subject to me. It interests me to the nth degree, their problems. If it was within my authority you'd see how quick I'd underwrite the youth of the many beautiful states of the country. (p. 105)

Rosenberger's actions in the play affirm this benevolent resolve. Although dying of cancer, he takes a sincere interest in the young protagonists as soon as he meets them, inquiring about the cause of the death of Steve's mother. Rosenberger recognizes that Steve's preoccupation with his parents' death and with his lost past, more surely than the adversity of the job market, has prevented him from making something of himself in the present. Unlike Fay, who has the strength to escape her past and withstand the pressure from her father to return to it, Steve remains fettered by nostalgia and unable to grow. The older man, realizing that death must be accepted as part of a cyclical process, and regretting his own failure to achieve a home—"I always liked a clean, wholesome home. I wasn't lucky" (p. 167)—decides therefore to devote his wisdom and experience to helping Steve and Fay build one of their own. The concept of home, inevitably associated with death, thus becomes more than a philosophical abstraction in *Night Music;* here, through Rosenberger, Odets's central ideal is made possible.

The Rosenberger character presents a powerful contrast to the figure of Jacob in *Awake and Sing!* In the earlier play this man with the bright vision of the future is comically undercut at almost every turn; Jacob is a dreamer and an extravagant talker but not an active agent of change, and his suicide is presented as a negative gesture that has no lasting effect on the life of the Berger family. Rosenberger, on the other hand, is able to utilize his dying self in the service of the future he dreams of, investing his young protégés with positive values that they will integrate into their own lives. Steve may be a confused young man, but unlike Ralph he is strong and aggressive, and Rosenberger's message will not be wasted on him:

> *You* are ignorant. Because your fight is here, not across the water. You love this girl? And you mean it? Then fight for love! You want a home? Do you?—then fight for homes! Otherwise, excuse me, you are a rascal and a liar! (pp. 234–35)

This prescription of striving for love and home points the way past Steve's emotional inertia, establishing the goal of future stability as an inspiration for resolving personal difficulties as well as a challenge to the larger society to transcend the current economic and political upheaval.

The concept of futurity is given specific incarnation at the end of the play when Rosenberger joins Steve and Fay at the New York World's Fair; in his stage directions Odets has the Trylon and the Perisphere figures showing in the background of the scene. The fair functions in one respect as a place removed from the real world situation of 1939, but its utopian serenity remains largely an illusion, as Odets is well aware. The reappearance of Roy, the young man from the park, who informs Steve that he has, indeed, joined the army, provides, in Odets's words, "a specter, an image of Steve's war thoughts." The war is real and it is absorbing the energies of the present, as the repeated intrusion of such incidental figures demonstrates. Still Odets insists, through Rosenberger, on the nobility of the fair's intention and on the potential of his young protagonists to overcome the wastage of the times in which they live. Odets exploits the imagery of the fair to emphasize that despite looming adversity, mankind persists in the capacity and the imagination to build the fair as a monument to the dream of the future, and that the people's ability to enjoy and appreciate this visionary impulse is a step toward realizing that dream. Like the cricket who sings his songs in the night, the human music of dreams and romance can triumph over frustration and despair; as Steve says to Rosenberger, "I'm a real harmony boy in my heart" (p. 179)

The play concludes at the airport, where Steve is waiting for a plane to the West Coast when he learns that he has been fired by the movie company. The loss of his job has, ironically, a liberating effect on Steve, who thereupon commits himself at last to Fay. The play then concludes on a note of jubilant optimism as he exclaims, "Make way! This girl's got a crush on me. Make way!" The final stage direction reads, "Overhead the airplanes are zooming and singing," and the familiar image provides a final point of contrast to *Awake and Sing!* There airplanes serves as a symbol of escape for Ralph, representing an immature character's urge to dream himself out of a situation that he cannot handle; Ralph's wish to fly is as unrealistic as his sudden declaration that his life is going to change. In *Night Music*, however, the flight image is celebratory, confirming that Steve has won his struggle with himself. Odets here fuses the concepts of futurity and harmony in one final sound image of progress and music. For the first time in the thirties, Odets's characters do, in fact, awake and sing and thereby achieve transcendence. Art, aspiration and experience merge in the wish fulfillment of romance.

It is appropriate that *Night Music* was Odets's final play for the Group Theatre, for it is, in many respects, a thematic summary of all the plays that preceded it, albeit lacking their depth and sophistication. In this flawed work, Odets manages at least to make the affirmative statement he had been struggling toward for so long. When it closed, the Group Theatre folded. Conceived as an artists' forum that might play a part in changing society, the Group had found itself more and more isolated as the mood of America changed. Left-wing theater groups, such as the Group and the Federal Theater, simply collapsed. Ironically, Odets the artist was finally able to synthesize the concept of home just as the Group, his spiritual home, was to dissolve. Along with many other Group members—Franchot Tone, Lee J. Cobb, Elia Kazan, and Harold Clurman—Odets soon gravitated to Hollywood, and from this point on, the dream of home would forever elude him.

6

The Melodramatic Vision
Clash by Night (1941)
The Country Girl (1950)

Not to be born surpasses thought and speech.
The second best is to have seen the light
And then to go back quickly whence we came.
> —Sophocles, *Oedipus at Colonus*

Most of Odets's work was a confession. He told us of his anguish at sharing those values in our civilization that he despised. He beggged for protection from the contaminations against which he always raged and which he realized infected him.
> —Harold Clurman, 1963

While *Clash by Night* was running on Broadway, Odets published an article in the *New York Times* describing the genesis of what he called "the trio play." Quoting from his journal the recorded thoughts that later evolved into *Clash by Night*, he explained:

May 19: Every time you refuse to live a relationship with another person to its most potential depth you are committing a sin against yourself and the other involved. . . . It is one of the rock bottom vices which infest American life from top to bottom. . . . Much better to refuse a relationship wholly, never starting it, than to deal half heartedly or less with it. Rather live alone than keep yourself shut to the man or woman with whom you spend time. . . . Eschew once and for all relationships which are not humanly productive, but first make an effort to make them so.[1]

The emphasis on relationships links the play to *Rocket to the Moon* and *Night Music.* The subject was still very much on Odets's mind when the play was in its formative stages, for his marriage to Luise Ranier had finally ended in divorce, and the Group Theatre was in disarray, soon to dissolve. Originally he planned to produce the play himself, working from the Group Theatre offices, with Luther Adler and Sylvia Sydney in the lead roles. But when he could not find sufficient backing, Odets turned to Billy Rose, and the play finally went into production with Tallulah Bankhead as the star. Only two members of the Group, Art Smith and Lee J. Cobb, were in the cast, although Lee Strasberg did direct.

Clash by Night had an extensive pre-Broadway run. It opened in Detroit on October 27, 1941, and then moved on to Baltimore, Pittsburgh, and Philadelphia. Reviews of the play early in the tour were favorable, if not enthusiastic, but the production began to experience problems, especially with the cast, as the tour continued. Bankhead was uncomfortable in her part and some cast members complained about Strasberg's direction. Further spoiling the play's reception was a suddenly distracted national mood: *Clash by Night* opened in New York on December 27, 1941, three weeks after the attack in Pearl Harbor. The reviews were mostly negative and the play closed on February 7, 1942, after only forty-nine performances. Odets now had back-to-back flops; there would be no more plays from Broadway's "Golden Boy" until 1949, when he returned from Hollywood to write *The Big Knife.*

Clash by Night and *The Country Girl,* like *Rocket to the Moon* and *Night Music,* focus on marriage, stressing the difficulties of human relationship. But the later plays evince a different generic emphasis. Neither *Night Music's* magical atmosphere, conjuring true romance with a "happily ever after" ending, nor the pervasive symbolism of *Rocket to the Moon,* propelled by the muselike character Cleo Singer, finds any counterpart in the harsher realism of these later works. *Clash by Night,* like *Rocket to the Moon,* links economic hardship and summer heat to form an oppressive backdrop, but the world of this play remains unrelievedly sordid. Here no Cleo Singer appears to provide a glimpse of possibilities beyond the immediate setting. Trapped again, as much by their own natures as by Depression adversity, the characters are uniformly unappealing; this is the only Odets play in which no character can inspire audience sympathy.

Again Odets poses a love triangle, but this time the outcome is to be violent: the playwright does not put his characters gently aside as in *Rocket to the Moon;* here he destroys them. *The Country Girl,* too, involves a love triangle, but this play more nearly echoes *Night Music,* for here Odets distances his story from the banality of ordinary life by locating the nexus of the play in "the theater" itself. This theatrical setting infuses the action with some of the otherworldly atmosphere of *Night Music,* but now the aura of magic must yield to a more realistic psychological focus.

What links the two later plays is that in both Odets is dealing in melodrama, externalizing the struggle between opposing moral forces. Whereas, in tragedy, man is portrayed at war with his own nature and, although the experiences of the tragic hero may have public repercussions, the struggle remains essentially private, melodrama is directed outward rather than inward: man is warring not against himself but against other men or conditions of the everyday world. As Robert B. Heilman points out in his sensitive study of melodrama, the stresses exist "between rather than within people."[2] In the theater, as in life, the tendency here is to "translate the opposing players into heroes and villains,"[3] and this relocation of conflict makes the dramatic experience easier on audiences. Inward conflicts are often difficult and painful to deal with, and, as the tragic hero demonstrates, they are to be resolved only amid the direst of consequences. In melodrama the dualities are portrayed beyond the self, and the audience is invited to participate in a struggle that is presented as good vs. evil and to watch as it proceeds to either destruction or triumph. More complex melodramas, such as Odets's, do not, of course, seek so straightforward an effect. Certain characters evoke differing responses to various situations, delaying the audience's judgment of them and blurring distinctions of good and evil. However, the basic premises of melodrama do prevail, objectifying the moral conflict, and so, unlike the experience of *Golden Boy* or *The Big Knife,* it is easy for an audience to distance itself from the characters and judge them. In *Clash by Night,* particularly, the characters so thoroughly lack insight or understanding that it is tempting simply to feel superior to them.

Clash by Night presents a world similar to that of *Rocket to the Moon.* The action of the play spans three summer months; the heat is insistent, affecting the characters' behavior. For some, a walk on the beach provides the only comfort and relief. Alcohol replaces water as the drink that quenches physical thirst, although it does not carry the symbolic weight that water has in the earlier play. Again a love triangle provides the central conflict, but it is the wife who is dissatisfied with the marriage and decides to have an affair. This play concerns characters of a lower social class than those in *Rocket to the Moon;* they are not professionals (dentists and chiropodists) but laborers, and the Depression economy affects them more profoundly. Jerry Wilenski is on the verge of losing his job throughout much of the play and eventually does so. His friend Earl is unemployed when introduced, but he does find work as a movie projectionist during the course of the play. Jerry's father has no job, and two other characters work only sporadically.

More pessimistic than *Rocket to the Moon, Clash by Night* is Odets's most damning study of human relationships and his most violent full-length play. It is also his most despairing work. The play takes its title from the last line of Matthew Arnold's "Dover Beach," and that poem serves as an important gloss on Odets's play because its themes, imagery, and its movement from a sense of enclosure and security to a climate of openness and danger mirror the development of Odets's dramatic confrontation. This poem contains thematic elements common to much of Arnold's mature poetry: the power that a universal law exerts over personal desire, the inadequacy of romantic love, and the transient nature of human life. All of Odets's plays focus on similar concerns, although the love theme was most compelling to him at this point in his career.

In the opening images of "Dover Beach," there is a sense of solace and composure that eventually yields to despair and alarm. At the beginning of the poem Arnold emphasizes words such as "calm," "fair," "tranquil," and "sweet," and these adjectives are reinforced by various images of enclosure: the sea between the straits, the bay between the cliffs and the window from which the speaker looks out framing the scene. The picture the poem evokes is of two people standing in a room looking out on a scene that mirrors the security within: the vast cliffs, the "fair" moon on the bay, and the tide. Nature, the speaker, and his love appear to be one. Then, quite suddenly, sound breaks the tranquil mood. The speaker hears "a

grating roar" and the stillness of the scene changes to one of movement, even hostility, as the waves "draw back and fling" the pebbles;
this eruption of violence prefigures the poem's closing phrase, "ignorant armies clash by night," which supplies the play's title. Another
section of the poem that must have struck Odets is Arnold's reference to the "sea of faith"—the poetic reference is to an ocean
enclosing the land and protecting it. Arnold employs the image to
contrast two time periods: the age of faith now gone, obsolete, and
the modern sensibility, which must deal with an absence of faith.
The poetic movement is significant here in that the physical imagery
has changed from a spatial dislocation to a temporal one.

Odets devises a similar structure in his play. Like *Golden Boy* and
Night Music, Clash by Night has an open structure, employing four
locales: the porch of the Wilenski house, the inside of the house, a
pavilion facing the beach, and the projection booth of a movie
theater. Despite this movement from inside to outside, no place
offers the secure haven that Arnold finds in the room with his love.
The "turbid ebb and flow of human misery" permeates the play at all
levels, as does death, which is another central motif. The one image
in the play that corresponds to the security of the lovers in Arnold's
poem is, characteristically in Odets's world, merely a mental projection, an unrealizable ideal akin to poetry or music. Jerry Wilenski, at
the end of his rope near the end of the play, speaks of his longing to
his father:

Poppa . . . I know what that song means you play. We had those Christmas
cards when I was a boy—a little warm house in the snow, yellow lights in the
windows . . . remember? It was wonnerful . . . a place where they told you
what to do, like in school. . . . You didn't have to have no brains—he told
you what to do. I wished it was like on the Christmas cards again, so nice an'
warm, a wonnerful home. . . . No, I wished I never grew up now![4]

Jerry is referring to a song that his father, a Polish immigrant, often
plays on his concertina; his image of security, then, is associated with
music, which is linked to the concept of "home" lost to his father,
and as he now realizes, to himself as well. The beginning of the
speech recalls Joe's and Lorna's ideal in *Golden Boy,* a place where one
can't be hurt. But Jerry is no Joe Bonaparte, for his understanding of

himself and of the world around him remains limited. He is not looking forward in a Utopian reverie, but dreaming of reversion to a womblike state. Childlike by nature, he is linked in this regressive tendency to his friend Earl, who eventually becomes his rival and antagonist in part because of the crude emotional nostalgia they share.

The play's action revolves around Jerry and Mae Wilenski. Jerry, a sporadically employed carpenter, is good-natured and generous but essentially unintelligent and immature. Mae is a bored housewife; having recently given birth to a daughter, she remains restless. In *Rocket to the Moon* Belle claimed that her childlessness was a prime cause of her dissatisfaction, but motherhood does not seem to fill the emotional gaps in Mae's life. Into this uneasy situation comes Earl Pfeiffer, a friend of Jerry's, who moves into a vacant room in the Wilenski house, thus setting up the romantic triangle situation that is to destroy the marriage and lead to the violent death of this domestic intruder.

Brief synopsis makes the play sound like simple, sordid melodrama, but Odets strives to invest his material with greater substance, using Arnold's poem as a guide to tell a story of ruined lives set against a backdrop of social deprivation and world war. Unfortunately, neither of these collateral elements is developed sufficiently in connection with the central characters to add much resonance to their suffering. While many of the characters complain about economic conditions, their basic unhappiness clearly lies deeper. Mae, for instance, complains about "living on the installment plan," but it seems obvious that more money would not bring the fulfillment lacking in her marriage. Likewise, the war is only a peripheral issue. Only Jerry's father, a minor character who says little, shows any concern about it; to the others it seems worlds away, irrelevant to their day-to-day lives. The antagonist in this melodrama is not so much the hostile world surrounding the protagonists as the innate inability of these people to maintain relationships, a pervasive dissatisfaction at the core of existence itself.

Most of the play takes place at the Wilenski home, either on the front porch or inside. The opening scene is expository, establishing immediately the nature of the relationship between Jerry and Mae. Jerry's childlike, elemental appreciation of nature is demonstrated in his opening comment, which also echoes the opening lines of "Dover Beach": "Look at it! The moon comes out an' then it's very beautiful. . . . you can't pay no admission price nowhere to get a sight like that moon shinin' down on the sea." Equally telling is Mae's response to Jerry's question, "What are you thinkin'?"

An old song was running through my mind. "I'm the Sheik of Araby, this land belongs to me. At night when you're asleep, into your tent I'll creep." (p. 4)

Mae's reference to this popular song betrays her dissatisfaction with her marriage and her life, indicating she seeks sexual adventure and excitement as an antidote to her dull existence. Odets has evoked Arnold's images at the beginning of the play only to undercut them. From the vantage point of the Wilenski's porch looking out onto the moonlit night, romance is not the answer; Mae and Jerry's relationship will not stand against the hostile energies of a world in turmoil.

This mood of contrast and disharmony is maintained by Odets as the scene continues. Jerry and Mae are joined by their friends Peggy and Joe, an engaged couple who can't marry because of economic conditions. Peggy, like Jerry, is awed by the moon, and she, too, echoes "Dover Beach": "The night is so calm. The moon is coming up." Her remark is soon followed by the sound of Jerry's father playing his concertina within the house. The moon and music are thus linked, as they are in *Golden Boy;* both are linked also to the subject of "home" when Jerry explains the song to Joe, "It's a Polish song . . . about the little old house, where you wanna go back, but you can't find out where it is no more, the house" (pp. 10–11). The setting of this scene further develops these various poetic strains: the Wilenskis are on the porch—Mae complains that it is not screened in and does not protect them from the bugs—seemingly suspended between the moon and the interior of the house. They are caught physically between two unattainable ideals.

Into this symbolically charged conversation Odets injects the specter of death. Jerry's observation of the night sky leads him to an abrupt sensation of mortality:

I was thinkin' of the stars an' how far away they are, an' that you feel pretty small in the world by comparison. Even when you're dead, the stars go on. (p. 4)

Later Peggy associates the serenity of the natural scene with her feelings after the recent death of her mother: "It's so calm . . . quiet. . . . This is the way I felt when I made the three day retreat at the convent, after my mother died" (p. 11). Mae's reaction to this wistful musing again emphasizes her prosaic nature: "Living in a convent would make my hair stand up. I'd much rather go to the spaghetti house twice a week" (p. 11). Later she asks that Jerry tell his father to stop playing the music.

In disassociating Mae from these interrelated poetic motifs, Odets is passing judgment on her. Like Bessie in *Awake and Sing!* Mae is shown to be a woman who remains unmoved by natural beauty or romance. Although her dissatisfactions and her yearning for escape are understandable, she can evoke no real sympathy from the audience. After Joe and Peggy leave, Mae continues to voice her discontent, referring acidly to Peggy's desire to marry:

She makes me laugh! Can't wait to plunge her hands in the family wash! Can't wait to be steamrolled flat! And he's got the nerve to sit there and refuse the offer! (p. 15)

When Jerry expresses his dismay over his wife's remarks, she calls him "dumb." He then tries to distract her by again mentioning the stars, but Mae is not interested and goes inside. Having thus characterized the malaise of Jerry and Mae's marriage, Odets next introduces Earl, the catalyst of the play's action, who will quickly disturb the atmosphere of comparative calm.

A close friend of Jerry's, Earl arrives in the first scene to visit. He is immediately attracted to Mae, asking if she was ever a show girl. Initially she has seemed put off by his brash manner, but this question pleases her. Earl then tells Mae about his marriage that ended in divorce; he is very bitter about his ex-wife:

It took me six months to be poisoned by that woman, an' six years to get over it! Hives, rashes an' blisters! We began with a toast and ended with a funeral oration! Divorce is like the other person died, I keep saying she's dead, she's dead. (p. 36)

Earl's description of his marriage seems a much harsher version of Mae's own feelings about hers. Earl declares that "a man's just a bum without a woman" and this remark evokes some sympathy from Mae. When Jerry returns from his beer-buying errand, he again refers to the moon, and Earl's response—"I'm no nature lover—the hell with it!"—links him ominously with Mae. Oblivious to the ready affinity between his friend and his wife, Jerry innocently offers Earl the extra room, and so the stage is set for the cataclysm that provides the play's melodramatic climax.

Scene 2 takes place several weeks later, moving the characters outside to a pavilion facing the beach, where Jerry, Mae, Earl, Peggy, and Joe are out for an evening of drinking and dancing. Again, it is extremely hot, and Earl, celebrating his success in getting a job, is treating everyone to drinks. During this scene Earl and Mae are left alone for a time, and their mutual attraction is openly acknowledged. Earl tells Mae that his mother died the year he was born, thus revealing himself as another Odets character who never had a real home and is searching for one; like the other motherless figures in the earlier plays, he seems to be seeking in Mae a combination of mother/wife. (In this respect he most closely resembles Steve Takis and Moe Axelrod.) Earl is fond of the word "delicious," and like Moe, who thought of Hennie as his "orange," he associates Mae with a mother's breast. Odets, however, does not develop this theme further in *Clash by Night,* leaving its potential psychological significance buried in the onrush of plot. Mae then confides in Earl her dissatisfaction with Jerry:

He thinks I'm a Red Cross nurse—you have to watch him every minute! He doesn't know there's a battle of the bread and butter. He expects his wife to fight those battles! He says money isn't everything. Maybe not, but it's ninety nine point nine of everything! I guess the truth is he's a momma's boy. (p. 74)

Clearly, in dismissing Jerry as a "momma's boy," she fails to recognize symptoms of that same condition in the man she is flirting with at the moment. When Earl responds, "Who isn't?" Mae asks, "Are you?" but he evades the issue by changing the subject.

Mae longs, as she says, for a paradise, impressed on her memory in the popular song "Avalon":

I used to sell sheet music in the dime store. A place called Avalon . . . no worries there, sort of flowers in the winter. I don't know how all that stuff gets in a song, but it does. (p. 25)

Mae also reveals a wistful admiration for her father, "the great Johnny Cavanaugh—with the smoke pearl studs!" Again, however, Odets fails to elaborate on this suggestion of a latent father fixation, and Mae simply goes on to tell Earl of her one true love, a Pennsylvania politician, whose heroic masculinity continues to shape her ideal of manhood:

Confidence! He gives you confidence, and he never breaks it down! He fights the blizzards and the floods for you. He gives you consideration, at least as much as he gives the baseball scores, or the Tears of St. Lawrence! He makes her more of a woman instead of less. . . . he beats the world off when it tries to swallow her up! (p. 77)

Later she again describes the man of her dreams in images that recall *Golden Boy:*

I guess I'm hold-over from another century! Didn't there used to be big, comfortable men? Or was it a dream? Today they're little and nervous, sparrows! But I dream of eagles. (p. 78)

Obviously Mae is longing for a strong, impressive man like her father or her former lover, but Odets quickly drops the subject with the bare implication that Jerry does not give her what she needs.

Earl then forces the issue, picking up Mae's suggestion that she doesn't love her husband and boldly demanding, "Could you go for me?" Suddenly, in this pavilion overlooking the beach, the clash of ignorant emotions is about to begin. The eternal note of sadness is sounded, and the potential destructiveness of the energies here unleashed is emphasized, once again, by an allusion to death, as the proprietor of the pavilion mentions that "yesterday a little girl drowned right off here" (p. 57). Jerry later echoes this, ironically invoking the protection of one traditional solace that Odets, as well as Arnold, knows is missing from the modern world:

An' yesterday some poor little girl drowned right here. . . . No one knows what's gonna happen next. Lucky we got our religion. (p. 62)

Chaos looms from within and without. In Odets's allusions to Earl's and Mae's needs, one for maternal comforting, the other for male domination, it is apparent that their natures are not compatible; neither will find the haven he seeks in the other.

The climate of dangerous tension is heightened by the introduction of Jerry's uncle Vincent Kress, who is described in naturalistic terms as "a small active terrior-like person" (p. 53). This is a most unsavory character, a pornographer, a voyeur, a hustler, an anti-Semite, a fanatical chauvinist. He represents for Odets the kind of fascist mentality that results from economic and social deprivation. When Earl asks him if he is working, he replies, "Would be if my name was Berkowitz. . . . What's happenin' in this country!" (p. 54). His despotic mentality is revealed when he deprecates his nephew's concern for his wife's unhappiness: "Jerry, that's so much liverwurst, that love business! I tell you, give 'er the whip!" (p. 205). In *Golden Boy* Carp's remark, "A man hits his wife and it is the first step to Fascism," was made in a joking way; here, the circumstances prove its seriousness. Later in the play, Kress, acting like an Iago figure, will convince Jerry that he has no choice but to kill Earl. The introduction of this sinister character in the second scene outside the house serves to confirm and focus the variety of menacing notes struck in the play so far: Mae's betrayal of her marital discontent and the implied invitation to Earl's advances, the references to drowning, and the nagging pressure of economic hardship. Figuratively represented in the person of Jerry's father, who has to be carried out drunk from the bar, all these ominous developments describe a world disintegrating from within and without.

Scene 3 takes place in the kitchen of the Wilenski home. Jerry, reading the paper, is disturbed by the news of another girl's drowning, a continuation of the death-by-water motif that haunts the play. Unlike the revitalizing elixir of *Rocket to the Moon*, water here is unredemptive, death-bringing. Mae, characteristically, ignores this natural omen and instead renews her angry diatribe on the poverty of their lives. Jerry leaves for work as she sinks into this usual bad mood, whereupon Earl enters from his room and again speaks to her about his needs. In a typical Odetsian lament, he declares, "I don't enjoy my life. I enjoy only the dream of it" (p. 99), and then follows this up by expressing a wish to be "unborn." The self-absorbed characters in this play are capable only of such nihilistic gestures, generally expressed with some violence:

You're like me, that's what it proves. You were born an' now you'd like to get unborn! That's why I drink this varnish, lady—to get unborn! Perpetual motion—born, everybody's getting born! Two strangers hit the hay one June night and suddenly there *you* are! Well, why not get *un*born the same way?. . . . wouldn't that be delicious? (pp. 103–4)

He complains that his wife never made him a home—"I had ideals about a home"—and insists on his need for love. Frantically he implores Mae, "The blues for home, for home sweet home, but where is home?" (p. 105). By the end of the scene, after struggling to resist, she enters his room to make love.

The action of the rest of the play follows quickly after this climactic betrayal. In the final scene of act 1, Jerry learns the truth about Earl and Mae. He manages to control his anger and wants to forgive Mae, and becoming very childlike, at one point calling her "momma," he asks for her forgiveness. Mae responds that she is tired of babying him and intends to stay with Earl. Jerry can only respond, "You're bad, both bad," and leaves the house.

When act 2 begins Jerry has been gone for three days. Earl wants Mae to leave with him, but she refused to go until she can say good-bye to Jerry. When Jerry finally returns he tells Mae that he is willing to forget the past and start over again. Mae refuses, insisting that she must reach out for happiness. Jerry's reaction, then, is to pass out, passively refusing to cope with the collapse of domestic order. In the next scene, however, Vincent Kress persuades his nephew to act:

You're twice his size. I'm only half his size an' I wouldn't have it! With my hands—like that—he'd struggle in my hands—no mercy!—no, no! Then throw him off to one side for the rats to nibble on! (p. 206)

The play soon concludes in the projection booth of the movie theater where Earl works. Jerry confronts Earl in a spirit of forgiveness, but Earl, not understanding, seizes a wrench and precipitates a struggle during which Jerry kills Earl.

Throughout the play, Odets attempts to counterbalance the pessimism of the main story with a romance involving Peggy, a part-time schoolteacher, and Joe Doyle. Harold Clurman regarded these lovers as a "kind of ideological afterthought,"[5] and he is right, for neither character really comes to life. Joe, particularly, sounds more like a mouthpiece for Odets's ideas than a fully realized character. Peggy demonstrates some more sympathetic qualities, but she, too, remains wooden and unconvincing. Peggy, like Jerry, is attentive to the moon and stars, and she is able to revive her spirits by walking along the beach. It is Joe, however, who delivers the play's longest speech, which provides a rather didactic summary of some of the play's important themes:

Listen, sweetheart, you don't make a point when you say you're afraid—we're *all* afraid! Earl, Jerry, Mae, millions like them, clinging to a goofy dream—expecting life to be a picnic. Who taught them that? Radio, songs, the movies—you're the greatest people going. Paradise is just around the corner. Shake that hip, swing that foot—we're on the Millionaire Express! Don't cultivate your plot of ground—tomorrow you might win a thousand acre farm! What farm? The dream farm! Am I blue? Did you ask me if I'm blue! Sure, sometimes. Because I see what happens when we wait for Paradise. Tricky Otto comes along, with a forelock and a mustache. Then he tells them why they're blue. "You been wronged," he says. "They done you dirt. Now come along with me. Take orders, park your brains, don't think, don't worry; poppa tucks you in at night!" . . . And where does that end? In violence, destruction, cripples by the carload! But is that the end for us? No, sweetheart, not while a brain burns in my head. And not because we're better than them. But because we know the facts—the antipicnic facts. Because we know that Paradise begins in responsibility. (pp. 217–18)

Odets here is blaming the dreams perpetuated by popular culture for filling people's heads with the wrong dreams and the wrong ideals.

This argument is reiterated in the final scene in the projection booth, as the juvenile dialogue of the movie being shown—a love story—is counterpointed against the gruesome action onstage. Ironically, the gimmick only suggests that Odets's play is not much more meaningful than the average film, or the cited popular songs, "The Sheik of Araby" and "Avalon." The attempted criticism of popular culture is ambitious, but the terms of the charge are not fully explored in this play. Characterizing the movies and radio as a cause for discontent rather than a symptom is an issue Odets has not, in fact, addressed here; nor does the equation of such popular escapism with the onset of fascism find any echo in the plot of *Clash by Night*. Furthermore, this speech confuses the real problems at hand: Is Odets excusing Mae's affair with Earl? What is it about Joe and Peggy that places them above society's values? Because Odets has established no adequate connection in the play between the personal and the social, his sudden attack on the popular culture is as vague as his treatment of economics, fascism, and war.

The fact that Odets fails to develop the thematic complexities of the world outside of the play seriously undercuts its dramatic thrust. What most seriously hampers its effect, however, is the miscalculation of the characterization of the three central characters. In her review of *Clash by Night* Rosamond Gilder wrote of Mae as

the incarnation of the type that exists everywhere . . . of the desperate and the discontented, seeking always for something unachieved; seeking security and finding it demanding; seeking peace and finding it dull; seeking love and finding it dangerous.[6]

Nevertheless, Odets indicates little interest in and no sympathy for Mae's personal predicament. When introduced, she is singing "The Sheik of Araby," indulging her unhappiness in dreams of adventure and excitement. While she seems to know what she wants in a man, one "who will give her confidence" like her father or the Pennsylvania politician, Odets never makes clear why she ever married Jerry, or why she is now attracted to Earl, who is, on the evidence of his own words to her, as emotionally regressive as Jerry. It appears that Mae has never really tried to "live in a relationship wholly" with Jerry, but the reasons for her refusal to do so are not even hinted.

Her harsh treatment of Jerry throughout the play, finally, must destroy any incipient sympathy for her situation, and she degenerates into a kind of shrewish siren whom not even her moments of tender mothering can redeem.

Similar in certain ways to Hennie and Bessie in *Awake and Sing!* and Belle in *Rocket to the Moon,* all strong women who have married weak men, Mae is accorded none of the mitigating circumstances that qualify the other women's unpleasantness. Belle is shown to have been victimized by her father's relationship with her mother and emotionally frustrated by her inability to have a child. Her marriage problems are clearly rooted in the past and supported by a psychology that Odets develops in the play. She is, moreover, represented as vulnerable, especially at the end of the play, and capable of compassion, as in her relationship with Cooper.

Hennie, though like Mae in her willingness to abandon her family for another man, does have the excuse of having had her marriage imposed on her by her mother, and if she never emerges as a very sympathetic character, there is yet a sense of entrapment in her personal dilemma. Why a woman like Bessie would marry a man like Myron is problematic, yet in spite of her many faults of temperament, her strength and determination to keep her family both together and afloat make Bessie an admirable figure. Mae, however, displays no sense of responsibility beyond herself, no sense of family despite her careful attention to her infant daughter. Her hesitation about having an affair with Earl seems motivated less by loyalty and responsibility than by calculation as to whether Earl is worth the risk. Odets, in sum, does not provide Mae so much a sympathetic character as a potentially sympathetic motivation.

Jerry, too, is a problem. Thirty-seven years old, he seems more a child than an adult. He is sensitive in an elemental way, very good-natured and warm, and Odets obviously intends him to be the emotional protagonist of the play. But Jerry is too stupid, brutish, and essentially unperceptive to be taken seriously as a mature man. It is nearly impossible to identify with him, so he remains a merely pitiable figure, a victim of his own ignorance. Having practically arranged the affair between Earl and his wife, he is dumbfounded when Mae yells at him, with some justification:

You come around with your friend, a man I've never seen before! You jump up and down, like a kid with a new toy—practically push me into his bed! (pp. 152–53)

Jerry so naively trusts Earl and Mae that he never even suspects what is going on between them until his uncle tells him about it. When at last he confronts Earl and Mae about the affair, they have just returned from the amusement park with a teddy bear that Earl says reminds him of Jerry. At the conclusion of this scene Jerry picks up the teddy bear; Odets's stage directions emphasize the reflection of his infantile nature:

He picks up the teddy bear from the table, several times bending it at the waist—a doleful "Momma, Momma" answers him. He discards the teddy bear and snaps out the kitchen light. (p. 164)

During that confrontation scene Jerry remains basically inarticulate, and in a later scene when Mae tells him that she is leaving him, he passes out. Jerry is readily manipulated not only by Mae and Earl, but also by his uncle Vincent Kress, who easily convinces him to kill Earl at the end of the play.

Odets tries to mitigate the weakness of Jerry's character by placing some of the blame on economic hardship as a source of his emasculation. At one point Jerry does bemoan his uneasy situation, and his fears find some support in the sad example of his father:

You are just in the world on a rain check, as I see it. Nobody knows what'll happen next. Everything boils down to worry . . . nobody don't sleep a whole night's sleep no more. You could wake up some day an' find you're an old man with a tool kit under your arm an' they don't want you—not even your wife. (pp. 126–27)

Again, this is not a wholly convincing justification for the man's annoying passivity, for Earl and Joe are as much affected by the Depression's adversity, but neither seems so thoroughly incapacitated. Once more, the outer and inner worlds are not reconciled. Jerry recalls Lenny in Steinbeck's *Of Mice and Men,* a strong, sweet, childlike man; he is, unfortunately, not a figure to engage an audience's sympathetic identification.

Earl, like Jerry, is an aging child, though not as innocent, trusting, or simple. Joe remarks that Earl has "a lot of bluster and then a boyish grin." And, as an outsider, he does try to project a self-assurance that he cannot sustain; his occasional arrogance puts Mae off at the beginning. Like Jerry, Earl is looking for a home, complaining that his wife never provided him with one and lamenting for the security lost when his mother died. (In this he is linked with Steve Takis of *Night Music*.) However, it seems clear that Earl will not find this emotional haven with Mae, for despite his exterior he is not the "confident" man Mae longs for, but an immature soul, desperate for attention and quick to lapse into self-pity. When Jerry kills Earl at the end, he is at least saving his friend from another disappointing marriage.

Earl is another character whose connection with the socioeconomic world of the play is vague. Again Odets never successfully integrates the economic reality of Earl's life with the psychological. His search for a mother figure seems to be his sole motivating force. At the beginning of the play, when he is out of work, he seems only nominally affected by it. When he gets a job, it affords him the opportunity to buy drinks for his friends and gifts for Mae, but this success does not alter his attitude or his behavior.

In *Clash by Night* Odets attempted an ambitious exploration of the contemporary scene, encompassing fascism, democracy, economics, the war, and the effects of popular culture on the democratic psyche, and placing all of this within the context of human relationships. His notes indicate the philosophical breadth of his concept:

August 8: . . . The theme is taking shape in my mind, intensely personal but generally significant feeling behind it. The theme . . . has to do with the need of a new morality, with a return to voluntarily assumed forms in a world of democracy where there are no forms but plenty of appetite and irresponsibility. . . .
October 21: Part of the theme of this play is about how men irresponsibly wait for the voice and strong arm of Authority to bring them to life. . . . Nothing stands for Authority and we wait for its voice! . . . The children are looking for the father to arrange their lives for them![7]

He planned, further, to shape his play around the poetic vision of the great Victorian intellectual who also saw his world entering into an age without values, blindly bridging the gap between culture and anarchy. Hoping to give all this theoretical material shape within the melodramatic form, Odets changed the relationship between his themes and his characters from the dynamic interplay that animated his slice-of-life plays of 1935. In those early works, the vitality and mechanics of family life were real; the effects of economic hardship intensified family relationships, and the people seemed powerfully realized because of Odets's careful meshing of character and motivation.

In *Clash by Night* there is much melodramatic confrontation, as various figures conflict with one another, but the characters never seem to connect. They demonstrate no real relationship to each other or to the world they live in. They do not come together as a unit; no one has any understanding of the other, and it seems they never will. These people have desires that they can barely understand, but how these urges relate to their lives or to the larger world is beyond their scope. The triangle of Mae, Jerry, and Earl in no way concerns the story of Joe and Peggy. The possibility of social redemption, which broadens the scope of the other plays, does not exist here. These characters are merely trapped by circumstances; indeed, the social overtones merely falsify the play.

In utilizing the melodramatic form to emphasize the episodic conflict between individuals, Odets sought to distance the audience from his characters in order to draw attention to the various thematic threads he was attempting to weave together into the fabric of the play. Unfortunately, in creating a group of wholly uninteresting and unsympathetic characters, he destroyed the element of audience identification altogether, leaving only the spectacle of a simple melodramatic triangle with an unconvincing violent conclusion. Odets instinctively saw a play in *Clash by Night,* but he neglected to endow his characters with any intellectual or emotional harmony to redeem the ugliness of their story. One of Odets's great talents as a playwright being his ability to create full and sympathetic characters, *Clash by Night* stands alone as his only play where no such characters exist. In abandoning this special aspect of his talent, he condemned this play, which in conception was one of his most ambitious, to be his greatest artistic failure.

With the failure of *Clash by Night* Odets hit the low point of his career: the Group Theatre had dissolved, he was divorced from Luise Ranier, and his first play produced outside the Group's auspices had flopped. He would work on only one more play before retreating to Hollywood. In 1942 he adapted Konstantin Simonov's *The Russians* for presentation by the Theatre Guild as *The Russian People*. Popular in Russia, where it was performed by the Moscow Art Theater, Siminov's play was exported as a piece of cultural propaganda used to solidify the Soviet position with the Allies; in England Tyrone Guthrie directed his adaptation of the play for the Old Vic. Odets altered little, except some minor stage business, retaining the plot and the characters of the original. His contribution was primarily in streamlining and colloquializing the language, rendering the dialogue more stageworthy than in earlier English versions.

The plot of *The Russians* offers a chauvinistic portrayal of the Russian people's heroic attempts to stave off German aggression, employing stock scenes of bravery and betrayal, as well as a love story. The characters are cardboard representations of basic good and evil types: the Germans cruel and vicious, the Russians (except for a traitor) loving, noble, and heroic. The resolution is entirely predictable. Reviews reflected the dichotomy of response experienced by critics who felt obliged to praise a patriotic play by an ally, yet recognized that the play itself did not deserve their approbation. As Gerald Weales points out:

The reviews are a study in the conflict between allegiance and aesthetics. With our Russian allies fighting so desperately, how could an American critic hurt their cause by hating their play? Never have so many critics tried so hard to be nice. There were two kinds of reviews: those that said the Russian front is great, therefore the play must be good, and those that said the Russian front is great, but the play is bad.[8]

Despite these attempts to recommend its political respectability, the play closed after only thirty-nine performances, its ill success attributable more to Simonov's wooden original than to the Americanized acting version Odets prepared.

Prior to adapting *The Russians,* Odets had gone briefly to Hollywood to write a screenplay for Warner Brothers on the life of

George Gershwin. That screenplay was not used, but a film of Gershwin's life, entitled *Rhapsody in Blue*, was released in 1945. According to its director, Irving Rapper, much of Odets's material was used therein, although he received no screen credit. Odets moved to Hollywood in 1943, and he stayed there for the next five years. In 1943 he also married Bette Grayson, and during his residence in Hollywood his two children were born: Nora in 1945, and Walt Whitman in 1947. He prospered financially, though most of the projects he worked on were never produced. For RKO he worked on adaptations of *Sister Carrie*, which was later shelved; *The Greatest Gift*, which after revisions by other writers was produced as *It's a Wonderful Life; All Brides Are Beautiful*, which was to have starred Joan Fontaine but was also shelved; and two other projects that were revised by others and released, *Sister Kenny* and *Notorious*. For Metro-Goldwyn-Mayer Odets worked on *The Whispering Cup*, which was shelved, and an original screenplay, *April Shower*, which was never produced.[9]

Odets's first writing credit during this stint in Hollywood was for *None But the Lonely Heart* (1944), based on a novel by Richard Llewellyn; Odets also directed the film. The novel depicts the career of one Ernest Verdun Mott, a boy of nineteen, his father dead in World War I, who struggles to find a place in the world where he can reconcile the conflicting urges of his soul. For the film Odets modified this character to suit the star, Cary Grant: Ernie is no longer "pimpled and puerile,"[10] but a mature man, charming and self-confident. He resembles many other Odets protagonists, brazen and rebellious, yet inwardly troubled, responsible, and loving. Ernie feels deeply the loss of his father, and although he projects a defiant attitude toward his mother at the beginning of the film, he gradually must acknowledge his deep-seated need for her. He addresses all the older men in the film as "Dad," and some of the older women as "Ma." Rebelling against the poverty of his home and the family business of selling secondhand goods to poor people, he has become a bum, wandering about the English countryside. He explains to his mother that he despises "cheating pennies out of devils poorer than meself." When he learns that his mother is dying of cancer, however, he resolves to stay home, to work in the store and take care of her.

A number of Odetsian touches link the film to important motifs in his plays. A characteristic emphasis is placed on music; one of Ernie's skills is tuning pianos, for he has a perfect ear for notes. One of the film's central conflicts involves Ernie's familiar attachment to a cellist and music teacher, Aggie (Jane Wyatt), and his more fervent love for Ada (Jane Duprez), a cash girl at a fun fair and former wife of a local mobster, Mordinoy (George Coulouris). The opposing values of music and money are represented thus in Ernie's involvement with these two women. At the beginning of the film, after an argument with his mother, Ernie remarks to a neighbor about the beautiful music coming from her radio and then promises to tune her piano. Shortly thereafter he is in Aggie's house, listening as she plays "None But the Lonely Heart" on the cello and is affected by its melancholy melody.

Next he visits the fun fair, where he turns off a player piano that is out of tune. There he first meets Ada and Mordinoy, who pays Ernie not to fix the piano and tempts him with more money if he will work for him. Mordinoy objects to Ernie's clothes, referring to them as "rags"; Ernie responds that they are the "emblem of his independence." To Mordinoy's offer of a job he replies that a man can "be a victim or be a thug" and he wants to be neither. However, Ernie's growing involvement with Ada, his desire to provide for his mother, and his increasing disgust over his poverty lead him at length to become part of Mordinoy's gang. Meanwhile, in a parallel descent to crime, Ernie's mother, anxious to leave her son some money, becomes involved with selling stolen goods, and for this she eventually goes to jail.

Ernie's conflict has much in common with that of Joe Bonaparte in *Golden Boy*. While working with Mordinoy, Ernie begins to dress well and is able to buy his mother a refrigerator and a radio. Mordinoy, in fact, is much like Joe's criminal mentor, Eddie Fuseli, ruthless and exploitive of other people. (Interestingly, George Coulouris's performance as Mordinoy closely resembles Joseph Calleia's portrayal of Fuseli in the film version of *Golden Boy*.) Near the end of the film Mordinoy tells Ernie, "I'm a machine. I ain't human. I believe in nothing." As *None But the Lonely Heart* takes place on the eve of World War II, he is probably to be taken as an exemplar of the Nazi-Fascist mentality: in one scene Mordinoy watches as his thugs rob and beat a Jewish merchant, Ike Weller, who is a close friend of

Ernie's family. Because of his association with Mordinoy, Ernie loses the love of Ada, who has sought to escape the unsavory gangland environment; she wants a more secure, more respectable life, and, echoing Mae in *Clash by Night,* has told Ernie earlier in the film that she needs a man who can give her "confidence." In that scene Odets pictures the characters speaking through a gate that suggests that they will never get together.

During the course of the film Ernie benefits from the influence of two father surrogates. One is Ike Weller (Konstantin Shayne) the kindly Jewish merchant, who is respectfully protective of Ernie's mother. He is a warm and loving man, much like Mr. Bonaparte and Leo Gordon. He counsels Ernie at one point that "the places of the world are empty and the human heart is everything." It is Ike who tells Ernie of his mother's cancer, and who, late in the film, bails him out of jail. Ernie's other surrogate father is Henry Twite (Barry Fitzgerald), who recalls A. L. Rosenberger in *Night Music,* serving as an almost supernatural guide figure by materializing every time Ernie needs advice or a friend. Henry is the first person Ernie meets at the beginning of the film, when he enters a cathedral and sees a memorial for an unknown soldier killed during World War I, thus associating him with Ernie's own dead father. He is there again after Ernie hears about his mother's cancer and when he hears that his mother has been arrested; Henry also delivers Ada's goodbye note to Ernie. At one point in the film he even rides past the family store on a wagon and gives Ernie a basket of fruit (another Odetsian motif) as a gift for his mother.

At the end of the film Ernie realizes that by joining Mordinoy's gang he has made the wrong choice; he must join instead with those who will "fight for a human way of life," he explains to Henry as they hear warplanes flying overhead. In a speech reminiscent of Odets's earlier plays, he tells Henry, "I'm dreaming . . . dreaming the better man. . . . Where is that clear human life the books tell us about when the world comes out of its midnight?" Henry, like Rosenberger, replies, "So, if there's a better world to be made, you young ones will have to make it." The film's final moments, then, follow Ernie walking alone; he peers through Aggie's lighted window, listening to the cello music.

None But the Lonely Heart was well received by the critics. It won several Academy Award nominations: Best Actor (Cary Grant), Best Supporting Actress (Ethel Barrymore), Film Editing (Roland Gross), and Musical Score (Hans Eisler and C. Bakaleinikoff); Ethel Barrymore won an Oscar.

In 1947, when HUAC was trying to establish the prevalence of communist propaganda in Hollywood films, Leila Rogers (Ginger Rogers's mother) called *None But the Lonely Heart* a film that "takes time out for a bit of propaganda treatment whenever director Clifford Odets . . . felt the urge." She also remarked that it was "moody and somber throughout in the Russian manner." Odets referred to these allegations in a letter to *Time* magazine, in which he bitterly denounced the committee:

> Shut my big unamused mouth if I don't think the Thomas Committee is a disgrace to the United States. . . . As for myself, Mrs. Rogers, Mr. Warner and any other witnesses who claim for me Communist Party membership are talking wildly thru their heresay. . . .
>
> Of course, everyone knows there is an un-American conspiracy existent in Hollywood. It consists in degrading and knocking out the brains of the entire American people by a relentless distribution of the hopelessly vulgar and neurotically superficial trash called the Hollywood film. The rare exception only proves the rule. But it will be some time before I am sufficiently unsexed to relinquish my very American dream of a nation of mature and great people to the cynical Hollywood conception of human life.
>
> In conclusion, I get damn tired of hearing crackpots here and in Washington constantly ascribing anything really human in films to the Communists alone. Why do they keep giving the Devil all the good tunes?[11]

On the strength of the critical reception of *None But the Lonely Heart,* MGM signed Odets to a lucrative contract to write and direct several films. He then spent a year under contract without any of his projects being accepted for production. Odets did receive screen credit on two other films in the 1940s, neither of them of much significance to his career. The first, *Deadline at Dawn* (RKO, 1946), was based on the novel of the same title by William Irish (Cornell Woolrich) and directed by Harold Clurman. It focuses on a sailor (Bill Williams) on leave in New York City, who must clear himself of a murder charge in a period of six hours if he is to get back to his base on time. He is aided by a dance-hall girl (Susan Hayward) and a philosophic cab driver (Paul Lukas) who finally confesses to the murder. The cabbie has most of the best lines as he philosophizes about urban existence.

In that same year Odets collaborated with Zachary Gold on *Humoresque* (Warner Brothers), based on the Fannie Hurst story and directed by Jean Negulesco. The project was originally intended as a remake of the successful silent film of 1920, the first picture to win the *Photoplay* magazine Gold Medal; however, the story was altered to give prominence to the character played by Joan Crawford. The original story and film concerns a mother's devotion to her son, who shows early talent for the violin and eventually becomes a great musician. In the 1946 version the emphasis is refocused on the impassioned romance of Paul Boray (John Garfield) and Helen Wright (Crawford), a wealthy married socialite who falls in love with Paul and insists on guiding his career. The love story is enacted against a background of violin music ranging from Dvorak's "Humoresque" to the "Liebestod of Tristan and Isolde" adapted for the violin by Isaac Stern (who actually plays the violin in the film). What was a drama about a mother's love for her son thus becomes a story of love too impassioned to survive. The climax of the film comes as Crawford, convinced, after a confrontation with Garfield's mother, that there is no longer any hope of possessing him, decides to kill herself: with the notes of the "Liebestod" in the background, her sequined gown blowing against the wind, she walks to the beach and into the sea. Indeed, Odets's script might be subtitled "The Golden Boy Variations," for he borrows heavily from his own earlier work, though varying the theme in a significant way. (Interestingly, John Garfield was Odets's choice to play Joe Bonaparte in the original stage version of that play.)

The film opens upon the New York skyline at night, then focuses on signs announcing a Paul Boray concert as passersby mill about; moments later a man pastes a "Program Cancelled" sign on the poster. Next there is a closeup of Paul's distraught face as he stares from the balcony of his apartment: Helen Wright, the woman he loves, has just killed herself, although the viewer cannot know this yet. His manager, trying to raise his spirits, points to a record and declares, "There's your biography . . . Paul Boray virtuoso! Artist!" The artist's need to sacrifice all for his art and the isolation and pain of the artist's existence, two of Odets's preoccupations, are thus stressed at the outset. Paul then gives voice to a longing for a return to his childhood, when his life was happy and seemingly uncomplicated, and this speech echoes many similar expressions of nostalgic regret in the plays:

All my life I wanted to do the right thing but it never worked out. I'm outside always looking in. Feeling all the time I'm far away from home. Where home is I don't know. I can't get back to the simple, happy kid I used to be.

The film narrative then reverts to Paul's childhood and follows his rise to prominence as a concert violinist. The extended flashback opens with Paul as a small boy; it is his birthday. His parents run a grocery store, and the family lives very modestly. Paul's mother (Ruth Nelson) is named Esther, which was the name of Odets's favorite aunt (he will use it again, for Noah's wife, in *The Flowering Peach*). She insists that her husband (J. Carrol Naish) must buy the boy whatever he wants for his birthday. Mr. Boray tries to interest his son in a baseball bat, but Paul insists on a violin. Frustrated and angered by his son's refusal to choose a more "normal" gift, the father takes him home with no present and maintains to his wife that the boy's interest in the violin will amount to nothing, and that even if he should develop a talent for playing, it would have no practical, commercial value. The mother, nevertheless, is sympathetic, and she immediately goes out herself to purchase the instrument. These scenes parallel Odets's own childhood experience: his father, disgusted by his son's aspirations toward acting and then writing, insisted that he be more practical, while Odets's mother attempted to encourage her son's dreams, though she was not a domineering and aggressive presence like Mrs. Boray. Unlike Odets's father, Mr. Boray betrays some sympathy beneath his blustering exterior, so he is, in much of his behavior, closer to Mr. Bonaparte than to Louis Odets.

Paul, unlike Joe, does not opt for success with the baseball bat, but singlemindedly pursues his art to the exclusion of all else. Like Joe, however, he is confident and brash, particularly about his talent; he is also anxious for success. His best friend Sid Jeffers (Oscar Levant) remarks to him, "You're suffering from the all-American itch. You want to get there first but you don't want to pay for the ride."—a very Odetsian line, though Levant probably wrote most of his own dialogue. Paul eventually meets Helen Wright, a wealthy but unstable socialite who decides to guide and finance his career. As they fall in love, Paul loses touch with his family and the values they represent. A scene in which Helen takes Paul to a tailor to choose more appropriate clothing for his concerts recalls a similar one in *Golden Boy*, wherein Eddie Fuseli buys new shirts for Joe. However, again unlike Joe, Paul refuses to dress as he is told: he accepts a new suit but insists on his own style. Like Louis Brant of "Victory," he is uncomfortable in "monkey suits" unless they are of his own choosing. The film, finally, provides an interesting speculation on Joe Bonaparte's possible fate had he pursued his musical career and married Lorna: Odets maintains here, as in "Victory," that art is all-consuming and admits no distractions, including love—except, perhaps, a mother's.

Negulesco's direction is fine, displaying some interesting *noir* touches and thematically suggestive editing. In one concert sequence Negulesco intersperses shots of Paul playing the violin—the standard, often-repeated shot in the film is a close-up on Paul's face, violin tucked under his chin—and of the three women in his life: his mother, Helen, and Gina, the young woman friend from their student days at the Institute, who represents a more stable love interest. The director cuts from Paul to a close-up of his mother, who then eyes Helen in her box, and then to a close-up of Helen herself. At a key moment in the performance, Helen's face fills the screen in an extreme close-up, wherein only her lips are seen, suggesting vividly her passion for the man. But the editing indicates also how isolated she is from Paul's world, for between her and the fulfillment of her desires are Paul's music and his mother. This shot of Crawford's lips is repeated at the end of the film as Helen is about to walk into the ocean to commit suicide; it enforces the connection between the nature of her love and death.

Oscar Levant maintained that this version of *Humoresque* was based in part on Odets's rejected script for *Rhapsody in Blue*. The film does bear only a slight resemblance to the original Fannie Hurst story and to the Frances Marion script for the silent version. The score by Franz Waxman, consisting of twenty-three classical pieces, received an Academy Award nomination.

By 1947 the first investigations by The House Un-American Activities Committee into the film industry had begun; by the end of November of that year, the Hollywood Ten had been cited for contempt and the blacklist was inaugurated. Perhaps in part because of the hysterical mood engendered in Hollywood by these developments, Odets returned to New York in 1948. His play about Hollywood, *The Big Knife*, opened in 1949, and *The Country Girl* a year later.

During his lifetime Odets tended to dismiss *The Country Girl*. He told Michael Mendelsohn:

Secondly, in a play like *The Country Girl*, which is relatively, in the body of my work, a superficial play, I knew just exactly how that play should become successful. I wanted to do a successful production. And in that case I trusted no one else.[12]

Odets's attitude toward *Golden Boy*, his other Broadway success, was similar: he considered it, too, a potboiler written primarily for money. Ironically, those two were to be the longest-running plays of his career.

The genesis of the play, Odets explained, happened by chance:

Very simply, I have thousands of ideas in my files; twenty or thirty plays outlined at a time. The important thing is what impels me to work on any one of them. In the case of *The Counry Girl*, the idea wasn't worked out very much. I happened to see Charles Coburn in New York and he mentioned he wanted to do a play. I looked in my files and got this idea and soon began to write. I soon realized that Coburn was too old for the triangle of the two men and the girl. Practically speaking, however, if Coburn hadn't mentioned wanting to do a play, I might not have started *The Country Girl*.[13]

In the fall of 1950 the play went into production, Odets and Lee Strasberg coproducing along with Dwight Deere Wiman. Odets himself directed, and he explained his directing philosophy this way:

To my mind, there are three ways to direct a play. First *critically*. That is, to analyze each scene and moment for the actors. Secondly, to direct it *synthetically,* to take the material of the play and create something new out of it by enlarging it. Thirdly, and the best way, is a combination of both. In the years I've spent in the theatre, I almost feel that it is better not to have the actors know too much of the philosophical overtones of a play. The affinity of the actor to the part is far more important. I'm against this business of philosophical nonsense where an actor with three lines wants to know what his motivation is to say "Hello" to the lead during a minor moment.[14]

The play opened in Boston on October 24, 1950, and in New York on November 10. The majority of reviews were enthusiastic, Brooks Atkinson of the *New York Times* proclaiming, "Clifford Odets has really got down to work. *The Country Girl* is the best play he has written for years, perhaps the best play of his career."[15] The play ran for 235 performances, and by the time it closed, it had been sold to the movies. It also received a London run in 1952 under the title *Winter Journey,* which had been Odets's original title for *The Big Knife.* The film version, released in 1954, was also successful, receiving nominations for seven Academy Awards, including Best Picture, Best Actor (Bing Crosby), Best Actress (Grace Kelly), Best Director (George Seaton), and Best Screenplay (George Seaton); Grace Kelly and Seaton's script were awarded the Oscars. The film version was altered slightly for Bing Crosby, changing Frank Elgin from an actor to a musical performer and singer.

The Country Girl is Odets's most insular play. The outside world and its problems have been so totally excluded here that, for the first time, an Odets play projects no social theme or wider implications. The world of the play is the theater itself, and most of the action takes place in the theater, opening during a rehearsal and concluding in the midst of a New York opening. This setting gives the play an atmosphere of fantasy: Georgie remarks at the end of act 1, scene 3, "nothing is quite so mysterious and silent as a dark theater . . . a night without a star." And this aspect of mystery infuses the play, wherein the human story is bound up with the theater itself.

The Country Girl presents another triangular situation, involving Frank Elgin, a fifty-year-old actor, his wife Georgie, who is in her thirties, and a director, Bernie Dodd, who is thirty-five. Once a star, Frank Elgin is now an alcoholic, unable to hold on to a job. Bernie

Dodd, who is directing a new play, remembers Frank's former greatness and so decides to cast him in the lead, despite the strenuous objections of the producer, Phil Cook. Georgie has, through the years, stood by her husband and cared for him, though when introduced she is packing to leave him. The revelation of her relationship with Frank and the evolution of her feelings for Bernie form the crux of the play.

The melodramatic tension derives from two central questions. The first, which sets the play in motion, is whether Bernie Dodd's confidence in Frank is justified: will Bernie be able to help Frank regain his confidence and rekindle his talent, thus making the play a success? The second, developing primarily in act 2, involves Bernie's growing attraction to Georgie and her increasing impatience with her husband's weakness: will she leave Frank for Bernie Dodd? The final scene resolves both questions, as Frank delivers a great performance at the New York opening, ensuring the play's success, and Georgie at last decides to stay with Frank. Thus *The Country Girl*, like *Night Music*, is Odets's second play to feature a conventional happy ending.

Although the play opens with Bernie's decision to take a chance on Frank and with Frank's audition for the part, it is, finally, Georgie who occupies center stage in the unfolding story. The play, indeed, suffers from some confusion of focus at times, resulting from Odets's occasional inability to clarify Georgie as the protagonist. Later Odets admitted to having changed the nature of her character a number of times while working on the play:

I wrote at least two or three versions of the play before showing it to anyone. No one saw it before the fourth draft. The differences in the versions were mainly rewriting of certain scenes pertaining to the dramatic structure. I didn't know until the second draft, for example, that Georgie wasn't a very destructive, bitchy woman. She really was in the first drafts. She had cancer too, and discovers in the middle of the play she hasn't much time to live. I wrote that out, however—How God-like. You give someone cancer, then take it away. Maybe playwrights should cure cancer, instead of doctors. Put a sheet of paper into the typewriter, take it out and cancer is cured.[16]

Georgie, however, is increasingly revealed as the central force in the struggle of wills, as Frank remains dependent on her, while, as the play progresses, she assumes a strong hold on Bernie as well.

The Country Girl opens in a darkened theater, illuminated by only a small light; music from a radio is heard in the background, and the musical motif is underscored as Bernie exclaims, "Where's that music coming from?" Music is thus associated from the outset with the darkened world of the theater; it will later be linked with Georgie as well. In act 1, scene 2 when she is introduced, Georgie occupies a small, darkened room lighted only by a lamp and a small window, as music is heard from a radio. The analogy of this setting to the opening scene confirms Georgie's place of importance in the play, for she is identified with music and the theater, facets of the power of art that drives the two central male characters and also draws them to her.

This musical/theatrical touchstone is used, in addition, to suggest her husband's estrangement from her and from the world of art she inhabits. When Bernie is trying to persuade Cook to let Frank read for the part, he remarks, "A little realism is of the essence." Then, when Frank enters, Bernie yells, "Shut off the radio"—invoking the characteristic Odetsian contradiction between the real and the musical ideal. Once a vital part of the theater but now banished from it because of his alcoholism, Frank is firmly associated with the real world and its attendant pains, which have come between him and his talent. In recalling his happier past, Frank refers less to his theatrical success than to the details of everyday life with Georgie:

I bought a fourteen-room house down in Great Neck the year we married. Never knew a better life. Swimming, boating, tennis, dinner at six—at seven she'd kiss me good-bye and I'd drive into town for my show. On matinee days she'd come in and we'd stay out late. Little spats and things, but it looked like a dream life to me.[17]

Frank, like many another Odets character, suffers from the disparity between his inner vision, a remembrance of when he flourished, in harmony with the theater and Georgie, and the harsh reality of his current life.

Bernie, too, cherishes an inner vision, bound up in the theater and memories of his youth. Speaking to Frank and Georgie in act 1, scene 2, he recalls having seen Frank in two plays:

I was a kid when I saw you give two great performances in mediocre plays— *Proud People* and *Werba's Millions*. I can get the same show out of you right now . . . if you lay off the liquor! I have more confidence in you than you have in yourself! (p. 30)

In trying to rescue Frank, apparently, Bernie is in some way trying to recapture a dream, as if by reclaiming the old actor's talent, he hopes to restore to the theater the magic he remembers experiencing there as a youth. He wants to forget the realistic, business aspect of the theater (represented by Cook) and immerse himself in the artistry of inspiration and performance. Late in the play Bernie says to Georgie, "I'm interested in theater, not show business. I could make a fortune in films, but that's show 'biz' to me." In Frank, Bernie sees an opportunity to revive his theatrical ideal. Echoes of Odets's own experience can be felt in Bernie's speech and in Bernie's character as a whole. After an exile in Hollywood where he worked in "show biz," Odets, too, longs to create real theater, to reclaim his true vocation and his real "home." *The Country Girl* thus can be read as an homage to the magic of theater, just as *The Big Knife,* which immediately preceded it, constitutes an attack on the antithetical "show biz."

Bernie, moreover, finds something of his father in this older man: in scene 1, he informs Unger, the playwright, that he can handle Frank because "my father was a lush—I have some background for the job." By reactivating Frank's confidence and his talent, he seems to be seeking to do for him what he never could do for his own father. Frank, as a dependent father figure, may therefore serve, in the context of the theater, to restore Bernie's sense of wholeness by resurrecting the father he lost.

In scene 2, when Bernie first meets Georgie, she turns off the music as Bernie enters. Her room is like the theater, dark and dimly lit, and, like the theater, it is a world beyond time, as she indicates: "Three clocks, a radio . . . and never know the time." Next to a picture of Frank, taken in his heyday, is one of her father. Later it will be made clear that Georgie feels orphaned, much as Bernie does, when she tells Frank in act 1, scene 4:

Take a lesson from my father, the late Delaney the Great. He didn't care
what people thought of him, no matter what he did. Played every vaudeville
house in the world. Didn't show up at home but twice a year . . . and those
two times he was down in the cellar perfecting new magic tricks. (p. 53)

For her, too, Frank functions as a father substitute; she seems to
have married in the hope that the handsome, dynamic leading man
could provide the strong masculine presence missing from her childhood. For Georgie, Frank represented thus the very spirit of romance:

You don't know what it is . . . meet, marry, elope . . . nineteen, romantic,
real cute, raised on too many books. Oh, my, I had such a naive belief in
Frank's worldliness and competence. Yes, I saw he drank . . . but that was
only a pathetic hint of frailty in a wonderful glowing man. (p. 105)

Like Mary Tyrone in O'Neill's *Long Day's Journey into Night,* she
married a dashing, older actor because she was looking for a home,
but the dream died and she never found one. In their efforts to
reform Frank and to seek for something forever lost, Bernie and
Georgie are therefore linked.

However, certain essential differences between them remain. Bernie, like many Odets characters, displays a gruff, arrogant exterior
that conceals a basic insecurity and loneliness. Proclaiming himself a
realist, hardened by life, he tells Georgie and Frank in act 2, scene 2:

I come from realistic people—I'm Italian. I'm not blind to Frank's condition—he's a bum! But I'm tough, not one of those nice "humane" people:
they hand you a drink and a buck and that's exactly where they stop. I won't
hand you a buck. (p. 31)

This toughness, he explains, derives from his experiences with his
alcoholic father, who has died "under subway tracks," and a bad
marriage. His attitude toward his ex-wife is reminiscent of Earl's:

Five months ago she invented a phrase, "the perennial bachelor," and went
to Reno to patent the invention! (p. 40)

He is, also, the father of a four-year-old daughter whom he barely

mentions. (One of the reasons offered for Frank's drinking and for
the disintegration of his marriage is the death of a child. In Odets's
earlier plays the loss or absence of children often wounds a marriage,
as in *Rocket to the Moon,* although children are not enough to keep a
marriage healthy, as in *Clash by Night* or *Awake and Sing!*)

Despite Bernie's bitterness, he remains boyish and idealistic, as
Unger, the playwright, tells Georgie:

Despite the talent, he's a dumb innocent kid in more ways than one. He's in
love with art, for instance, and would make it a felony that you are not. (p.
75)

Because of his wife's desertion, Bernie mistrusts women, taking an
initial dislike to Georgie. He believes Frank when he tells him that
Georgie is an alcoholic, incapable of dealing with their marriage, and
needs his care; Bernie is willing to see her as manipulative and
destructive, at one point calling her a "bitch." Twice in the play he
even addresses Georgie as "Mrs. Dowd," apparently identifying her
with the ex-wife whom he detests. Ironically, however, this repeated
misnaming hints, instead, at Bernie's subconscious attraction to
Georgie; by the end of the play he declares his love for her and
attempts to win her away from Frank. Pleading his loneliness and
rootlessness in the final scene, he tells her, "A job is a home to a
homeless man. Now the job is finished—where do I go from here?"
(p. 113). Then, passionately, he declares, "You could be a home for
me—that's real!" (p. 114).

The reiteration of the word "home" in Bernie's appeal for love
evokes another familiar Odetsian theme (see Moe, Steve Takis, and
Earl), while suggesting a submerged familial configuration in the
triangular situation that has developed among the principal characters. Considering Bernie's association of Frank with his father, it
may be that he responds here to Georgie as a mother figure, recognizing in the Elgins the potential home he has never had. Thus it
becomes significant that in act 1, scene 1, when Bernie and Frank
improvise a scene from the play together, Frank takes the paternal
role and Bernie, that of a young man in love with his granddaughter;
during that scene Frank calls Bernie "son." Then in act 2, scene 2
Bernie's dialogue echoes this relationship:

BERNIE: I want you to do something for the kid—
FRANK: What kid?
BERNIE: *This* kid! (p.102)

Thus regularly assuming a filial position in dealing with Frank, Bernie is at last drawn to Frank's young wife, whose qualities of loyalty and self-sacrifice appeal to him as a promise of security and maternal care.

Frank Elgin is an extremely insecure man, who is, as Bernie gradually discovers, dependent on his wife for whatever self-esteem he may have left. Once an acclaimed actor, he is now an apparently hopeless alcoholic. Like Odets himself, Frank is a man who has suffered a lengthy period of separation from his true vocation, and so his alcoholism may be construed as a metaphor for Odets's own removal to Hollywood. His explanation of his decline even mirrors Odets's career in some detail:

I knew it then—on the coast—I lost my nerve! And then, when we lost the money in '39, after those lousy Federal Theater jobs—! This is the face that once turned down radio work. What ever the hell I did, I don't know what! But I'm good! I'm still good, baby, because I see what *they think* is good! (p. 33)

Later Frank elaborates further, blaming Georgie for the disintegration of his life:

Then we had a child. . . . After that . . . every part I play, it's just like I ran off with another woman. I begin to drink myself. Don't ask me where the money went. She cuts her wrists, sets fire to a hotel suite—any time I'm on the stage she needs a nurse to watch her. And then, finally, we lost the child. You don't say, "Go to hell, goodbye!" do you? By 1940, '41—well, when you're in that situation you beat a bottle hard! (p. 45)

Once the toast of Broadway, Odets, too, began his decline with the end of the Federal Theater grants in 1939 and the dissolution of Group Theatre in 1940. Since that time, he, too, has been floundering. In Odets's case the lost child may have been the Group, and the home and talent repository it represented; or it may have been, simply, his talent: after his great successes of the thirties, *Night Music*, the adaptation *The Russian People*, and *Clash by Night* all failed. And just as Georgie remarks later that Frank went to Hollywood, where certain deals did not work out well, Odets's Hollywood career, too, was checkered with uncompleted projects and mediocre finished ones. Frank thus incarnates the painful disillusion of the older Odets, while Bernie represents the youthful idealism of his past.

Frank is dependent on other people's affection—Odets, again, was easily hurt by critical reaction to his plays, and often courted the critics—and utterly reliant on Georgie's support, desperately needing her to help him through the production in rehearsal. Symbolically, Frank needs Georgie (music) and Bernie (theater) if he is to regain his own artistry and the status he once enjoyed. Frank himself recognizes their contribution to his comeback when, in the midst of his triumph, he says:

I . . . I don't know how to say this . . . but no matter what happens, you have saved me, Georgie . . . you and Bernie. I think I have a chance. (p. 122)

Frank seems a most sympathetic character at the beginning of the play, weak but charming. However, when his lies about Georgie's alcoholism are revealed, the play's center of interest shifts to Georgie. Suddenly Frank seems a less-interesting character than his wife because his victory is not to be so hard won as hers, which must come from the marshaling of inner resources, while Frank's derives largely from the hard work and sacrifice of others. Georgie, finally, pronounces the play's central insights, and so it is the heroism of her loyalty, rather than the process of Frank's revitalization, which dominates the play.

Georgie's recurrent association with the music from her radio, and with the aesthetic idealism it represents, provides a reliable index to her feelings and to the sensibilities of those around her. In act 1, scene 5, during one of Georgie's and Bernie's arguments, Odets's stage directions read:

He looks at her carefully, with a polite charm, masking a certain scorn. Despite her awareness of his good sense, Georgie is somewhere disturbed by him. Thinking, she turned on a small radio. (p. 61)

Frank enters immediately after this action, and he, too, argues with her, shouting, "Shut the radio off." Frank's order echoes Bernie's of act 1, scene 1, and Georgie's turning off the radio duplicates her similar action in act 1, scene 2. Symbolically it is made clear that neither man can fulfill Georgie's need for music, for romance, because neither has the capacity or understanding to appreciate her.

In act 2, scene 1, which immediately follows, Georgie is again listening to the radio while she talks to Unger. He is typing a revision of the play, and Georgie is explaining to him why Frank started drinking:

I'd say bad judgment started him off. He had some money once, but you don't know my Frank—he wanted to be his own producer—eighty thousand went in fifteen months, most of it on two bad shows. I didn't know a thing about it—he was afraid to tell me. A year later we lost our child. . . . it was awesome how he went for the bottle. . . . he just didn't stop after that. (p. 74)

The music here underlines the counterpoint between Georgie's longing and the reality of her relationship to Frank. The conversation quickly changes to Bernie, thus juxtaposing the two men, as Georgie asks, "What's wrong with him? His wife?" (p. 74). Georgie's speech about Frank here revises Frank's similar complaint about her in act 1, scene 3, wherein he tried to blame his troubles on Georgie, as Bernie does on his ex-wife. The musical motif then continues when Unger asks, "Does my typing bother you?" and Georgie replies, "No. Does the music?" Again, the linkage of theater and music demonstrates the complexity of the relationship between Georgie's music (her romantic longings) and the mysterious theater world that both attracts and frustrates her in the guise of Frank and Bernie. Unger, the playwright, is the one male character who is not bothered by music—of course, neither is the playwright Clifford Odets, but realizing the musical ideal in life remains a problem for his three principal characters and a continuing concern for the artist as well.

One of Odets's most suggestive moments occurs later in the same scene. Georgie is alone, and Odets describes her private reverie in the following way:

Georgie remains standing at mirror; takes off her glasses, looks at herself; something poignant reaches out from image to reality. The radio has begun playing a waltz. Georgie begins to sway in its rhythm and, in another moment, she is waltzing alone, almost as if it were possible to waltz herself back to a better time. What she is murmuring to herself we can not hear. (pp. 82–83)

Bernie enters, interrupting her trance, and Georgie, flustered, asks for some aspirin, claiming to have a headache. A few moments later, the spell having completely dissipated she turns off the radio. When Bernie kisses Georgie at the end of act 2, scene 2, Odets's stage directions appear to refer to the scene just described: "Then she seems to come out of a sleep" (p. 109). At this point the strained relationship between the two ceases. Significantly, at the end of this scene, Bernie calls Georgie "Mrs. Elgin," indicating that she is no longer a substitute for his ex-wife or his mother, but a woman in her own right. Georgie, too, flowers, for she understands that she has found something special.

Despite her romantic idealism, Georgie proves herself both practical and perceptive. She recognizes the childish dependence of her husband, and she understands what attracted her to Frank and why her efforts to reform him have ended in defeat. Still, she suffers, as is indicated in her plaint in act 1, scene 4, when she tells Frank that she hasn't felt like a woman in ten years, to which he replies, "I suppose that's my fault?" Georgie's cryptic answer—"Summer dies, autumn comes, a fact of nature—nobody's fault" (p. 53)—encompasses both her contempt for him and her resignation to the inevitability of disappointment. She goes on to compare him to her father, who, thought an absent figure, at least exuded confidence: "Might not have married you, if I'd had a father. But he believed in himself, I mean—you don't. That's cost you plenty. . . . it's cost me as much" (p. 53). Unlike her mother, who seems to have accepted her husband's constant absences, Georgie has been finding life with Frank increasingly difficult; indeed, she is first shown packing to leave. Frank's chance to reassert himself in the new play convinces her to give the marriage one more chance. When he later wavers and considers leaving the play, she openly challenges him, "If you walk off this show too, you'll never see me again." During the course of the play Odets gradually reveals the extent of Georgie's sacrifice in this marriage, and so her threats to leave Frank do not alienate the audience's sympathy. Unlike Mae in *Clash by Night,* Georgie is someone who has committed herself wholly to her relationship, and we sense her frustration and despair.

Georgie not only understands her husband, but is able to see through Bernie as well. She calls him "Bernardo the Great," which echoes her calling her father "Delaney the Great." The association indicates that Georgie sees in Bernie the same excessive dedication to his "magic" that her father had, and it also suggests a similar inability to be a husband and father. In act 2, scene 1, she calls him a "boy" and tells him that, "Life is earnest, life is real, and so are invest-ments," implying that he has no real understanding of Frank or the reality of human commitment. Shortly before Bernie kisses her, during an argument about Frank's real nature, she tells him:

Mr. Dodd . . . we had a town idiot when I was a child. . . . he kept insisting that elephant's tusks come from piano keys. You are very obtuse and wilful, for a man who so relishes his own humanity. (p. 104)

When Bernie admits that he was wrong, she tells him, "Then you have learned something—ripeness is all!" (p. 107). Georgie, though no older than Bernie, is much the wiser.

Odets's psychological melodrama reaches its climax in the final moments of the last scene, when Bernie declares his love to Georgie, and she must make her choice. When Frank comes backstage after a scene, she tells him:

Frank, I certainly didn't want to bring up any of this tonight. But you did . . . so let's have the whole truth. I married you for happiness, Frank . . . and, if necessary, I'll leave you for the same reason. (p. 121)

And then adds:

And yet I'm sure that both our lives are at some sort of turning point. . . . there's some real new element of hope here. . . . I don't know what. But I'm uncertain . . . and you, Frank, have to be strong enough to bear that uncertainty. (p. 122)

When she hears the audience applauding Frank's third act entrance she exclaims, "He's handsome tonight," then begins "humming Frank's snatch of a tune," and gathers some tissues and towels to help dry him off when he returns. With these gestures she makes clear her choice: she has rediscovered the handsome Frank that she fell in love with, significantly reassociating him with music. Bernie comprehends her determination and bids her good night, remarking that she is "steadfast, and loyal . . . reliable." The play concludes with her words of encouragement to him: "Wrestle Bernie. . . . you may win a blessing. But stay unregenerate. Life knocks the sauciness out of us soon enough" (p. 124). Clearly, Bernie will most likely "win a blessing," and Georgie surely has won hers. All three share in the benediction, and Odets does so as well.

Within the world of the theater, Odets has fashioned a struggle involving art, idealism, and the fragility of human relationships, presenting three fully developed protagonists who are flawed but manage to learn, and who promise to emerge from the struggle stronger and better able to battle with life. Unlike those in *Night Music*, the central characters here do not need a Rosenberger to guide them, but all help each other and themselves. However lasting their sense of purpose at the play's end, and however realistic their hope to sustain it, Odets identifies in their final reconciliation a genuine moment of triumph and insight. The pessimism of *Clash by Night* has been purged; in *The Country Girl* he has achieved a vision of harmony.

7

The Political Vision
Waiting for Lefty (1935)
Till the Day I Die (1935)
"I Can't Sleep" (1935)
"The Cuban Play" (1935–38)
"The Silent Partner" (1936)

There was always, as a child, and right now as a man, something awesome to me about a tree . . . laden with fruit. . . . I think these things are related to the mechanisms of what is a poet, because the thing keeps a firstness. . . . I still do what I did when I was twelve years old and saw an airplane fly over the Bronx. . . . There's no time I don't lift my eyes and look up at the sky.
—Clifford Odets, 1961

In the fall of 1934, *New Theatre* and *New Masses* jointly sponsored a contest, offering fifty dollars for the best revolutionary play. Odets, then an unknown bit player with the Group Theatre, submitted *Waiting for Lefty,* which he had written in three nights in a hotel room in Boston. In January, his play was performed at one of the New Theatre League's Sunday night benefit performances by members of the Group Theatre. In February, the play was published in

New Theatre, and in March the editor of that journal, Herbert Kline, who was also one of the contest judges, cited *Waiting for Lefty* as the best entry, adding that the more than two hundred other entries were mostly mediocre.

When *Waiting for Lefty* premiered on January 5, 1935, also on the bill were Philip Stevenson's *God's in His Heaven* and the dances of Anna Sokolow. Odets, himself a member of the Communist Party at the time, occasionally directed plays for the Theater Union while also performing with the Group. One of the functions of the Sunday evenings being to provide entertainment for members of the Party-affiliated organizations and unions, he had decided to stage *Waiting for Lefty* for that audience. Luther Adler, who appeared in the play, remarked to Harold Clurman that "the Group has produced the finest revolutionary playwright in America."[1] Yet the effect of Odets's first produced work was to transcend the boundaries of the didactic revolutionary play. It remains today the only such play that is still read and anthologized, and it is generally recognized as a part of mainstream American drama. *Waiting for Lefty* was certainly the most admired play of its kind during the thirties. Clurman termed it, in fact, "the birth cry of the thirties," describing its premiere in *The Fervent Years:*

The first scene of *Lefty* had not played two minutes when a shock of delighted recognition struck the audience like a tidal wave. Deep laughter, hot assent, a kind of joyous fervor seemed to sweep the audience toward the stage.[2]

Stanley Burnshaw, in *New Masses,* wrote of the opening in a similar vein:

On Jan. 5, when the curtain rang down on the first performance of Clifford Odets' *Waiting for Lefty* the audience cheered, whistled and screamed with applause. One week later when the same actors had repeated their performances, the Fifth Avenue Theatre, packed to capacity with hundreds of standees, fairly burst with a thunder of hand-claps and shouting.[3]

Of course *Lefty* did play before primarily sympathetic audiences, and so this wild enthusiasm is understandable: its reception is analogous to that accorded to overtly religious plays by audiences united in their acceptance of certain beliefs. But the popularity of Odets's play went beyond such catering to the faithful, for even some of the more perceptive critics who found fault with the play nevertheless joined with the audiences in celebrating it.

After this auspicious opening *Lefty* was performed at countless benefits. The Group eventually brought it to Broadway, where it was presented with another Odets one-act play, *Till the Day I Die*, opening on March 26, 1935, at the Longacre Theater. Next it moved to the Belasco and ran for a week with *Awake and Sing!* While the Group was preparing its new season in the fall, this double bill reopened and ran for three more weeks before moving to Philadelphia for a five-week run. In addition, the play appeared almost simultaneously all over the country, performed mostly by workers' groups.

Not surprisingly, *Lefty* also aroused a good deal of hostility. In Boston the actors were evicted from the Long Wharf Theater as "Communists." Police broke up a production in Newark, and there were a number of arrests. Even after all the furor died down, *Lefty* remained a popular play with socially politically oriented theater groups. S. J. Perelman even parodied it in "Waiting for Santy," proving that the play had assumed almost institutional status.

Lefty takes its form from agitprop drama, a genre that became popular in the late 1920s and remained influential into the thirties. The term suggests the two functions of this type of play, agitation and propaganda; its function was to manipulate an audience in order to elicit a specific response. The plots of these plays drew on actual historical and social events and featured stylized, cartoonlike characters who represented certain fixed types: the boss, the worker, the imperialist, the fascist, etc. The political views of these figures were presented in a straightforward manner, often utilizing actual documents or speeches culled from newspapers and arranged in a way to engage the audience's emotions and then impel it toward a particular perspective on the issues. These plays were also designed to do away with some formal conventions of the theater, particularly the separation of actor and audience, for agitprop sought to merge the two and thus draw the audience into the play.

Lefty's transcendent use of the conventions of agitprop theater may be best appreciated by comparison with a typical example of the genre, *Dimitroff*, which was occasionally presented with *Lefty* and which also appeared at a Sunday night benefit by the New Theater League. This play was written by Art Smith and Elia Kazan (the latter a member of the Group, who appeared in *Lefty* as Agate). Like *Lefty*, *Dimitroff* was published in *New Theatre* (July/August 1934).

Dimitroff's aims are stated quite directly in its introductory note:

The story of this play is not primarily the story of Dimitroff. The hero of the *production* should be *mass pressure*. The *production-play* should be the account of how the pressure of the world proletariat forced the release of the class-war prisoners: Dimitroff, Taneff and Popoff. It should lead directly into the present mass-struggle to force the release of Thaelmann and Torgler.[4]

The play is composed of ten short scenes, many of which are devoted to the trial of Dimitroff and Torgler, Communist opponents of Hitler's government, who stand accused of setting fire to the Reichstag. The early scenes make clear that the central characters were framed, that the burning of the Reichstag was planned by Goering, Goebbels, and Hitler to appear to have been the work of the Communists. Actual speeches by Hitler and by Communist leaders concerned with the fate of Dimitroff are incorporated into the action. In a scene in prison between Dimitroff and his mother, the mother clarifies some of the aims of the play:

They say *Goering* will never let you go. You are too strong. He is afraid of you. He is afraid of all of us. Of the people. His government is the last stand of a wild animal crazy with fear. It is almost time. The people will rise and overwhelm him.[5]

At the end of the play Dimitroff himself addresses the audience:

We have been saved by the world pressure of the revolutionary masses. But *Torgler* is still in prison and *Thaelmann* is held in chains. We must not falter now. *We must fight fascism with undiminished strength and courage. We must free our comrades. Free all class war prisoners!!*[6]

The play concludes with a call to action meant to unite the audience with the actors in proclaiming these demands:

AUDIENCE: Free all class war prisoners!!
DIMITROFF: Free Torgler!
AUDIENCE: Free Torgler!!
DIMITROFF: Free Thaelmann!!
AUDIENCE: Free Thaelmann!!⁷

Lefty adopts and explodes this conventional format. Based loosely on
a contemporary event, it is composed of eight short scenes, including
the expository sketches that open and close the action but are not
designated as scenes in the text (In *Six Plays of Clifford Odets*, 1939,
one scene was excised); it concludes with a dramatic call for a strike.
But while Odets's play shares surface similarities with the typical
agitprop play, it diverges significantly from the formula in scope and
purpose.

When first published in *New Theatre*, *Waiting for Lefty* was subtitled *A Play in Six Scenes Based on the New York City Taxi Strike of
February 1934*. However, the strike was a thing of the past when the
play premiered, and *Lefty* makes scant reference to what actually
took place. It lacks the historical immediacy of a play like *Dimitroff*,
and the specificity of detail. What *Lefty* attempts, rather than simply
to comment on a particular issue, is to highlight a generalized
attitude not only about labor conditions but about the World War II
period, the effect of the Depression on personal relationships, and anti-
Semitism. And while the play ends, like *Dimitroff*, with a call to
action—

ALL: STRIKE!
AGATE: LOUDER!
ALL: STRIKE!
AGATE AND OTHERS ON STAGE: AGAIN!
ALL: STRIKE, STRIKE, STRIKE!!!⁸

—its aim is to achieve not an immediate result, but a more symbolic
call to arms. Odets exploits the agitprop device of linking actor and
audience in a hortatory finale, but he joins them more broadly,
almost as a family sharing common values and a similar consciousness. This communal focus is what accounts for the play's
lasting appeal, for *Lefty* is agitprop drama that resists identification

with any specific, time-bound problem. Gerald Rabkin comments perceptively on the play's inclusive method:

> It swept all of a liberal persuasion into militant participation, at least in the theatre, by virtue of the precision with which Odets enunciated the Depression malaise. Odets' achievement lay in his ability to humanize the agitprop without forgoing its theatricality and didacticism. He succeeded not only in presenting the conversion to militancy of a series of taxicab workers, but in forcing the audience to see in the plight of these characters a reflection of their own social predicament.[9]

This technique of implication is enforced by the diverse nature of the characters: in the six "episodes," only two of the central characters are members of the proletariat; the others are of middle-class origin—a chemist, a doctor, and an actor. All are forced into militant action by social circumstances that victimize them all. Furthermore, these characters transcend agitprop stereotyping. Fuller, more individualized, and recognizably human, they retain the cartoonlike dimensions of agitprop figures, but their distinctive personalities make their words more compelling. Not precisely realistic, they are clearly creations of a genuine playwright, not a political agitator.

Because Odets began writing *Awake and Sing!* before he composed *Lefty,* it might appear that he was experimenting with dramatic form in eliminating the proscenium arch in this play. However, while Odets would experiment with realistic conventions throughout his career, this was not a case of deliberate iconoclasm. Like other agitprop plays, *Lefty* was written to be performed in union halls and so its construction was not stage-bound. That it ended up on a Broadway stage was a tribute to its popularity, but its experimental flavor when performed in such a setting is only accidental.

The play opens in a union hall where Harry Fatt, a union leader who is accompanied by a gunman stage left, is trying to persuade a gathering of cab drivers not to strike. Fatt's speech is directed toward the audience as well as the workers, and it is designed to turn both groups of listeners against him. Then, as the action unfolds, the "six or seven men in a semi-circle" come forward in turn to speak, and their stories are acted out on stage while the other members of the cast remain silhouetted in the background. The ensuing scenes thus take place simultaneously in the memories of the speakers and in the present moment at the union hall. The audience is drawn into what seem like real descriptions of past events, while retaining a vague consciousness of the union meeting setting at the same time. This illusory effect is broken in episode 4 when Odets abruptly rturns to the present in the hall as Tom Clayton is introduced to warn the drivers against the proposed strike.

While the action is framed by the immediacy of the meeting, the true power of the play is contained in the six episodes that provide its thematic center. Herein Odets introduces character types, themes, and symbols that are to recur in his later plays. The two best scenes present domestic dilemmas: "Joe and Edna" (episode 1) and "The Hack and His Girl" (episode 3) hint at Odets's signal ability to catch the pulse of family life, soon to be demonstrated at full length in *Awake and Sing!*

The first episode is introduced by Joe, one of the seated workers, who rises to speak after Fatt, and the focus shifts to a scene between Joe and his wife Edna. When Joe returns home to find that the furniture has been repossessed, Edna expresses her disgust at their poverty and tries to persuade Joe to strike for higher wages. Discovering that she can't do so, she threatens to leave him and thereby prevails. This scene is built around the motif of embrace, initially a thwarted realistic one, as Joe seeks to dismiss the loss of the furniture by attempting to embrace Edna. She refuses, exclaiming bitterly, "Do it in the moves, Joe—they pay Clark Gable big money for it." (This concept of film images cheapening and damaging the lives of real people, reiterated in episode 3, is to be explored in greater depth in *Awake and Sing!, Clash by Night,* and *The Big Knife.)*

Joe then anticipates Leo Gordon of *Paradise Lost,* asking Edna, "What can I do?" Unlike the later play, however, this activist work offers a ready rejoinder to such a declaration of helplessness: Edna insists that Joe work for a strike. Joe's capitulation to "conditions" is thus directly countered by her call to action. A typical Odets male, Joe would choose to sidestep his responsibilities, remarking, "I wish I was a kid again and didn't have to think about the next minute." But Edna reminds him of his own kids who have neither proper food nor clothing, and in her lament introduces what will become a major symbol in Odets's work:

> But damnit our kids get colds one on top of the other. They look like little ghosts. Betty never saw a grapefruit. I took her to the store last week and she pointed to a stack of grapefruits. "What's that!" she said. My God, Joe—the world is supposed to be for all of us. (p. 10)

The house lacks fruit; the dreams of a good life have been undercut by the Depression and by the exploitation of the workers, and, as a consequence, the family is suffering. Joe remains hesitant until Edna threatens to leave him for a former boyfriend, raising the possibility of a literal destruction of his home. This prospect at last stirs him to act, and the scene ends with an embrace, symbolic rather than physical, as Joe goes out to find Lefty Costello and espouse the activist cause.

Episode 3 develops similar themes, though here Odets presents not a husband and wife but a young couple unable to marry for lack of money or prospects. The scene opens upon Florence, who is waiting not only for Sid, but for a culmination of her dreams, and her attitude of expectancy echoes the waiting motif that pervades the play. Her brother warns that she must not marry Sid, who "ain't got nothing," adding that he himself cannot afford to support two families. Florence, like many Odets heroines, declares that "I gotta right to have something out of life. . . . I want romance, love, babies. I want everything in life I can get." But the Depression has dug a chasm between romance and reality, and the resulting debasement of marriage provides a theme that Odets returns to in *Awake and Sing!, Paradise Lost,* and *Clash by Night.* The heroines either find it difficult to achieve a love match at all, or, as in episode 1, discover too late that even a happily concluded marriage is likely to turn sour because of poverty. Odets exploits such sentimental calamities to underscore his vision of a world out of sync with what should be.

In this scene it is the woman who seeks escape through romance. When Sid arrives she wants their meeting to be "like in the movies," and here the lovers do embrace and kiss. But it is only a temporary gesture, for Sid points out later (echoing the original title of *Awake and Sing!),* "We got the blues, Babe—the 1935 blues." Recognizing the impossibility of their dreams, the young man then delivers Odets's indictment of the hopeless condition of the lower classes, equating the bosses' exploitation of the workers with the government's manipulation of the war situation. Sid is particularly distressed by his brother's volunteering for the navy.

Take this gun—kill the slobs like a real hero, he says, a real American. Be a hero! And the guy you're poking at? A real louse, just like you, 'cause they don't let him catch more than a pair of tens, too. On that foreign soil he's a guy like me and Sam, a guy who wants his baby like you and hot sun on his face! They'll teach Sam to point the guns the wrong way, that dumb basketball player! (p. 21)

The scene concludes with the couple dancing to the music of a phonograph; it is a quiet moment, one of profound loss. (It anticipates a similar moment in *The Country Girl.*) Briefly, through music—Odets's frequent symbol of the ideal—the lovers embrace, but the moment cannot be sustained. The episode ends in despair as both realize that their relationship must end. Departing from the typical agitprop formula, this scene develops, in the parting of the lovers, a poignant dramatic thrust that overwhelms the economic subject. It is a standard situation, typical of thirties drama, but Odets infuses the scene with power through careful molding of character and dialogue.

Episode 2 functions as a bridge connecting 1 and 3 through its evocation of economic pressure in the testing of individual will. Rather than dramatizing directly the conditions motivating the drivers to strike, this scene recounts how one man became a cab driver after losing his job as a laboratory assistant. The fervently pacifist theme of this story prefigures Sid's antiwar speech in episode 3, placing the local issues of the play in a wider context.

Offered a raise and a promotion by the industrialist Fayette (whose name echoes that of Fatt; both roles were played by Russell Collins in the original production), the protagonist, Miller, learns that he will be required to spy on an eminent chemist. The firm is doing research on poison gas (Sid's remark, "I'm rat poison around here," provides a verbal echo in episode 3) for use in the next war.

Fayette declares callously that war is business—"If big business went sentimental over human life there wouldn't be big business of any sort!"—and that "the world is an armed camp today." Miller, however, is a pacifist because his brother, who "could run the hundred yards in 9.8 flat" (he anticipates Ben in *Paradise Lost*), was killed in the last war, and he resists his employer's corrupt reasoning with growing resentment as Fayette attempts to coerce his cooperation with bribes and then threats. At length, the scene, which has opened on an informal note as Miller compares Fayette's office to a Hollywood set, thus suggesting, as elsewhere, that there is something false, hollow, and perhaps treacherous about it (and the room's opulence also contrasts sharply with the lack of furniture in the preceding scene), now concludes dramatically as he punches Fayette in the mouth, thus repudiating the offer of complicity, and with it, his job and the whole capitalist ethic. Like the two episodes it bridges, Miller's story culminates in a symbolic gesture of alienation, signifying the breaking of ties to the hopeless passivity of an exploited working class.

The first three episodes, designed to elicit audience sympathy, undermine Fatt's control of the meeting. Fatt responds in episode 4 by introducing Tom Clayton, a labor spy who seeks to dissuade the workers from striking. Abruptly unmasked by his own brother as a hired union breaker, he is expelled from the meeting. The brother reveals that Clayton's real name is Clancy, and the final image in his unmasking speech echoes episode 1:

Remember his map—he can't change that—Clancy! Too bad you didn't know about this, Fatt! The Clancy family tree is bearing nuts! (p. 25)

Rather than the health—and happiness—giving fruit that Odets regularly associates with a well-ordered society, this tree bears only nuts, the antithetical symbol of sterility and oppression. This episode also pursues the blighted-family motif of episodes 1, wherein a family is threatened with dissolution, and 3, where a potential family cannot be formed; here, brother turns against brother, and the family tree is literally torn apart.

The final two episodes are the weakest in the play. Episode 5, "The Young Actor," was dropped from the 1939 Modern Library edition of *Six Plays of Clifford Odets,* though it was included when the play was originally published in book form in 1935. (The cast list indicates that the scene may have been dropped when the play moved to Broadway in September 1935.) In this episode the indictment of the businessman as oppressor and war entrepreneur shifts to his incarnation as Broadway producer, but the treatment here is handled more comically than in the rest of the play. Mr. Grady, the producer, is of the shallow, uncultured, and coarse type that Odets would later develop into Marcus Hoff in *The Big Knife.* An unemployed actor named Philips has come to his office seeking the role of a soldier in a new play. He feels that his experience in working with some well-known theater companies will impress Grady, but he finds the man interested only in physical appearance:

Nobody interested in artists here. Get a big bunch for a nickel on any corner. Two flops in a row on this lousy street nobody loves you—only God, and He don't count. We protect investments: we cast to type. Your face and height we want, not your soul, son. And Jesus Christ himself couldn't play a soldier in this show . . . with all his talent.[10]

At the moment more concerned about the surgery being performed on his dog than about the plight of Philips, Grady is clearly a grotesque version of the industrial bosses whose inhuman priorities reduce their employees to soulless bodies "cast to type" in physical servitude.

The ideological thrust of the scene is conveyed rather crudely in Grady's stenographer's advocacy of the positions and precepts of the Communist Party:

STEN: Stop off on your way out—I'll give you a copy. From Genesis to Revelation, Comrade Philips! "And I saw a new earth and a new heaven; for the first earth and the first heaven were passed away; and there was no more sea."
PHIL: I don't understand that. . . .
STEN: I'm saying the meek shall not inherit the earth!
PHIL: No?
STEN: The MILITANT! Come out in the light, Comrade.[11]

Odets told Michael Mendelsohn that the scene was pulled because it was "untypical"; in addition to its aberrant comic tone and car-toonlike characters, it constitutes the play's most direct Communist statement. Odets originally wrote it in response to pressing profes-sional and social concerns, but his awkward handling of the episode reflects his discomfort even then with overt doctrinal representation. Pehaps, too, the artist in him was more than a little embarrassed by the woodenness of its expression.

The last numbered scene, "Interne Episode," dramatizes the per-vasive oppression in the form of anti-Semitism. Young Dr. Benjamin is informed by his superior, Dr. Barnes, that he is being fired because he is Jewish. Such discrimination prevails in spite of the presence of Jews on the hospital's board of trustees; as Barnes remarks, " . . . doesn't seem to be much difference between wealthy Jews and rich gentiles. Cut from the same cloth." Raising the issue of "class distinction" as the doctors discuss the case of a charity patient, their dialogue stresses again the evil consequences of the capitalist system, corrupting even the hospitals. Increasingly incensed, Barnes de-clares:

Doctors don't run medicine in this country. The men who know their jobs don't run anything here, except the motormen on trolley cars. . . . In a rich man's country your true self's buried deep. Microbes! Less. . . . Vermin! See this ankle, this delicate sensitive hand? Four hundred years to breed that. Out of a revolutionary background! Spirt of '76! (pp. 27–28)

Benjamin first introduces and then rejects the possibility of going to Russia to work in socialized medicine, deciding instead that his true mission is to remain in America. Determining to drive a cab to keep alive while he studies and learns how to fight back against the tyranny of wealth, he caps his pledge of defiance with a radical clenched-fist salute that brings the scene to a close. The cumulative tension of rebellion generated in this succession of sketches culmi-nates at last in Agate's exhortation to his comrades: "Tear down the slaughter house of our old lives! Let freedom really ring." His speech is interrupted by the announcement that Lefty has been killed, shot in the head, which further excites the crowd. The play then con-cludes with a rousing call to strike.

Although *Lefty* is still read and anthologized today, it is generally

valued as little more than a curious memento of a particular theatrical moment. Unarguably the best American agitprop play of the
thirties, it retains its distinction not because it is a great play—it
isn't—but because it represents a uniquely successful molding of the
form to create a well-made and unified work. In analyzing its political and emotional power, it is important to recognize Odets's skillful
orchestration of factual material, symbol, and character development
to achieve an unusually dramatic effect. This play remains significant
also as the first expression of Odets's distinctive style and themes,
although here his personal and aesthetic concerns are subjected to
ideology. As his later, full-length plays assumed more subtlety and
greater depth, with his political convictions remaining on the fringes
of the action, the change disconcerted and confused his critics and
his public. The public perception and expectation of Odets (and
even Odets's expectations of himself) would never merge comfortably with the private artist, and this dichotomy of political and
aesthetic inspiration was to plague him throughout his career. Thus
much of Odets's artistic life was determined by his first and most
famous play.

The economic success of *Lefty* inspired the Group directors to
bring it to Broadway, and, since that play runs for less than an hour,
Harold Clurman asked Odets to write a companion piece for it.
Odets complied, finishing *Till the Day I Die* in five days. This was
one of the first anti-Nazi plays to reach Broadway, its most significant predecessors being Elmer Rice's *Judgment Day* and S. N. Behrman's *Rain from Heaven,* both presented in 1934.

Rice's play, like *Dimitroff,* was inspired by the 1933 trial of the
German revolutionary Dimitroff over the charge of setting the
Reichstag fire. It is essentially a courtroom melodrama highlighted
by the protagonists's defiance of the proceedings. Unlike Kazan and
Smith, Rice displaced the setting to an undesignated Balkan country
and then ended the play with Judge Slatarski, who will not bend to
the totalitarian government, shooting Visnic, a thinly disguised
version of Hitler, and shouting, "Down with Tyranny! Long live the
people!" Such fervid wish fulfillment only undercuts the genuine
significance of the actual story, which was sensational enough in its
own right.

Behrman's play, on the other hand, is, like much of his best work, essentially a drawing-room comedy, here undermined by a dissonant horror of fascist brutality. At the play's end one of the central characters, a Jew, vows to return to Germany to fight the evil on his home ground; this determination links him to *Lefty*'s Dr. Benjamin, who decides to remain in America and join the dissident forces there.

Unlike its antecedents, Odets's anti-Nazi play actually takes place in Germany. It is based on an actual event detailed by a German writer, F. C. Weiskopf, in a letter for the *Neuen Deutschen Blatter*, which was translated and printed in *New Masses* in the column "Voices from Germany" in 1934. The letter tells the story of a German Communist arrested for underground work. Tortured by the police, he tells them nothing and is subsequently released. However, his comrades, suspicious of the early release, shun him, and he is eventually arrested a second time. Again tortured and mocked by the Nazis for being abandoned by his comrades, he again remains silent and is again released. But this time the Nazis follow him and arrest whomever he speaks to. Realizing that he is thus acting as an involuntary traitor, he asks his brother to shoot him; his brother consents.

Odets utilized many of the details from this story in his play, including the details of Nazi torture and the Nazis' method of manipulating the man as a traitor to his own cause. One significant change is that Odets's protagonist must shoot himself, for his brother refuses to do it. Nevertheless, the play in its details so closely mirrored Weiskopf's letter that the latter threatened a suit. The case was settled out of court, with Weiskopf receiving $250 and 25 percent of the future income from the play.[12] Despite these extensive borrowings, *Till the Day I Die* is manifestly an Odets play. Indeed, it displays so many of Odets's personal preoccupations that its purpose as an anti-Nazi statement is finally overwhelmed by the variety of thematic corollaries. Ironically, *Till the Day I Die* demonstrates a closer affinity to *Golden Boy* and *The Big Knife* than to *Waiting for Lefty* or Weiskopf's letter.

The play centers on Ernst Tausig, a violinist and a Communist revolutionary who works in the underground movement to destroy the Nazi regime. An idealist with an artistic soul (represented by the violin), Tausig, unlike Joe Bonaparte or Charlie Castle, refuses to yield to the repressive system that threatens his creative spirit.

Whereas this yielding causes a tragic conflict that ultimately destroys the two later protagonists, Tausig remains faithful to his ideals and is destroyed anyway. For this reason Tausig's downfall naturally inspires a greater sense of despair; that his story displays neither the rallying power of *Lefty* nor the tragic scope of the later plays betrays a corrosive ambivalence, within the playwright, about the kind of play he was trying to write.

One of the play's basic problems is the presentation of Tausig, who, though endowed with a touching love for the violin and an ennobling concern for truth and justice, essentially serves as a mouthpiece for the Communist cause. Many of his speeches have the ring of propaganda, and therefore he remains a rather flat character, less interesting in fact than some of the minor figures around him. Throughout most of the play he is simply the central target of the weakness or evil of others, his only significant act being the suicide that ends this victimization. In *Lefty*, Odets dramatized how adversity effects change in various characters; here, the protagonist's character has already crystallized, and the play can only chronicle the brutality of the Nazis who harass him to his death.

The action opens in a small room where the underground is printing leaflets. Odets underscores the atmosphere of tension created not only by the Nazis' hounding, but also by the Communists' fear of informers. The scene introduces Ernst Tausig, his brother Carl, his girlfriend Tilly, and Baum, the printing-press operator. The danger of their work is emphasized and counterpointed by music images, as when Tausig complains, "Not to have touched a violin for six months? Incredible!"[13] Carl answers this with an oddly practical endorsement of the value of music:

When I walk in the streets I sing. That makes them say "He's above board, he can't be doing underground work." But they don't know I'm singing because I know where we'll be some day. (p. 109)

Tausig then enlarges on Carl's theme when he describes his vision of the future:

My present dream of the world—I ask for happy laughing people every-where. I ask for hope in eyes: for wonderful baby boys and girls I ask, growing up strong and prepared for a new world. I won't ever forget the first time we visited the nursery in Moscow. Such faces on those children! Future engineers, doctors; when I saw them I understood most deeply what the revolution meant. (p. 112)

Baum, like Tausig, complains, "I used to be crazy about tulips," indicating that he, too, is divorced from his symbolic ideal—Odets will use flower images similarly in *Night Music*—by the current political crisis. The grouping of these motifs serves, ironically, to complicate the scene, for by inserting Carl's avowal of pragmatic policy in his singing among the other men's unadulterated tributes to music and flowers, Odets seems to hint of some inherent flaw in the revolutionary movement as well as in the system it opposes. The true dreamers' visions of a future utopia are abruptly shattered, then, when the scene closes with the sound of the secret police banging at the door. Odets's stage directions emphasize the unmusical nature of the Nazis: "In the dark between this scene and the next the shrill sounds of a half dozen whistles, variously pitched, slowing with hysterical intensity" (p. 113). Sound registers in the real world of this play in shrill, distorted notes; only in Tausig's mind is there harmony and beauty, and the lyric idealism of his mental vision contrasts ominously with his brother's more mundane song in the street. Thus the musical motif is used to differentiate the two men, preparing the way for Carl's denunciation of his brother at the play's end. This apparent discord even within the protagonist's family signals Odets's disenchantment with the movement he is ostensibly championing.

In the scenes with the Nazis, Odets undercuts audience expectations by introducing farce and even pathos in his portrayal of the enemy. In scene 2 he presents Popper, a fat detective "in a brown trench coat and brown derby," who is having trouble with incompetent orderlies and is revealed, while interrogating Tausig, to be not very competent himself. The scene has a slapstick quality that minimizes the potential danger to the protagonist. Popper's menace is further deflated by his superior, Schlegel, who eventually takes over the questioning. Schlegel is one of the more interesting characterizations in the play. At first depicted as villainous, he is then shown to be a music lover, asking Tausig about Beethoven's Violin Concerto.

When Tausig answers that he knows the piece, Schlegel commits one of the play's most alienating acts (and the most violent in all of Odets's work): he takes a rifle and slams the butt down on Tausig's fingers, breaking them. (This scene prefigures the breaking of Joe's hands in the ring in *Golden Boy* and Bessie's destruction of Jacob's records in *Awake and Sing!*) Nonetheless, Odets later attempts to humanize Schlegel by having him bemoan the fact that the Germans are afraid to attend a concert of the lieder of Hugo Wolf. It is revealed also that Schlegel is homosexual, and in a genuinely moving moment he admits to his lover, Adolph (!), that "I'm lonely, I've got no one in the whole world." He then adds, "Hitler is lonely too. So is God" (p. 119).

Scene 3, also brutal and rather farcical, takes place in a barracks where prisoners are being tortured. Odets illustrates the senseless, degrading violence of the troops who beat up prisoners mercilessly to win bets. The violence of their actions is presented here as so casual and banal a mode of conduct as to condemn any group's blind obedience to the dictates of a leader.

In the fourth scene Odets introduces an even more equivocal Nazi, Major Duhring, who is part Jewish. Secretly admiring Tausig, this man is uncomfortable before him, seeking to rationalize his own position:

Why I am in a Nazi uniform happens to be unimportant. A realistic necessity. I am married into one of the finest old German families, Nordic from the year one. The work I do for the National Socialists harms no foe of the Nazi state; in fact I am inclined to believe that if the truth were known, my work may often be interpreted as a positive hindrance. . . . I will not deny the justness of the scorn in your eyes. This may cost me my head. . . . I'm not sure I care. (p. 130)

Duhring then warns Tausig of the tortures yet to come:

It's possible you may forget your proletarian task. Don't smile. A man's made of flesh and bone. They'll inform your comrades through subversive means that you've turned stool pigeon. Before you know it your own unit papers will be passing the word along. In a few months—no friends. No home. (p. 133)

At the conclusion of the scene Duhring shoots Schlegel, who has threatened to expose his Jewish origins, and then he shoots himself, prefiguring Tausig's eventual suicide.

These scenes in the Nazi offices serve two important functions. Perhaps surprisingly, they portray two Nazi officers as cognizant not only of their own better selves but also of Tausig's heroic idealism. Their responses, opposite but equally extreme, demonstrate some residue to humanity, however perverted and betrayed, as Schlegel's anguished perception causes him to turn on Tausig, while Duhring's turns him against himself. A more subtle subversion of the play's political intent, however, is the fact that Duhring's warning about Tausig's betrayal by his friends will prove accurate. One significant difference between Odets's and Rice's plays is that Tausig is to be destroyed not only by the Nazis but by his own comrades as well. Both groups deny the man's individuality, treating him as a faceless, expendable pawn in the contest of ideologies, much in the same way that the two Nazi officers allowed their own humanity to be subsumed in allegiance to a cause. (This depersonalizing tendency would later form the essence of Odets's complaint about the Communist Party in his testimony before the House Un-American Activities Committee.)

In scene 5, where Tausig, badly beaten, returns to Tilly's room for some rest, he remarks, "I know that till the day I die there is no peace for an honest worker in the whole world" (p. 139). Tilly returns a rather Chekhovian answer, which is to be belied by the play, "Let us hope we will both live to see strange and wonderful things." Learning both that Tilly is pregnant with their child and that a resistance movement has formed in France, Tausig then exults, "Our work is bearing fruit."

This hopeful exchange between lovers is countered, however, in the following scene, in which Tausig is tried in absentia by his comrades on the charge of being an informer. As one member puts it, "He must go on the blacklist. . . . For our purposes he is deadly, dangerous" (p. 144). Tilly makes an appeal on behalf of Tausig, reminding those present that they have known and worked with the man for years and declaring that she does not believe him to be a traitor. Then Stieglitz, a leading figure in the movement, who has been recently released from a detention camp, rises to speak, but

soon becomes inarticulate, his mind destroyed by years of incarcera-
tion. Once brilliant, now a defeated man though still devoted to the
cause, he serves as Tausig's stand-in in the scene; his appearance adds
force to Tilly's words and stimulates further audience sympathy for
Tausig.

As Stieglitz leaves the meeting hall, however, Carl takes the floor
to speak against his brother, and his action mirrors the betrayal scene
in *Lefty*. Here, transition from pity to condemnation is abrupt and
jarring, making Carl's words sound heartless even as he proclaims
the revolutionary credo. While Carl speaks, a violin and piano duo
are heard playing a Mozart sonata in the background, and the
contraposition of the music with the denunciation of a brother
creates a dramatic emotional conflict through Odetsian symbolism.
Asking, "Is there time for music today? What are we fighting for?"
Carl espouses the harsh, unsentimental reasoning of the party line:

Yes, it is brother against brother. Many a comrade has found with deep
realization that he has no home, no brother—even no mothers or fathers!
What must we do here? Is this what you asked me? We must expose this one
brother wherever he is met. Whosoever looks in his face is to point the
finger. Children will jeer him in the darkest streets of his life! Yes, the
brother, the erstwhile comrade cast out! There is no brother, no family, no
deeper mother than the working class. (p. 147)

Despite the vehemence of this rhetoric, which galvanizes the meeting and turns the vote against Tausig, a profound ambivalence
pervades this scene, as if Odets desperately wants to advocate the
larger sense of brotherhood that the party represents, but cannot
quite countenance Carl's betrayal, his denial of his brother's humanity, and his inability to believe in his innocence. Again, the musical
counterpoint enforces the family connection, for Carl remarks that
this was "the first piece by Mozart my brother and I ever played
together." The sundering of an ideal (home)—in which Odets believed deeply—for one that he seems to question invests the scene
with a tension that confused the thematic thrust of the play; the
subtext simply belies the test. In this light the stage directions that
conclude the scene are also significant:

He sits now. The music finishes before anyone speaks. The vote is called for. All raise their hands in assent except Tilly. She looks around at the others. One of the men is eating small nuts loudly. Her hand slowly comes up. (p. 147)

In the betrayal scene in *Lefty*, the accuser dismisses his disgraced brother with the scornful comment that the "family tree is bearing nuts"—an Odetsian curve, the symbolic opposite of fruit. Now Odets introduces nuts again as if to answer Tausig's joyful question in scene 5, "Our work is bearing fruit?" The damning reply emerges here as first Carl and then Tilly vote to blacklist him. Odets may have wanted to depict Tausig as a martyr, but he seems instead a victim of political abstraction.

The final scene protracts this mood of ambivalence, closing the action with a confrontation between the two brothers. Tausig, his hand amputated, recognizes the necessity of his blacklisting, but he is determined to persuade his brother that he is not a traitor. When Carl notices the smell of perfume on his brother, Tausig explains:

They gave me money. It falls out of my hands. . . . I passed the store the other day and it was in the window. Perfumed soap. I bought some. A man must have something. It smells like flowers. (pp. 152–53)

The allusion to flowers recalls Baum's nostalgic reference to tulips in scene 1; the echo indicates that Tausig retains his personal memories and that he maintains his idealism to the end. Producing a gun, he asks his brother to shoot him, but Carl refuses, insisting that Ernst must kill himself. As he does so, the final words of the play are exchanged by Carl and Tilly:

CARL: Let him die. . . .
TILLY: Carl. . . . *(Shot heard within.)*
CARL: Let him live (p. 154)

The eulogistic concept that Ernst will live through his death anticipates Mr. Bonaparte's final words, spoken over the body of his son in *Golden Boy*, "Come, we bring-a him home . . . where he belong." Also Teagle's epitaph for Charlie Castle, "He . . . killed himself . . . because that was the only way he could live."

Unlike the later protagonists, Tausig is not a divided soul, but a wholly committed, unchanging idealist. Odets's attempt to vindicate his hero through suicide/martyrdom demonstrates his desire to end the play on a note of transcendence, to highlight the party's best qualities above all else. Nevertheless, the play's memorable moments spring not from such efforts at propaganda, but rather from the glimpses of a deeper artistry evidenced here in embryonic form: Odets's pungent dialogue, his ability to delineate character with a minimum of detail, and, most notable, his creative ambivalence about political causes and their effects on individuals. Carl, for instance, is ironically linked with the Nazi Schlegel, for both are driven to sacrifice their humanity to ideology; Odets enforces the parallel by having Tausig display for his brother the stump of what was once his hand, smashed by Schlegel and eventually amputated. Even Tausig's final vision of the future, pure agitprop, seems strained here, unlike Agate's curtain speech in *Lefty*. In fact, by this time this hero is a crushed and broken man, his personal maxim having been delivered much earlier in the play: "A man must have a place." This desperate affirmation of the claim of common humanity is clearly nearer to Odets's own view than any cause or movement.

The critical reception of *Till the Day I Die* was mixed. The left-wing press was harsh, but mainstream critics, particularly Richard Watts, Jr., of the *New York Herald Tribune,* were kinder. The play ran for 136 performances after its March 26 opening, the length of the run probably owing more to the success of *Lefty* than to its own popularity. Like *Lefty,* this play had trouble with censors. In Phila-delphia, the New Theatre was threatened with revocation of its license if it staged the play, and when Will Geer produced the play in Los Angeles, he was severely beaten by "Friends of the New Ger-many."

In 1935 Odets also wrote a monologue, "I Can't Sleep," for Group actor Morris Carnovsky. It was presented at Mecca Temple under the auspices of the Marine Workers' Committee and the American Union against Reaction on May 19, and again on May 26 at a Gala Theater Night for the New Theatre League. Odets's fourth produc-tion of 1935, this work, three pages long, was written in one night in his apartment, and it was later published in the February 1936 issue of *New Theatre.*

The monologue is delivered by Sam Blitzstein, who is asked for money by a beggar on the street. He first refuses and then returns to offer some money, which the beggar then refuses. This unleashes a series of reflections and reminiscences from Blitzstein. The playlet's most powerful moments come when Blitzstein reveals his inner loneliness; he is a worker but he is not so much concerned with working conditions as with his alienation from his wife and children:

> Even my wife don't talk to me. For seven years she didn't speak to me one word. "Come eat," she says. Did you ever hear such an insult?! After supper I go in my room and lock the door. Sometime ago I bought for myself a little radio for seven fifty. I'm playing it in my little room. She tells the girls not to speak to me—my three daughters. All my life I was a broken-hearted person, so this had to happen. I shouldn't get a little respect from my own children! Can you beat it?![14]

His personal isolation yields, finally, to a realization of his connection with his displaced fellow man, symbolized by the beggar:

> Maybe I would like to say to a man, "Brother," But what happens? They bring in a verdict—crazy! It's a civilized world today in America? Columbus should live so long! Yes, I love people, but nobody speaks to me.[15]

Next he turns to recollection of his childhood in Russia, where his brother was killed in the 1905 revolution, and then to tender memories of his mother:

> My mother worked like a horse. No, even a horse takes off a day. My mother loved him like a bird, my dead brother. She gave us to drink vinegar we should get sick and not fight in the Czar's army. Maybe you think I didn't understand this.[16]

The speech concludes upon his demand for recognition by his "brother," the beggar:

> I watched last week the May Day. Don't look at me! I hid in the crowd and watched how the comrades marched with red flags and music. . . . I hear them crying, "You forgot, you forgot!" They don't let me sleep. All night I hear the music of the comrades. All night I hear hungry men. All

night the broken hearted children. No place to hide, no place to run away.
Look in my face, comrade. Look at me, look, look, look!!![17]

This identification of his symbolic other in the beggar constitutes a
fundamental change in Blitzstein, for it is an awareness he has been
avoiding, much like Leo Gordon in *Paradise Lost*. This short piece
thus insists that the members of the middle class awake from their
apathy and unite with their displaced brethren.

"I Can't Sleep" displays the eccentric Yiddish speech patterns that
Odets uses so effectively in *Awake and Sing!* and *Paradise Lost,* and
later in *The Flowering Peach*. Also, it interestingly mirrors the playwright's concern over merging his personal vision with political
reality, casting the debate in terms of Blitzstein's private vacillation
between personal memory and current conditions, the inner life, and
the outer world. Odets achieves a purposeful combination of the
two in this monologue, though, characteristically, in a short note
appended to Carnovsky, he complained about the conclusion:

Dear Morris,
   This last paragraph goes off a little, I think. But it can be fixed when I'm
not so tired—four in the morning now. Will get it to you this way and fix it
up when my mind's fresher.[18]

As in *Till the Day I Die,* there is certainly more of Odets to be found
in the personal experiences than in the political rhetoric. The piece
was written shortly after the death of his mother, which shattered
Odets, while Blitzstein's strained relations with his wife and three
children mirrors the situation in Odets's home, where he grew up as
the oldest of three children raised in an atmosphere of parental
estrangement.

Odets's feelings over his mother's death inform another short
piece, "Remember," which he wrote for the Negro People's Theater
and presented on October 19, 1935, at the Manhattan Opera
House. Writing and directing this project in a week, Odets described
the play as dealing with the "horrors of home relief." When a relief
investigator comes to the run-down tenement of a black family to see
whether the family is entitled to aid, the young daughter reveals that
her father works one day a week, invalidating the claim. Shortly

thereafter a neighbor arrives, announcing that the mother has died in a charity hospital. In his grief, the father then denounces a society that permits a woman to die for lack of care, concluding by exhorting his daughter to "remember, remember, remember all her life" the evils of the system that killed her mother and to fight against those responsible for her misery.[19]

In June 1935 John Howard Lawson asked Odets to head a committee, under the auspices of the League of American Writers, to investigate labor and social conditions in Cuba. Fulgencia Batista and his president, Carlos Mendieta, had recently ousted president Ramon Grau San Martín and established a dictatorship; their regime was solidified when they forcefully ended a general strike in March. Moved by Lawson's appeal, Odets agreed to go on the trip. When the American Commission to Investigate Labor and Social Conditions in Cuba set sail on the *Oriente* on June 29, Odets was the titular chairman. Not until they were about to reach Havana did Odets discover that he had been chosen for his publicity value and that the real head was Conrad Komorowski, who, as Odets later told HUAC (see chapter 8), he assumed was a Communist because Komorowski was so efficient and professional in his work. Odets also learned then that the delegation was not actually going to investigate anything, but was sent to Cuba to be arrested. When the boat docked, the delegation was detained in Tiscornia Prison Camp overnight, and sent back to New York the next day. If only from a publicity angle, the trip was a success. The treatment of the delegation elicited protests and telegrams to Secretary of State Cordell Hull, and the group was welcomed at the pier on July 6 by several hundred people.

The trip produced an article by Odets for the *New York Post* on July 5, in which he described the group's adventures:

As we dock in Havana, police and reporters swarm aboard the Oriente and lock us in the smoking room. We suspect our baggage has been examined on the way down. . . . All the time we are surrounded by Cuban secret police, by army and navy guards and by musical comedy detectives in straw hats.

The reporters tell us they are "waiting for Lefty" and inform us that a

Cuban delegation of fifty organized to meet us has been arrested. But the city, we are told, is plastered with leaflets about our trip.

Secret service men are brutal in their handling of our two Negro delegates. The whole place bristles with guns. Paul Crosbie, one of the delegation, tries to insist on our rights as American citizens, but nobody listens.

A fight develops among the different groups of guards. The harbor police want us. So do the national police, a much tougher bunch. . . .

The significance of the whole outrageous affair is clear.

The Mendieta-Batista dictatorship here is afraid of an honest investigation.

The American people must realize that now after what has happened.

So our mission on behalf of the Cuban people has been fruitful even though we were not allowed to investigate anything.

The trip also prompted Odets to write a number of pieces about American collusion with the Mendieta regime, focusing much of his attack on US Ambassador Jefferson Caffery. Odets also collaborated with Carleton Beals on a piece for *New Masses* and on a pamphlet, "Rifle Rule in Cuba," in which he contributed an essay, "Machine Gun Reception." The experience was the impetus for a play, never produced, originally called "Law of Flight," later changed to "The Cuban Play."

Odets began writing "The Cuban Play" when he was in Hollywood working on *The General Died at Dawn*. He struggled with it on and off for three years but was never satisfied with it. A proposed Group production never materialized, which was fortunate, for this is surely his most lifeless work. Odets himself recognized the central weakness of the play: in a framing sequence a character called Author complains that he cannot write a play about Cuba because he is unfamiliar with the land, the geography, and the people. Not knowing how they live, what they eat, how they speak, he can neither conceive their interior lives nor create real characters and vital images. Odets most likely abandoned his play for precisely those reasons.

This draft work displays an intricate structure, as Odets employs discrete platforms and levels for the various actions, as well as the play-within-the-play device. The frame scene opens with a Cuban revolutionary trying to convince a famous American author to write a play about Cuba. When the Author resists, offering excuses to put off the man and his subject, the Cuban counters by declaring that Americans' failure to protest their banks' support of fascism in Cuba is weakening the future of democracy in the US. Odets designs this scene primarily to provide the historical background for his protest, allowing the Cuban to deliver an extended lecture on recent Cuban history. It begins with President Gerado Machado, a puppet of the American bankers, who is thrown out of office when he "decides to do some work for himself." Dissatisfied with the people's choice, President Roosevelt sends thirty warships to Cuba to enforce the dictatorial government of Sergeant Batista, who forms an alliance with President Mendieta and curtails all civil liberties; writers and students who protest are shot. The Cuban's story draws the Author into Cuba's delemma, and so leads into the main story of the play.

The action represents the experience of Antonio Lorca, a character based on the anti-Batista guerrilla Antonio Guiteras; Odets chose the name Lorca in homage to Federico García Lorca, who had been killed by Franco's forces in Spain in 1936. The opening scene establishes that Lorca, like Guiteras, held three cabinet positions under President Grau San Martín, and Odets's protagonist eventually meets a fate similar to that of the historical figure. Guiteras and a close associate, General Carlos Aponte, were killed in May 1935, as they were about to leave for America, while in "The Cuban Play" Lorca and his close friend General Del Gado are ambushed as they prepare to leave for Mexico to obtain more guns for the revolution.

Odets also highlights the founding and growth of the Young Cuba (*Jovan Cuba*) movement to counter the Batista dictatorship. Lorca's philosophy of nonviolence brings conflict with his chief antagonist within the guerrilla forces, Primo, who advocates terrorist tactics and is opposed to the inclusion in the movement of divergent ideologies, such as those of "communists, socialists and reformists." Whatever drama the play possesses, and there is very little, stems from this ideological dispute and from Primo's and Salzedo's desire to support a workers' strike against the government. Lorca feels that the time is not right for such a step, that the workers lack real unity and, most important, enough arms to make such an action successful. By the end of the play, however, the pro-strike sentiment has swept events from Lorca's control. The strike is crushed by the government, and hundreds of workers are killed.

Odets attempts to complicate the action further by opening the main plot with a confrontation between Lorca and Rojas, an ex-schoolmate and one-time idealist, who is now an officer and high-ranking official in the Batista-Mendieta regime. Because of public pressure Rojas frees Lorca from prison, but promises to find him and kill him—the next time he sees him, he adds, will be in the "morgue at Mirramar." Lorca castigates Rojas for selling out: " . . . you desired materials. You wanted to live a lewd and lavish life. You became a renegade" (act 1, scene 2).[20] Lorca feels that Rojas loves him and hates him at the same time, and later in the play it is revealed that the only woman Lorca ever loved was Rojas's sister, who was killed by Machado in 1929. Thus is composed the standard Odetsian struggle between the idealist and the materialist, but Odets is invari-ably more successful with this theme when he internalizes it in a single protagonist. In this play the characters remain cardboard heroes and villains, and a potentially interesting situation therefore can generate no energy.

Odets's purpose, however, is explicitly didactic, and the play fails primarily because its plot exists merely as an excuse for its rhetoric. The key passages, accordingly, are the opening scene wherein the Cuban revolutionary delivers his historical prologue, and a dialogue between the idealistic Dr. Hevia, a friend of Lorca's, and a car-icatured American businessman named Beebe, in which the two men discuss American economic policies regarding the sugar industry. While Beebe is extolling America's lifting of the Platt Amendment, which forbade Cuban trade with countries outside North America, Dr. Hevia counters that this apparent liberalization is just a sham, for America will merely lower its tariff on Cuban sugar and allow its businesses to unload millions of dollars worth of surplus goods on Cuba. Another important scene presents the final confrontation between Lorca and Primo, during which the philosophy of non-violence is given its most articulate defense. Terming Primo a ro-mantic and an individualist, Lorca asserts that "society exists for our making. But it must be made, not destroyed by a bomb." He goes on to explain, in almost Chekhovian terms, that progress is measured in inches, that societies must evolve over years of hard work and struggle: "Progress implies unspectacular work, patience, realism, thought and planning" (act 2, scene 10).

Even the melodramatic moments that Odets exploits to some

effect in other political/labor plays are not effective here. A scene between Lorca and his dying mother, who cannot believe a fine man like Roosevelt would sanction what is going on in Cuba—she dictates a letter to him while dying—is embarrassing. Lorca's own death in Del Gado's arms while gasping "A . . . A . . . A . . . Avalon" is equally awkward. Earlier Del Gado, who enjoys listening to music on a phonograph (the identifying mark of an Odetsian hero), has played a recording of "Avalon" and remarked that it "sounds like a wonderful place (act 3, scene 3). Lorca then went on to define his dream of Avalon as of a place where there would be food for all, where women would be the equal of men, and where there would be land enough for all—a familiar Odetsian refrain. Equally familiar is the imperative that Lorca must die, a martyr to his unrealizable ideal. (Odets would use the Avalon image in a similar, and rather more effective way in *Clash by Night,* a play that shares the extreme pessimism of this effort.) At length "The Cuban Play" closes with the deaths of Lorca and Del Gado and the triumph of Flores, whose final instructions are to take the bodies to the morgue at Mirramar (an early title for the play).

Perhaps it is unfair to criticize this play too harshly; it is only a draft. Most of Odets's drafts are very long and required extensive pruning before reaching final form, and this one is no exception. It is so full of lengthy speeches, its message repeated so often, that one cannot imagine an audience actually sitting through it. On the other hand, Odets's experimental approach to the formal arrangement of dramatic motifs would not be matched for inventiveness until *Night Music.* There are, moreover, two effective comic scenes, one between two American businessmen contemplating Havana at night, and another wherein Del Gado, the play's most fully realized character, entices a paymaster to hand over his money and his gun. These successes, however, come too late and deliver too little to save a play that would surely have lost its audience long ago.

The outcry surrounding the Cuban adventure subsided after a final protest rally on July 10, where Odets shared the podium with Carleton Beals and Roger Baldwin of the American Civil Liberties Union. Despite the publicity value of the expedition and his own lighthearted piece for the *Post,* Odets was angered at his treatment by the party. He learned that the Communists knew the trip was potentially dangerous and so substituted Odets for Mother Bloor, who was originally scheduled to go. In protest against this ill-usage, Odets resigned from the Communist Party after only eight months of membership.

Odets's major attempt at a labor play was "The Silent Partner," a project on which he worked for a number of years but which was never produced or published. It was put into rehearsal in 1936, while Odets was in California, but since Harold Clurman felt the play presented too many problems and remained dissatisfied with Odets's revisions, the play was eventually shelved in 1937. As late as 1939 Odets still had hopes of revising and producing it. Many members of the Group, especially Morris Carnovsky, were impressed by the play, but Clurman doubted that a New York audience would pay to see a play about a strike by that time and predicted that the cost of the play would be prohibitive. (There were over forty parts.) Furthermore, he feared that production of this work would foster the notion that the Group was a "Red theater." Clurman's objections won the day. In his preface to the six plays published in 1939, Odets felt that "The Silent Partner" should have been included instead of *Rocket to the Moon* because he felt it more rightly belonged with that group of plays: "Of the two it was conceived and written first. Revisions have changed it, but in terms of inner and outer progression it belongs among the first six, part and parcel of a 'first period' group. Theatre exigencies being what they are. . . ."

In *The Fervent Years* Clurman writes perceptively about the strengths and faults of the play

I read his new play almost immediately and found it at once his most ambitious and his most incomplete script. It had a great theme. Through a strike situation in an industrial area, identified as the twin cities of Apollo and Rising Sun, Odets showed an old order of benevolent capitalism that had grown lame, a new order of monopolistic capitalism that was growing vicious (or fascist), and a still unorganized and spiritually unformed working class. What Odets was trying to say was that the old world of money and power was fast becoming decrepit and desperate, while the new world of the future, which belonged to the mass of people, was in America still raw, unclear, undisciplined, mentally and morally clumsy.[21]

He then comments further:

No play of Odets had a wider scope, a greater variety of characters, or more exciting scenes. But the play, intuitively sound in its basic perception, was very weak in all its central characters and situations. . . . His play revealed more instinct than accomplishment, more rough substance than created form. . . . If he could imbue these central characters with the life he meant them to have, this would be his most important play and he would indeed be the writer everybody hoped he would become. He needed to work hard rather than to push the play into production.[22]

Odets himself told Michael Mendelsohn that in this play he had tried to achieve a "heightened realism, a very tense fullness and richness . . . naturalistic and yet existing on a symbolic level."[23] He had tried for a similar duality earlier with *Paradise Lost* and achieved much better results; unfortunately, this play does not succeed on either level. The central problem here is that his characters never really come to life, but remain basically mouthpieces, types who neither grow nor evolve. In addition, the symbolic structure too often simply distracts, interfering with the play's forward movement.

The plot revolves around a strike that has been forced on the workers in their efforts to form a real union as opposed to a company union; this has led to dismissals. When the play begins, the strike is in its ninth week.

The play opens and closes upon images of death. It begins in a cemetery, where some workers are awaiting others to discuss further strike strategy. The scene has an ominous, forbidding air about it as the strikers wait nervously for their comrades, one signaling the others with his bicycle bell. The twin towns symbolically named Apollo and Rising Sun are under siege by the company and political bosses, making it difficult for the workers to get together. The setting is dominated by a "tree of sickly foliage which is higher than the cemetery wall" and, to the left, a marble cross. The blighted (fruitless) tree symbolizes the plight of the community, while the cross is not so much a religious artifact as a representation of the concept, central to Odets, of brotherhood and communion. The two will apparently have to merge symbolically if the world of the play is to revive. Odets also introduces images that he will later expand on in *Rocket to the Moon* and *Clash by Night:* the action opens on July 1; the land is parched by the heat, and there is no rain. Again Odets is trying to portray an Eliot "Waste Land," an America destroyed by big business, which here has assumed fascistic dimensions, victimizing the workers by not allowing them to congregate and, soon, bringing in armed deputies and scabs to control the towns. In "The Silent Partner" Odets thus picks up the thread of *Lefty,* presenting the industrial establishment as so gigantic and powerful as to oppress and control in a totalitarian way the lives of the people. The play's title is taken from a remark attributed to Andrew Carnegie: "Where the wealth of a nation is honorably accrued, the people are always a silent partner." Odets's use of the phrase is obviously ironic, for in this world of business there can be no honor.

One of the central characters, a strike leader whose name was revised from Love to Lovelace and whose first name is, interestingly, Cliff, is shot by scabs and dies at the end of the play. His last words—"Tell them, tell them, boys and girls, remember us"—recall Ernst Tausig's final speech in *Till the Day I Die.* Like Odets, Lovelace was seeking in this era of social disintegration the ideal of a sustaining community. (This was the quest that had led Odets to the Communist Party, which he left while working on this play.) The blood sacrifice of Lovelace, then, is similar to the murder of Lefty, as both are martyrs to a cause. Odets's linking Marxism with Christian imagery consecrates the values of the party, while suggesting his residual guilt for having left it.

Lovelace is one of two brothers, and Odets describes him as the more intellectual and introspective of the two. In the final scene, where his coffin is on view in his home, it is surrounded by books. At one point in the play he remarks that he does not "feel like a man," and, anticipating *Rocket to the Moon,* comments, "Most of us live like icebergs . . . three-quarters under water. We need to learn to live differently. . . . Personally I believe in the life of trees" (act 2, scene 3).[24]

His brother, Christie, who is hotheaded and fearless, shouts scornfully after his brother's death, "Stay on your knees! Cry out to your mother! Ask her to get me bullet proof skin for an hour!" (act 2, scene 4). During the course of the play Christie turns away from the woman who loves him, Pearl (also Odets's mother's name), because marriage is impossible in such depressed times. Pearl, however, replies, "What is the strike for? If it is not for love. . . . If it is not to get married, what's it for? If it's not for babies what's it for?" (act 2, scene 3). This connection between love, procreation, the strike, and the movement is underscored by Lovelace:

I was a seven months' baby, and all my life I was looking for that extra two months. I felt unborn, incomplete. The church didn't help, reading didn't— maybe having children and a wife might have—but organizing a union did. I tell you this: the strike is a mother. I'm born now.

Odets's use of symbolic names, images, and props is labored, though sometimes provocative. More troubling are the characters, who remain merely symbolic. Like the Gordon children in *Paradise Lost,* they are too firmly rooted in the image network Odets created for them ever to take on the realistic dimension that he hoped to develop as well. The antagonists, the corporation representatives who are drawn in equally bold strokes, are presented as one-dimensional, violent, fascistic chauvinists; even their names are woodenly emblematic, particularly Pope (an ironic anti-Christ) and Fink. In act 2, scene 1, at a meeting at the home of the head of the factory, Mr. Gracie (!), they enunciate their attitudes about business and the strikers. Pope declares, "Friends, American business is going places, and we can't stop for small birds. We can't permit progress to be stampeded." Later in that same scene Fink comments, "The easiest thing would be if we could get all troublemakers in a detention camp. Hitler's not so dumb as we like to think a foreigner is."

Straddling the two worlds is Gracie, whose family founded the company but who is now merely a titular head, since a New York corporation headed by a Mr. Drake actually runs it. Ironically referring to himself as "the Admiral of the Swiss Navy," Gracie is essentially humane, but although he sympathizes with the strikers, because of his position, he is impotent. He does nothing but drink and complain. In some respects he resembles Major Duhring in *Till the Day I Die,* exposing his fears, doubts, and concerns in a letter to his son. Admitting that "life begins to terrify me," he indicates his sympathy with the workers: "The strikers have much right on their sides. In some things they're wrong, but their demands are not unjust." He concludes in defeat:

The plant has been taken away from me. It's an age of speed-up and monopoly, and only the biggest fish, sharks, can roam the once free ocean. The minnows are swallowed without dressing, whether they be small capitalists like me or workers at the machine.

Gracie is constantly hounded by his younger manager, Cutler, who was once a worker but has betrayed his roots. Now essentially a spy for Drake, he watches over Gracie and reports back to New York. After dictating his letter, Gracie says to him, "You're a weed that crowds out the cultured plant. You won't give off a flower for six generations." Cutler replies, "I'm not much interested in flowers, Mr. Gracie," and this rejection of a favorite Odetsian image effectively damns him.

As the action slowly builds to a confrontation between the workers, the scabs, and the armed deputies sent by the corporation, Odets utilizes some standard conventions from strike plays. There is a worker, Crane, who does not believe that the bosses will use violence and so advocates reason. In the first scene, he says, "No one is going to be shot. This is not the African jungles. We're living in one of the greatest states in the union. This is the twentieth century." After an attack by the scabs, he adopts a more militant position and fights with his comrades. As in *Lefty*, Odets also includes a scene in which a worker is exposed as a spy.

However, "The Silent Partner"'s most impressive scene, successfully combining realism and symbolism, is act 2, scene 2, entitled "It Is Propaganda"—in a nod to Bertolt Brecht, all the scenes in the play are titled—which takes place in Corelli's bakeshop, also used as a relief station for the workers. Here the women are waiting for a shipment of milk sent by local farmers to help the starving workers and their families. Many of the women are tense, worrying that the guards will not let the milk be delivered. They also discuss whether the strike is accomplishing anything, and one, Mrs. Finch, feels that the workers should agree to the company's offer and go back to work. Most of the women support their husbands, and Odets emphasizes their solidarity by having them distribute apples and sing. When the milk is finally delivered, Odets's stage directions emphasize the almost mystical power of the scene.

All the women are standing motionless, focused on the milk cans. Their eyes and mouths making love to the milk. Slowly Roxie comes forward to one of the milk cans and looks down at it as she will in later life at her first baby. Suddenly she falls to her knees, throws her arms around the can and begins to sob. This is something which all the other women understand.

Company thugs then enter and pour milk into the gutter. This action radicalizes even Mrs. Finch, who declares, "May any man who votes to end our strike burn in hell forever! Forever!" This scene, with its merging of symbol and character, makes clear that only through communal cooperation can the children be fed and a life of dignity and brotherhood be restored. The possibility of paradise appears to be within grasp.

Odets's manuscript provides two endings for the play, both taking place in Lovelace's house as his mother distractedly looks for a shoe box to hold her dead son's shoes. The first ending is affirmative, as one striker's wife, who was injured by a scab, and who has been in what is feared to be a terminal coma throughout the play, suddenly takes a turn for the better. Her recovery thus balances the death of Lovelace. In the other, more muted, ending, Mrs. Lovelace makes an emotional speech about her dead son, insisting that the company meant her son "no harm," and, with the jazz music of a carnival calliope in the background, lamenting, "The children, the children, they know and the parents don't. So they think. What is it the young ones want, the world in one bite? They won't listen till the end of the earth . . . the young fools. . . . children turn a body's heart to stone." The protagonist is thus reduced to a sacrifice to a cause that will not benefit from his death. Here Odets's pessimism about mankind's capacity for real change sabotages a play whose form demands a more positive resolution.

"The Silent Partner" is an occasionally interesting play, primarily because of its ambitions; it is also at times an effective one. More often, however, it seems static and lifeless, with no very compelling characterization and too much didactic bombast. Conceived as an expression of his own political and private ideals, it is rooted in Odets's desire to merge polemic and personality in a grand artistic vision; unfortunately, like the tree in its first scene, the play is overgrown with "sickly foliage."

8

The Final Testament
The Flowering Peach (1954)

Music can be heard! The backdrop is illuminated by the burning
castle and reveals a wall of human faces, questioning, grieving, despairing. . . . As the castle burns, the flower bud on the roof bursts
open into a giant chrysanthemum.

—Conclusion of Strindberg's
A Dream Play

The two years following the opening of *The Country Girl* were
difficult ones for Odets. Shortly after it closed, Odets and Bette
Grayson were divorced and then, in May 1952 he was called to
testify before the House Committee on Un-American Activities.
Before the committee Odets reviewed his political past, admitting
his membership in the Communist Party and naming names of
friends and associates who had been members when he was. Odets
confessed that he had been a Party member "between six and eight
or nine months" during the year 1935, after which he had left the
Party because he could no longer respect its "cultural" bias:

If I can't respect these people on a so-called cultural basis—that is, as literary
or theater critics, I don't know what I am doing here. I remember telling
you that, when my plays came out, they received fantastically bad notices,
although a play like *Waiting for Lefty* was widely used, not only by the
Communists but by all liberal organizations and trade-union movements. I
not only disagreed with their critical statements of my work, but I disagreed
with their critical estimates of anybody's work, writers that I didn't know,

like Steinbeck and Hemingway. I had a great number of fights about that. And I simply thought, This is not for me, there is no reason for me to be mixed up in there. I am a playwright. I have established myself as a playwright. I have a great deal of work to do. I have enough to say out of my own mind and heart, and I had better leave. This would be the general attitude under which I left.[1]

Much of the questioning concerned Odets's trip to Cuba, in June 1935, as chairman of the American Commission to Investigate Labor and Social Conditions there. Odets acknowledged his participation in that commission, but then detailed his disillusionment with that enterprise as well:

I was only nominally the chairman of this committee. When I got on the boat and the committee started for Cuba, I discovered—should I say, to my disgust—that this man actually was the expert and I was the idealist, so to speak. I was the idealist who had some kind of publicity value and he was the expert on Latin-American affairs. He spoke with such authority and such knowledge that I simply supposed, if there were other Communist Party delegates on this commission, that he was the top one.[2]

Later claiming that he was indignant over his treatment and expressing embarrassment over his own lack of "sophistication," Odets did explain to the committee his motivation for making the trip:

The purpose that attracted me was that there were oppressive measures taken against thousands of intellectuals and college students. They were thrown into jail, under the previous Machado regime, which was a horrible regime. I was glad to go down. If nothing else did happen, we would dramatize what the issues were down there. Of course, the stories that were coming out were very garbled. No one knew what was happening. I frankly think that, later, the American Embassy straightened out the whole thing and was a salutary and moderating influence.[3]

Much of the rest of his testimony concerned his disagreement with the Marxist practice of imposing philosophy on writers, a concept that Odets found abhorrent:

I didn't respect any person or any party or any group of people who would say to a young creative writer, "Go outside of your experience and write a play." I knew that, as fumbling as my beginnings were, I could only write out of my own experience. I couldn't be given a theme and handle it. It was not my business. It meant to me, if I may say it this way, a loss of integrity. And so I persisted in going along on my own line and writing what did come out of my true center. And whenever this happened, I got this violent opposition in the press, and I became further disgusted and estranged.[4]

He went on to deny as utterly ridiculous the charges that he had interwoven Communist propaganda into his films:

I go to Hollywood to make an honest living, writing entertaining scripts. I have never gone to Hollywood as a propagandist. I think nothing gets by anybody in Hollywood. I don't think Hollywood has ever made a movie with left propaganda in it. And I think the whole matter of social messages from Hollywood [is] something that really cannot happen. All scripts are carefully written and rewritten and gone over with fine combs in Hollywood, and I never in my life had any intention of going to Hollywood and making a two-million-dollar picture which was a propaganda picture.[5]

In his concluding statement he explained his participation in what the committee considered "Communist front organizations," employing typical Odetsian musical images:

the lines of leftism, liberalism, in all of their shades and degrees, are constantly crossing like a jangled chord on a piano. It is almost impossible to pick out which note is which note. I have spoken out on what I thought were certain moral issues of the day, and I found myself frequently on platforms with Communists that I did not know about then but evidently are now known Communists. Many of these people have some very good tunes. They have picked up some of our most solemn and sacred American tunes and they sing them. If I as an American liberal must sometimes speak out the same tune, I must sometimes find myself on platforms, so to speak, with strange bedfellows. I have never wittingly, since these early days, joined or spoken on an exclusively Communist program or platform. I see that one must do one of two things: One must pick one's way very carefully through the mazes of liberalism and leftism today or one must remain silent. Of the two, I must tell you frankly I would try to pick the first way, because the little that I have to say, the little that I have to contribute to the betterment or welfare of the American people could not permit me to remain silent.[6]

Murray Kempton cynically wrote that Odets confessed to the committee in order to save the movie version of *Clash by Night*, which was released that year,[7] but Odets was not involved in the making of that movie, so that seems unlikely. In a very negative article on Odets, Malcolm Goldstein wrote that "had he not given in, it is unlikely that Hollywood would have filmed *The Country Girl*,"[8] but this reasoning also seems simplistic, for Odets's reputation on Broadway in 1952 was stronger than it had been in fifteen years. If he was interested only in Hollywood money, he would surely not have waited until 1955 to return there to claim his rewards. Whatever his reasons for testifying as he did, they must have involved more than bald economic self-interest.

Odets felt that his appearance in front of the committee was misunderstood, that he had been unfairly lumped with the many "friendly witnesses." In fact he hectored, criticized, and badgered the committee, although he was forthcoming about his own past and his distaste for the Communist Party, particularly its tendency to dictate matters of style and content to writers. The irony, of course, is that Odets was producing scripts on demand for Hollywood at this time; in his own mind he differentiated between what he considered art and the screen work that he produced as a professional and that he would come to describe as craft. However, he was also critical of the committee itself and refused to denounce the Communist Party as revolutionary.

Distraught that so many condemned him solely on the basis of what was reported in the press, Odets even kept a copy of his voluminous testimony, insisting that all of it should be read to provide a balanced picture of his actions. Odets did, in fact, name six names, including former Group members J. Edward Bromberg and Elia Kazan, but at the time he felt that he was sidestepping the committee by giving the same names revealed by Kazan a month earlier (Kazan had named Odets and ten others).

Despite these explanations and rationalizations, Odets never successfully reconciled his acquiescence with the image of himself as a hero of the left and a spokesman for revolutionary change, but remained profoundly affected by the abuse heaped upon him. His creative side never really recovered, and this experience in an important way explains his subsequent inability to write for the theater: of his numerous attempts at plays after 1952, only *The Flowering Peach*, which opened in 1954, was completed and produced. His film work for the most part remained anonymous as well, for Odets preferred rewrite jobs and polishing jobs, which brought no screen credit. His name appears on only three films after 1952.

This last play began as an idea for an opera, which Odets discussed with composer Aaron Copeland in 1953. When that project collapsed, Odets developed it instead as a play, basing the characters of Noah and his wife on his favorite uncle and aunt in Philadelphia, as he explained during an interview in Boston:

This uncle of mine is very voluble, very human. It occurred to me that here was a man of flesh and blood who was the Noah of the play. It's important for me to know how my people speak. I said to myself, wait a minute, Noah had three sons, it was a family life, I know family life. There are children and parents, with ambitions, with disappointments, with anger and love. In the play, these people think like us, speak like us, they're a distillation of modern and biblical. Noah's wife became my Aunt Esther. The Bible doesn't give the names of Noah's wife and daughters-in-law. But anyone can see that there is great love for Noah and Esther in the play.[9]

The Flowering Peach went into production in 1954, with Robert Whitehead producing and Odets again directing; then while Odets devoted himself to making extensive revisions, Martin Ritt, who played Shem, took over the direction. Opening in Wilmington, the play had runs in Baltimore, Washington, and Boston, where it was given a new second act, before opening in New York on December 28. The reviews were friendly but not enthusiastic, and the play closed on April 23, 1955, after 135 performances. *The Flowering Peach* was never published in any formal sense: an abridged version appeared in Louis Kronenberger's *The Best Plays of 1954–1955*, and the acting version published by The Dramatist's Play Service is the only complete text available. The published play is divided into nine scenes, although the stage production was played in two acts, the first act ending as the flood begins (scene 5 of the published version).

The Flowering Peach is Odets's retelling of the biblical story of Noah and the Flood, and it is his only play without a contemporary setting; the stage directions state that the action takes place "Then.

Not now." In some respects Odets's resort to a biblical setting seems a logical extension of his usage of the theatrical setting in *The Country Girl:* late in his career he apparently preferred to confront his social and psychological concerns in more controlled environments. In one case the theater, and in the other myth, provided him manageable arenas for the exploration of his own moral and aesthetic dilemma, as well as his continuing inquiry into the place of the self in the world. *The Flowering Peach,* like *The Country Girl,* is a play of reconciliation.

In other respects, however, *The Flowering Peach* recalls the dramatic milieu of *Awake and Sing!* and *Paradise Lost:* once again Odets is dealing with the nuclear Jewish family. Despite the biblical setting, Noah's family seems a modern brood, intimately related to the Bergers and the Gordons. There are the characteristic family tensions and quarrels. Noah, like many of Odets's older Jewish men such as Jacob and Mr. Gordon, is presented as a dreamer and idealist, while his wife Esther is a realist who is at odds with her husband's personality yet remains affectionate and loving beneath her hard exterior. Thus, although a sympathetic figure like Mrs. Gordon, Esther functions like Bessie, as the force that keeps her family together. Odets also individualizes Noah's three sons, Shem, Ham, and Japheth, and the three daughters-in-law, whom he names Leah, Rachel, and Goldie. In so returning to a familiar emotional medium, Odets fashioned some of his most memorable characters and regained the warmth, tenderness, and humor of the best of his early work. As Harold Clurman pointed out, this last play exhibits "the kindness and intuitive brother feeling he brings to all the themes he treats."[10]

The story of Noah and the Flood has, of course, been exploited often as a dramatic subject. Medieval religious plays retold the tale a number of times, most notably in *The Wakefield Noah* and *The Chester Deluge.* These plays were essentially expressions of faith, justifying God's ways to man. Both present Noah's wife as hard and shrewd: in the former Noah threatens to beat his wife for not believing in God's commandment, while in the latter she is presented in a more comic way as a woman who won't leave her friends and so must be forced onto the ark. Although the religious thrust of these plays is alien to Odets's purposes, both proceed, as he did, by presenting Noah as a pious, idealistic man and his wife as a foil to him.

Other and more important parallels can be found in Marc Connelly's *The Green Pastures* (1930) and in Andre Obey's *Noah* (1934). Connelly's play applies selected motifs of Hebraic/Christian biblical myth to the Southern black experience, written in dialect and charged with sentiment and humor. In the first part of the play Connelly introduces heaven before the Creation, Adam and Eve, the story of Cain, and the Noah story, fashioning a tableau of man's sinning and punishment by the Flood; the new world will be founded by those virtuous few who have survived the Flood. Connelly's Noah is a simple black preacher who is visited by God; Noah's wife offers him a chicken dinner, after which God reveals his plan to Noah. The scene evolves humorously, emphasizing Noah's simplicity and goodness. The comic highlight is reached when Noah tries to persuade God to allow him to take two kegs of "likker" on the ark, while God insists, "I think de one kag's enough." In the final scene devoted to the Noah story (scene 10), Noah is described as drunkenly pulling on a cord as if he were in a steamboat race, suffering the affectionate ridicule of his wife and children. The Noah story occupies only three scenes in *The Green Pastures,* but Connelly's treatment introduces such motifs as a humorous tone, Noah's drunkenness, dialect speech, and the affectionate family circle, all of which Odets's version would echo.

Another important aspect of *The Green Pastures* in relation to Odets's play was Connelly's theme, particularly in the second part of the play, wherein Connelly changes focus from a concern with reforming man to an examination of human nature. The "lawd" comes to see mankind as weak but nonetheless a race of people who can hope in the midst of catastrophe and who can show courage and compassion despite suffering. Man, as Hezdrel tells God, learns to be wise "through suffering." God eventually learns that even he must suffer and accept man as he is. *The Flowering Peach,* too, is centrally concerned with man's nature, although Odets's Noah, a saintly man, is the one who must come to grips with the contradictory nature of mankind and learn to accept it. He must learn to accept his own limitations as well, and in this important respect he is akin to

Connelly's God figure, for God as such does not function as a character in Odets's play.

Odets's version, however, is closest to Andre Obey's *Noah,* which was first produced on the New York stage in 1935, the year of Odets's own greatest success as a playwright. The two plays display a number of significant parallels. Obey, too, emphasizes the family unit, especially in his characterization of Noah's three sons (who play no part in the medieval plays and are of little importance in *The Green Pastures*). Obey's Noah, like Odets's, is an idealist and a devout believer in God, and he, likewise, has trouble, especially while on the ark, convincing his sons of God's authority and the need to believe in him. Obey's Noah has absolute faith in the new world, while yet sharing with Odets's Noah a basic distrust of human nature. He tells Shem at one point, "Eternity frightens you! You, you puny mortals. You morsels of men. They are not ready for this new timeless world."[11]

In both plays the Noah character is given extended scenes in which he is talking to God and thinking to himself; in both God remains an offstage presence, unheard. Both also feature a central conflict between Noah and one son: in Obey's play Noah has trouble with Ham, who is skeptical about God and openly hostile and cynical; in Odets's play it is Japheth, who is, however, presented not as a bad son but as a rebel against a God willing to destroy the human race. In *The Flowering Peach* part of the debate between Noah and Japheth revolves around the need for a rudder for the ark, and this practical conflict provides a concrete symbol exemplifying both men's views of the nature of God's authority. In *Noah* this is a question the protagonist himself ponders, but it is not central to the play's meaning; it seems likely, however, that Odets borrowed the device of the rudder from Obey.

The key scene in *Noah* that depicts the conflict of faith is act 3, scene 1, in which a storm threatens the ark. The family regards the storm as a sign that Noah is wrong about everything and that God has deceived him; Noah's wife sides with the children in the debate. When the dove brings the olive sprig, the argument is dropped, but Noah remains disturbed, feeling that, because of his family's persistent doubts, the whole experience has been a failure and nothing has been learned. Obey's play concludes with the ark on top of Mount Ararat. The children leave, exulting in finally being free of the ark, and ready to divide the world between them. Noah's wife has grown childish and cannot face the new life. Noah is left alone to talk to God, acknowledging the difficulty of his struggle and his inability to understand completely all that has happened, but satisfied that he has done well enough. He asks God for a sign that he, too, is satisfied, and the play concludes with the appearance of the rainbow.

Odets's play is similarly concerned with the opposition of human nature to God's ideal. The debate between skepticism and faith, however, is more pronounced, and while both plays end with the rainbow's symbolic benediction, Odets's conclusion is more comic. Obey's vision leaves Noah finally alone on the mountaintop, contemplating the rainbow as an emblem of the tragic and cyclical rhythm of existence. In Odets's play, on the other hand, although Esther has died, Noah still has his family, and he will live out the rest of his life with Shem; his reconciliation is less ambiguous because less lonely.

The two plays share a preoccupation with the family unit, making it the modern link with the biblical narrative. Both plays assume a real relationship between the individual human being and his God, and both stress an awareness of death and rebirth as part of the cycle of human life. Both Noah figures are capable of change, and both playwrights thus project visions of man as a developing moral being because of his personal relationship to God. In each case the biblical tale provides a classic context for the pursuit of modern psychological and sociological meaning.

The Flowering Peach opens on a note of negation: Noah's first word is "No!" In the midst of a dream, he is responding to the revelation that God will destroy the world. His first speech is composed of a series of nos, repeated until his wife manages to rouse him. The earth is suffering from a heat wave; the drought motif recalls at once *Rocket to the Moon* and *Clash by Night,* but the world of this play is on the verge of actual destruction, and the rain that is to come will eradicate rather than revive it. Clearly this theme of destruction was intended as an allusion to the dropping of the atomic bomb, the

Flood being an entirely appropriate image for what had happened in Odets's world a few years earlier.

Revealing to Esther that God told him that "the earth is corrupt and filled with evil and greed,"[12] Noah remarks that his "soul is sick," a phrase he will repeat throughout the play. Noah, one of Odets's idealists, is sick with despair, appalled by man's transgressions and God's judgment. He even cautions God with comic earnestness later in scene 1: "You're talking a total destruction of the whole world an' this is something terrible" (p. 11). Unsure of his ability to carry out God's commandment—"I'm too old, everybody should laugh in my face! I ain't got the gizzard for it" (p. 11)—he is convinced by an offstage roll of thunder. Odets thus humanizes Noah, making him a rather cranky and often drunken character, much like Connelly's virtuous buffoon.

The motifs of negation and destruction in the opening scene are balanced, as usual in Odets's work, with images of beauty and the ideal. After Noah's cries of no and his hesitant speech with Esther about the ark, he hears music, the offstage signal for God's presence, and he moves away from his wife to talk to God. This association of music with the deity makes it a somewhat more complex symbol than it is elsewhere in Odets's work. His God supplies for Noah the Odetsian ideal, the measure of all things, wherein Noah reposes complete faith. But as the philosophic argument of the play will demonstrate, a God who is willing to destroy the world is clearly an ideal to be questioned. By the end of the play, Noah must revise both his opinion of man and his relationship to his God.

Two other concepts are introduced in scene 2 as images of the ideal. One is *Shabbos*, the Jewish Sabbath, the day of the week sanctified by God, designated as a day of rest and prayer. Noah's family gathers together for the Sabbath meal as Noah tells them of his vision. When this revelation provokes argument among the sons, Noah quiets them by reminding them that it is the Sabbath. The very notion of this ritual day is at odds with the sins of man, which have provoked the Flood: man is to be destroyed because he has strayed from the ideals that the Sabbath represents. Shortly after Noah exclaims, "Shabbos is comin'. . . . quiet in the house" (p. 19), the stage directions read, "The sky is aflame and colors the room." God manifests himself in these colors, as he will at the end of the play in the rainbow, sanctifying the day. Then suddenly appears the Gitka (an animal invented by Odets), which the rest of the family thinks is a mouse, but which Noah recognizes as an emissary from God. It begins to sing "a worldless, sad, and delicate song," and with the song all the animals appear outside Noah's house, standing peacefully in readiness to board the ark. Now everyone understands that Noah has, indeed, been touched by God, and the scene concludes with Noah intoning "the traditional words over the candles." In this fusion of images the first two scenes of *The Flowering Peach* provide one of Odets's most beautiful compositions, a moving evocation of the connection between music and holiness as a counterpoint to the more violent action to follow. At the second scene's end, only Japheth, who will rebel against God's dictum, stands outside of the family group.

These scenes are also effective in contrasting the divine ideal with earthly reality. Odets juxtaposes Noah with his wife Esther, who, like earlier Odets heroines, acts as a foil to her husband's otherworldly preoccupations. Esther deals in the here and now, the practical matters of caring for a house and children. When Noah is involved in his visitation from God, Esther can only interpret his strange manner as a drunken stupor and recommend that he eat breakfast. When Noah then tells her about the Flood, Esther simply warns him to stop talking nonsense and do something useful, like killing the mice in the house. Shortly afterward, she asks Noah, "Answer me a question, a *realism*—why should we be saved?" and Noah responds, "This is not a 'realism'! God's ready to destroy the whole world, so she wants a 'realism'!" (p. 8). Esther's characteristic insistence on realism thus establishes the contrary mode needed to offset and intensify Noah's final words, "I'll tell you a mystery." In part, the play's dramatic tension hinges on the seemingly antithetical nature of these two perspectives.

Noah's chief antagonist in the play is not his wife, however, but his youngest son, Japheth. Noah and Japheth are, in fact, much alike, as Odets emphasizes in a stage direction, describing them as "two outcasts in the more competent and fluent world" (p. 13). Rachel, whom Japheth will eventually marry, says to him, "You're just like your father," while Shem, the oldest son, rightly calls both his father and his brother "fanatics," for both are wholly devoted to their beliefs.

However alike in temperament, these familial antagonists support opposing spiritual concepts, and their essential differences must be clearly recognized if the play's resolution is to achieve the resonance that Odets intended. Japheth believes in man, not God. His faith, unlike his father's, lies not in an idealized future, but in one in which man might reach beyond himself to build a better world, though still not a perfect one. His man-centered philosophy is most vividly expressed in his response to Rachel's question, "What do you believe in?":

Those roads down there! The patterns they make! They're not cobwebs, those roads, the work of a foolish spider, to be brushed away by a peevish boy! Those roads were made by men, men crazy not to be alone or apart! Men, crazy to reach other! Well, they won't now. (pp. 49–50)

Japheth can be described as reality's extremist, while his father is a champion of the ideal. Allying himself with God and the associated motifs of music and Shabbos, Noah demands that his world conform to a standard of piety that is far beyond the potentially real. Just as he refuses to accommodate man's imperfect nature in his vision of a virginal future, so Japheth seems unable to accept any idea larger than man himself. Both have much to learn, and both, Odets makes clear, need to change.

Japheth's protest against his father's righteous God, then, creates a serious rift between them. In scene 2 when Noah tells his family of God's plan, Japheth exclaims, "Someone, it seems to me, would have to protest such an avenging, destructive God!" (p. 19), and this is not far removed from Noah's own initial reaction, "You're talking destruction of the whole world an' this is something terrible—!" Noah, of course, has reluctantly acquiesced, but Japheth will not accept such a God and so must oppose his father. For Noah, Japheth's refusal to obey God means that he is a bad son: at one point he shouts, "Disrespect to a father is disrespect to God!" This equation thus draws the larger implication of their dispute, placing it in the context of archetypal father-son conflict.

Declaring that he cannot live with God's edict, Japheth resolves to die with the rest of mankind. The crisis resulting from this decision changes Japheth, who is at first portrayed as a diffident, stuttering boy, intimidated by his two older brothers and in awe of his father. But his determination to defy God's catastrophic judgment affects him deeply, and in scene 3 Japheth seems physically transformed, displaying a new poise: Odets's stage directions read, "This son is no longer a boy. There is a responsible and mature air about him" (p. 25).

The disagreement between these familiar antagonists begins on a comic note in this scene as father and son argue about the correct pronounciation of "tiger," Noah insisting on "teeger." However, debate soon turns more serious as Japheth asserts the need for a rudder for the ark, whereas Noah contends that this is unnecessary, that God will guide the ark. This dispute will persist throughout much of the play. Noah also expresses anger at Japheth's unmarried state, because the new world will require population, but Japheth remains unimpressed with this reasoning:

And what about the bushels of babies who will die in the flood? Since you bring it up . . . is this vengeful God the very God I was taught to love? (p. 29)

Disgusted, he leaves at the end of the scene but returns in scene 4 to help finish building the ark "for the family, not for God" (p. 33). In fact, it is Japheth who does most of the work on the ark, for the rest of the family lack the necessary skills. The debate over Japheth's decision continues, but he remains unmoved. This father-son struggle comes to an abrupt and rather anticlimactic end in scene 5, which concludes the first half of the play. As the rain starts to fall and the family must board the ark, Japheth still insists on staying behind, when a suddenly rejuvenated Noah strikes Japheth, knocking him unconscious. He is carried aboard.

Noah's transformation has occurred at the end of scene 4. Again he is asleep, and God's visitation is announced by the singing of a bird. When Noah awakens, he has become a younger man: "His eyes are eagle-bright, his reddish hair shows only one streak of gray, and his beard is smaller but growingly alive!" (p. 42). The father's reinvigoration neatly complements his son's equally dramatic maturation in the earlier scene, for Noah must be physically ready to contest with Japheth in the second half of the play, during which God will remain absent until the final moments. The play's focal conflict is thus refined to the point of father-son debate for the remainder of the action.

The two continuing conflicts that provide the terms of this doctrinal debate are the argument over the rudder and the problem of Japheth's marriage. The question of building a rudder was introduced in scene 3, Noah insisting that, "The good Lord steers the ark, not us" (p. 26), while Japheth claimed that man must guide his own destiny. This argument is resolved in scene 7 when, after hitting a floating house, the ark begins to sink. The family begs Japheth to repair the ark, but he replies with retaliatory irony that all is in God's hands. Noah, finally, yields, remarking that Japheth will use his own judgment, to which Japheth replies, "To use my own judgment, Poppa, I'd have to trust myself." Noah's poignant response, "*Why* don't you trust yourself?" (p. 73) then decides the issue, conceding that man's own efforts may be required to ensure his survival when no divine rescue is at hand.

The opposition of father and son is quickly reanimated, however, over the problem of Japheth's marriage choice. Noah hopes that Japheth will marry Goldie, a woman who saved the young man earlier in the play and who has been invited to join the family on the ark. But Japheth loves Rachel, the estranged wife of his brother Ham, while Ham has fallen in love with Goldie. All the young people want to make the exchange. Noah, however, refuses to sanction this trading of partners, as an offense against God, and he claims ancient authority: "It stands in the books for a thousand years." Esther, ever the practical foil to her husband's fanatical orthodoxy, pleads with him to allow it "for the sake of happiness in the world." Noah's reply is typical:

That's foolish, Tuchter! First place, he won't permit such marriages, the God I know. And secondly, He won't let nothing happen to you, the God I know. (p. 79)

Esther's subsequent death at last teaches this zealot that perhaps he doesn't know God anymore, and so he relents:

Jaaphieee! I have trouble. Sonny, help me. I'm in trouble. Children, the whole night is ahead to give thanks to Heaven. Go better now every husband should kiss each wife, as Mother wanted. And I'll go kiss mine and close her eyes. (p. 81)

The specific points of argument between Noah and Japheth thus exemplify a standard generational conflict as well as the theological-philosophical controversy engendered by their predicament. However, the dramatic tension of their situation derives from the strong emotional bond between them. Like his father, Japheth cries out in his sleep to God. When Noah is in trouble, at the outset of the play, it is Japheth he asks for. Later, this "favorite son" begins to question his authority, Noah becomes distressed, and Japheth defends his position by appealing to his father's love:

Because I insist upon a rudder? I can't help it—a rudder is vital to the health of the Ark. Would you want me to lie? (p. 29)

When Esther dies, Noah weeps in Japheth's arms. Rachel points out qualities that she finds in both Noah and Japheth, "love, wrath, gentleness," all positive characteristics. Both father and son are dreamers and idealists, and their spiritual kinship is further under-scored by the following exchange:

NOAH: God never said we should steer the ark! Tomorrow first thing you'll take it off!
JAPHETH: And God didn't tell you to invent the hoe and the rake and yet you did!
NOAH: I was a youngster then—what did I know? (p. 68)

Odets indicates that Japheth is right, both about the rudder and about marrying Rachel, but Japheth's position is not allowed to become the decisive one in the ongoing family drama. Clearly both men must temper their views, and the motif of necessary attitudinal change dominates the final two scenes of the play. Odets's implication is that idealism such as Noah's sincere faith may rigidify into a callous piety unless it can be adapted to changing times and novel situations, while rebellious skepticism such as Japheth's may degenerate into a bleak cynicism without some steadying influence of philosophic perspective. At the end of the play Noah elects to live out the rest of his days not with Japheth but with Shem, his capitalist son, because, considered with comic practicality, "It's more comfortable." But Japheth has Noah's blessing—"I pray a beautiful soul shall enter your baby" (p. 84)—for the best hopes for the new generation reside in Japheth and his unborn child.

If the emotional tie between this father and son provides an important human dimension for this modern version of the biblical tale, an equally affective element is supplied in the marital relations each man enjoys with a woman whose personality complements his own. Despite the frequent arguments between Noah and his wife, there is a real tenderness in their dealings with one another. Odets characterizes Esther's gibes at Noah as "harmless," gentle taunts that he has "heard for so many years that he no longer has ears for them" (p. 6). This habit of mockery connects Noah's family to Odets's earlier contemporary Jewish families who also quarrel constantly but take no offense from the exchange of sarcastic remarks. The relationship of Noah and Esther most nearly recalls that of the Gordons in *Paradise Lost,* for both wives display impatience at their husbands' idealism, as well as genuine affection and respect for their principles. After sixty years of marriage, Noah clearly loves his wife, and he even recognizes the rightness of much that she says. His reaction to her death at the end of the play is one of the most poignant moments in all of Odets's work.

Japheth's evolving relationships with Rachel links him further to his father, for this, too, is an authentic love story. As Japheth's confidence in himself grows, so does his capacity for love and his ability to express it. By scene 6 he is able to declare his love for Rachel:

JAPHETH: Rachel, I love you and want to marry you.
RACHEL. I would marry you . . . but your father won't permit it.
JAPHETH. Ham was right—you're changing. Well, I'm changing, too—And my father—innocent and stubborn as he is—HE'LL have to change! (p. 59)

Like Japheth, Rachel is at first a youngster lacking in self-confidence. Troubled by her unsuccessful marriage to Ham, she feels unloved by the rest of the family as well. With some encouragement from Esther, however, she eventually responds to Japheth's ardor and asserts her own feelings in agreeing to marry him. Her love will benefit him as well, for Rachel resembles Esther in her admiration for Japheth's idealistic intensity, but she is also practical and realistic. After his declaration of faith in mankind in scene 5, she replies with expedient logic:

If you think people should reach each other . . . the ark is the only place they'll do it now. . . . Japheth, I beg you to think! There is idealism now in just survival! (p. 50)

The echo of Esther's characteristic pragmatism in such exchanges indicates that Rachel's influence will provide the same necessary humanizing balance in Japheth's marriage as can be seen in his parents' relationship. Noah's eventual blessing on their unborn child thus confirms Odets's implication here that man is indeed the measure of things and that the human heart is a surer guide than the law.

This emphasis on human diversity and vitality is elaborated further in Odets's portrayal of Noah's family. Shem and Ham, the other two sons, are types rather than fully delineated characters like Japheth. Ham, as in Obey's play, is presented as a cynic. He is also a drunkard, like his father, but he is not a good husband, and it is not surprising that he can't forge a relationship with the more serious, sensitive, Rachel; instead, Ham is immediately attracted to Goldie, a loose woman. Shem, on the other hand, is the archetypal capitalist. Unlike Morty in *Awake and Sing!* however, Shem is presented as a respectful and obedient son, despite his entrepreneurial zeal. In charge of overseeing his father's business property, he cannot resist moneymaking schemes even in the face of divine judgment. Before the Flood he sells off thirty thousand shekels' worth of land and then hides the money; when Noah learns about it from a tax collector, he is shocked, exclaiming, "Money is unholy dirt on the ark," and Shem can only reply, "*But what am I without my money?!*" (p. 37). Japheth must eventually knock Shem unconscious to get the key to the house where the money is hidden, an act that anticipates Noah's stunning blow to Japheth to get him on the ark.

While on the ark Shem endangers everyone by making and storing manure briquettes to be used and sold as fuel after the Flood. When the manure unbalances the ark, Noah demands that he throw it overboard—"With manure you want to begin a new world?" (p. 64)—while Esther, suggesting that Shem's hoard will benefit the family, defends him. The surface conflict here between individual enterprise and the ideal of community serves the wider purposes of the play's philosophical argument by elaborating Noah's despair over the imperfection of "human beings." The paradoxical duality of physical and spiritual elements is here given its most overt treatment. Man's society, Odets acknowledges, is built in part on a foundation of manure, but his ultimate emphasis falls upon the interdependence of body and spirit, lust and love, the holy and the unholy, for in this manure can grow the flowering peach, the redemptive image that gives the play its title. The discordant variety of life itself, vividly represented in Noah's family, will give rise at last to the new growth that will ensure the future. This acceptance of imperfection within the context of human community, paired with the cautionary emphasis on the grounding of idealism in reality, constitutes Odets's secular gloss on the biblical myth of divine judgment.

The significance of the fruit tree is carefully prepared for during the course of the play. In scene 5, before the family boards the ark, Esther puts on a hat "decorated with fruits, berries, and flowers" (p. 45). As always, fruit is an important symbol in Odets's work, combining allusions to life, growth, sexuality, and nourishment, and Esther's wearing the hat accentuates her importance as a character. Odets obviously sympathizes with her realistic point of view and her desire that love prevail in the relationship between Japheth and Rachel. At the scene's end, as the family hurriedly boards the ark, Esther realizes that she has forgotten her hat and then Noah realizes that he has forgotten the gitka; both are quickly retrieved. The hat and the gitka are thus linked as significant and complementary symbols of the redemptive mission of the ark's passengers.

In scene 8 Odets crystallizes several symbols he has used throughout his career in realizing his most transcendent vision. Noah has sent out the doves in search of dry land. He and Esther have quarreled, and they have not spoken to each other for some time. Esther has been ill, confined to her room, and has not been seen in the play during scene 7 and part of scene 8. When finally she reappears, she asks for the hat; Ham's reaction is that his mother looks "like a queen." Esther requests of Noah, "Marry the children . . . for the sake of happiness in the world," adding that their happiness "is my last promised land" (p. 79). She then complains that the gitka has not sung for a long time. Her final words signal the approach of death: "I'll take the hat to shade my eyes. . . . Noah, I'll tell you a mystery" (p. 80). Soon afterwards the dove returns with an olive branch in her mouth, the gitka begins to sing a "mourning song," and Esther dies, her hat falling off. In her final scene Esther thus becomes an emblematic figure much like Noah: she has moved from asking a "realism" to telling a "mystery," and in her death the two points of view merge. Further elaborated by the gitka's song and a significant reference to the moon—that Odetsian image of idealized reality—this scene recalls the symbolic richness of *Golden Boy, Rocket to the Moon,* and *Clash by Night.* In this significant fusion of music, fruit, and the moon, Esther passes on her vital wisdom to Noah and the family.

The final scene, then, highlights a young peach tree "in profuse and handsome bloom," which is the play's legacy and also Odets's final image. (This symbolic appearance of the flowering tree recalls Strindberg's use of a flowering castle at the end of *A Dream Play,* another work of reconciliation.) Noah can finally bless Japheth's marriage, understanding Esther's vision and recognizing the short-comings of his own. His final words to God are a request that the world not be destroyed again, indicating that he has learned to trust himself, and the play ends on a note of prophecy, echoing Esther's final words as husband, wife, and Japheth merge:

But what I learned on the trip, dear God, you can't take it away from me. To walk in humility, I learned. And listen, even to *myself* . . . and to speak softly, with the voices of consolation. Yes, I hear You, God—now it's in man's hands to make or destroy the world—I'll tell you a mystery. (p. 45)

It is oddly fitting that *The Flowering Peach* turned out to be Odets's last play, for it takes him full circle from his first full-length work, *Awake and Sing!* Both plays focus on a Jewish nuclear family, both balance the comic and the serious, both deal with the conflict of idealized visions with the demands of the real world, and both project images of utopia. In the earlier play, however, the Berger family never achieved harmony or togetherness, and the worlds of Bessie and Jacob remained far apart, not realizable even in the next generation. Odets the young playwright was too angry and idealistic himself to reconcile viewpoints that he saw as irreconcilable. The later Odets is more chastened, more willing to comprehend and appreciate the paradoxes he was unable to face as a younger man. In an interview before the opening of *The Flowering Peach* he said:

I'm not a kid any more, I'm 47. And at this age I began to ask myself, what happened? Do you want to begin all over again? Who are you and where are you? I went through an examination of personal resources while doing this play. From all this came something, I think, that is very affirmative.

When you start out, you have to champion something. Every artist begins as if he were the first one painting, every composer as if there were no Beethoven. But if you still feel that way after ten or fifteen years, you're nuts. No young writer is broad. I couldn't have written "The Flowering Peach" twenty years ago. As you grow older, you mature. The danger is that in broadening, as you mature, you may dilute your art. A growing writer always walks that tightrope.[13]

In *The Flowering Peach,* accordingly, the basically unsympathetic Bessie has become the more understanding and motherly Esther. Jacob, the idealist who felt that he must kill himself to effect his vision, has become Noah, who is able to survive a cataclysm and learn from it. The Berger children, who ran away from their problems, have become Noah's children, who are able to overcome adversity and grow. Jacob's vision of "O Paradiso" could only remain in his head; ultimately it was only a song on a record that Bessie would break. The Berger house remained one "without an orange." In Odets's final play, however, the visions of paradise have become a possibility, because man has learned to understand his nature and trust himself. In such a world Moe Axelrod's dream, "Ever see oranges grow? . . . one summer I laid under a tree and let them fall right in my mouth,"[14] can become a reality. The peach tree can grow; indeed, it flowers.

The Flowering Peach elicited some cynical responses from critics. Malcolm Goldstein and Mordecai Gorelick saw the play as an apologia for Odets's willingness to comply with HUAC, particularly citing Noah's final decision to live with his rich son. While there is a biographical element in all of Odets's work, reducing the play in this way seems merely mean-spirited. Sensitively and carefully read, *The Flowering Peach* clearly reflects themes and images that had occupied Odets throughout his career; it also forms a logical extension of the vision he had been working out in *The Country Girl*. Harold Clurman also took a biographical approach to the play, but was characteristically more generous:

What is certain is that *The Flowering Peach* represents Odets in spiritual transition. The play's honesty and value in this respect consist in not coming to more specific answers than the conciliatory ones it illustrates. For all its ideas—which are abstracts of the pull and tear of the author's impulses—it is not really a "philosophical" play. It sometimes drifts as if it did not know where it meant to go. Yet in this looseness there is a certain advantage: the play never lies. Odets improvises on a theme, and through the ambiguities, stutterings, pronouncements, and random jokes we feel a man—immensely sensitive to the experience of his life and time.[15]

Brooks Atkinson's review of the play is perhaps closest to the truth:

Mr. Odets' new play is a beautiful one. His finest, in fact. . . . If you listen closely you can probably discover a message of hope for the sullen world of today. But Mr. Odets is not setting himself up as an oracle. He does not pretend to have the magic formula. Contemplating the long history of the race in terms of some disarming people, he is facing the world with respect and humility. *The Flowering Peach* is his testament to the endurance and native wisdom of mankind.[16]

Shortly after Odets's death it was revealed that the Pulitzer Prize jurors Oscar J. Campbell and Maurice Valency had both chosen *The Flowering Peach* for the prize. However, they were overruled by the advisory committee, and the award went to Tennessee Williams's *Cat on a Hot Tin Roof*.

One of Odets's first projects upon his return to Hollywood was a script called *Joseph and His Brethren* for Columbia. According to Bob Thomas, biographer of Harry Cohn, who was the head of Columbia Studios, Odets had written "what many had considered a monumental screenplay, but Cohn could find no actor of sufficient stature to

play Joseph." Cohn tried repeatedly to keep the project alive, offering it to Otto Preminger and then Frank Capra, but no satisfactory
deal could be worked out. Finally the project was written off at a loss
of $1,700,000.[17]

Odets's name appeared on three more films before his death in
1963. With Ernest Lehman he cowrote *The Sweet Smell of Success*
(United Artists, 1957), which was based on Lehman's novella. Its
central plot concerns the relationship between an ambitious press
agent, Sidney Falco (Tony Curtis) and an influential columnist, J. J.
Hunsecker (Burt Lancaster), with whom Sidney desperately wants
to establish a close relationship in hopes of furthering his own
career. In order to ingratiate himself, he agrees to break up a romance between Hunsecker's sister Susan (Susan Harrison) and a jazz
musician named Steve Dallas (Martin Milner); Hunsecker threatens
that he will not publicize Sidney's clients in his column if Sidney fails
to do so. Sidney then smears Steve by placing an item in another
column, claiming that he is a Communist and a marijuana user.

The smear gets Steve fired from his job, and when Steve accuses
Hunsecker of planting the item, it eventually breaks up the couple.
Outraged at this effrontery, Hunsecker next asks Sidney to plant
some marijuana on Steve and then arranges to have a policeman beat
up the musician and arrest him. Sidney's initial hesitancy about
going so far is overcome by Hunsecker's offer that Sidney take over
his column for three months while he takes his sister for an extended
trip. Susan eventually discovers her brother's duplicity, and one
night Sidney finds her about to commit suicide by jumping from a
window at her brother's apartment. As Sidney tries to prevent her, a
struggle ensues, and when Hunsecker returns suddenly in the midst
of this scene, he assumes that Sidney is trying to rape Susan. He
thereupon calls the police to arrest Sidney for planting the marijuana
on Steve, while Sidney vows to tell the world about Hunsecker's
crimes. The film thus ends on the implication that both Sidney and
Hunsecker will receive the punishment they deserve.

The film displays interesting nuances beyond the original story.
Hunsecker's characterization as a rabid chauvinist who attempts to
destroy Steve by imputing Communist leanings to him adds a new
political and societal twist to the columnist's corruption, and these
overtones were probably worked in by Odets. Odets also must have

contributed much of the dialogue, which effectively reflects the world of press agents and columnists. The slangy flavor of that very synthetic world is vividly represented in a speech, apparently Odets's work, in which Sidney explains his personal philosophy to his secretary:

Way up high, Sam, where it's always balmy! Where no one snaps his fingers and says, "Hey, Shrimp, rack up those balls!" Or, "Hey, mouse, run out and get me a pack of butts!" I don't want tips from the kitty—I sit in the big game and play with the big players. On you it's becoming, but you're old-fashioned, Sally. Ideals and manners—they burned those books last election! *My* experience I can tell you in a nutshell, and I didn't dream it in a dream: dog eat dog!

Other Odets lines energize the dialogue: "Watch me run a fifty-yard dash with my legs cut off"; Sidney refusing to speak on the phone, "If it's for me, tear it up"; and Hunsecker's sardonic line, "I'd hate to take a bite out of you. You're a cookie full of arsenic." In addition, the film develops an effective *film noir* atmosphere, as James Wong Howe, the cinematographer, expertly captures the underside of the New York night world. Nevertheless, *The Sweet Smell of Success* was the first box-office failure for the Hecht-Hill-Lancaster company, perhaps because it marked Burt Lancaster's first appearance in the role of an unredeemable villain; Tony Curtis, too, abandoned his usual charming image to play an unsavory character.

Odets's next effort was for Twentieth Century-Fox, *The Story on Page One* (1960), which he also directed. Carrying his only original story credit, the film is unfortunately predictable and dull. Its plot details the trial of Jo Morris (Rita Hayworth), for the murder of her husband and her lover Larry Ellis (Gig Young). A thirty-five-year-old widower, Larry is still dominated by his mother. (Mother-obsessed characters are common in Odets's plays, but the mothers have usually died when the characters were very young.) One night Jo's husband finds the lovers, draws a gun, and accidently shoots himself. The trial occupies most of the film, interspersed with some flashbacks depicting the love affair and the death of the husband. At length, a rather banal happy ending is granted, with the lovers, acquitted of the murder charge, leaving the court; Larry also seems to be breaking free of his mother's domination.

The Story on Page One evinces a basic similarity to *Clash by Night*. Each of these dramas concerns a love triangle involving a dissatisfied woman, and in each case there is a child that complicates the possibility of divorce. Each, moreover, climaxes in an act of violence, although the husband rather than the lover is its victim in the film. The film, unfortunately, shares many of the play's weaknesses as well. The protagonists are neither interesting nor sympathetic, and, as a result, in the courtroom scenes that take up most of the film interest centers more on the lawyers than on the defendants. The prosecuting attorney, vividly portrayed by former Group actor Sanford Meisner, epitomizes the cunning of a ruthless lawyer. His opponent, too, performs impressively, and the resulting dramatic impact of the courtroom scenes undercuts the central character study.

As in *Clash by Night,* Odets, perhaps recognizing how thin his story was, apparently felt compelled to add a social dimension. At the beginning of the film, the defense attorney makes some speeches about the inequality of justice, explaining to Larry's mother that the state is able to commit a great deal of money to obtain a conviction, while she cannot even afford an investigation. The potential relevance of this diatribe is quickly submerged in the courtroom pyrotechnics, however, as Odets once again sacrifices character and theme for melodramatic effect. *The Sweet Smell of Success* and *The Story on Page One,* on the other hand, share a common emphasis on unnatural family attachments, exposing Hunsecker's possessive supervision of his sister and Mrs. Ellis's smothering love for her son. In both cases Odets fails to reconcile these motifs of psychological aberration with his social themes, and, as a result, both films are confused.

Odets's last script, written for Jerry Wald (who produced *The Story on Page One*), was *Wild in the Country* (1961), directed by Philip Dunne and based on a novel by J. R. Salamanca. This film, which starred Elvis Presley, preceded the song-dominated musicals that characterized much of Presley's movie career, though even here, a few songs are featured. The story chronicles the maturation of a sensitive and rebellious farm boy with a talent for writing. After a series of mishaps, including a trial for manslaughter, he overcomes his past and goes off to college on a scholarship.

The plot develops a number of typical Odetsian themes, and its protagonist, Glenn Tyler (Presley) displays characteristics of several Odets protagonists. Outwardly brash and violent, he in fact possesses a sensitive and loving nature. He reveres the memory of his mother, who died shortly before his ninth birthday, and resents his father for making her life difficult. From his mother's influence he has developed a taste for literature and music, and he cherishes a guitar that she gave him and that his brother breaks during the course of the film. Glenn's recourse to music as an outlet for his longings recalls its similar use by other Odets characters: he sings to the various women in his life just as Steve Takis plays the clarinet to express his feelings for Fay Tucker in *Night Music*. And the conflict between his volatile temper and his artistic tendencies links him to Joe Bonaparte in *Golden Boy*.

This film, like *None But the Lonely Heart*, focuses on the protagonist's relationships with three women. One is his cousin Noreen (Tuesday Weld), who lives with her father and her illegitimate baby; Glenn's uncle hopes the cousins will marry. Noreen loves Glenn, seeing in him a chance to change her life, but he mistrusts his own wild instincts (and hers) and feels that she deserves a more settled future. She apparently represents to him an aspect of himself and his past that he wants to escape. His avoidance of this involvement thus mirrors the reluctance of Ada to become involved in *None But the Lonely Heart*, and when Glenn takes Noreen to a county fair where they dance and play games together, the episode recalls the fun fair in the earlier film. Glenn's other girlfriend is Betty Lee (Millie Perkins), who comes from a respectable churchgoing family. She understands his longings and appreciates his nature. In one scene in which they are flying a kite, Glenn remarks that he would like to fly. Echoing Odets's earlier play, Betty Lee tells him to take a "rocket to the moon."

Glenn, however, soon falls in love with his social worker, Irene Sperry (Hope Lange), an older woman who takes an interest in him and encourages his writing. For him she represents the care and tenderness he lost when his mother died; in Glenn Irene sees an image of her late husband, a playwright who died young (presumably a suicide) because of her inability to cope with the responsibilities of marriage. Glenn declares his love for Irene one night when they are forced to stay in a motel room during a thunderstorm. They are in separate but adjoining rooms, but Glenn comes into her room in a scene reminiscent of *Night Music*. The relationship between Glenn and Irene thus develops the Odetsian search for a mother figure, but the story concludes with Glenn going off to college to "find himself" before continuing his love affair with her.

At the end of his life Odets was at work on two projects. One was the musical version of *Golden Boy*, developed as a vehicle for Sammy Davis, Jr. As a result of this casting, the story's focus changed from the conflict of Joe Bonaparte, son of Italian immigrants, who must choose between the violin and boxing, to that of Joe Wellington, a black boxer who must decide between his desire to remain true to his roots and his need to make it in the white man's world. Joe's love for Lorna further complicates this conflict in that it now becomes the story of the love of a black man for a white woman. According to playwright William Gibson, who essentially rewrote the play, the draft Odets left behind required major reworking:

The driving line of the original play was of course there; Clifford had once said to me that he "never thought much of that play" but after viewing some semipro staging of it years later he "knew they'll never break it down," and his sense of its line was still unerring. But music in the theatre creates a profoundly altered time-world in the audience, material which in straight drama requires ten minutes of preparation can in a musical context be attacked instantly, and the text was that of straight drama, as yet undistilled to the concentrate which music compels. And Clifford, still working on the page, had not been privileged to witness the physical fact onstage of a Negro boy talking to a white girl.[18]

Much of Odets's story yet remains, including Joe's conflict with his father, although the father's motivation and character are vague and Mr. Bonaparte's lines often sound silly in the mouth of a black man from Harlem. Joe's relationships with Tom Moody and Roxie are the same as in the original, as is his association with Eddie Fuseli, here renamed Eddie Satin. Some of Odets's dialogue is retained and there are some new lines that sound like Odets, but much of the dialogue was essentially rewritten by Gibson, who acknowledged that lyricist Lee Strauss also contributed "some bits." The show opened in New York on October 20, 1964, over a year after Odets's death.

The other project Odets was working on was a television series, "The Richard Boone Show." In an article written for the *Los Angeles Times* on August 1, 1963, he explained how he became involved with that project:

To begin with, Jean [Renoir] said one night, over a poignantly delicate bottle of 1953 Chateau Lascombes: "TV, I don't think you understand, my dear Cliff, is, for a writer of your popular inclination, the medium of the future. It is fast, to the point, without frills, wide open for any technical innovations; and the audience is always waiting for you with open arms!" He had made a provocative point.

Only some few weeks later I found myself sitting (sans wine) with Dick Boone, a kindly, bluff acting man, who can be fearfully direct when rough-house or persuasion are needed. (Incidentally, Dick often reminds me of John Steinbeck, another friend; they seem cut exactly from the same textured tweed.)

Dick was talking about doing a television show together and I was playing the reluctant bride. It was only when he said, "But I don't think you understand. Don't you realize that together, with a hand-picked company of players, that we probably can make the first real theatre on TV?"—It was only then, according to Dick's later version, that I "jumped over the table!"[19]

The idea of a stock company no doubt appealed to Odets, perhaps reminded him of his days with the Group Theatre. The show's format consisted of ten regular actors in addition to the star who would appear in different parts in each original drama that would appear each week. Odets was to write four of the thirteen original scripts and, as editor in chief, supervise development of the other scripts.

Time magazine, which had featured Odets on its cover in 1939, debunked his signing on to work in television in an article in 1962, entitled "Credo of a Wrong Living Man." Proclaiming it

"doubtful that Odets's own pungency will manifest itself on T.V.,"
the article quotes Odets's defense of craftsmanship:

"There is the mistaken idea," he says in self-defense, "that if you stay on
Broadway and do plays—no matter how bad—this makes you a moral,
right-living man. Come to Hollywood, and this makes you a wrong-living
man. All the really great artists are professional craftsmen who write everything. But there is this idea in the U.S. that there's something nasty,
unsavory or immoral about doing professional craftsmanship."[20]

The article's writer then appends a characteristic sarcastic punch line:
"So much for people who wonder why he wrote a movie for Elvis
Presley."

Odets died before "The Richard Boone Show" premiered, but
two of his scripts were performed on the show, *Big Mitch* (December 10, 1963) and *The Mafia Man* (January 7, 1964). *Big Mitch,*
originally titled "North Star," focused on the relationship of a poor
Californian and his daughter. Disappointed when his daughter marries a rather dull accountant, Mitch decides to make a grand gesture
anyway and buys the newlyweds an enormous freezer (the brand
name is North Star). He then realizes that he will need to pawn or
mortgage everything he owns to make the payments on it; eventually
he must also take a job driving a cab. The freezer functions as a
symbol of Mitch's pride and of his hopes for a happy future for the
young couple.

Odets's other script, *Mafia Man,* was originally titled "Don't
Blow Bugles." The story begins in Italy, where Frank Ritchie, a
gangster, is living, having fled the United States some years earlier. It
is soon revealed that his son, ashamed of his father's past, has left
West Point. Ritchie decides to return to the States and testify against
the Mafia in order to restore to his son "an attitude to live." He
disguises himself as an invalid and asks an unemployed actress to
accompany him as his daughter. The plot then features a series of
murders and shootings, including one of an airsick Indian who
mistakenly takes Frank's wheelchair and is shot to death. Frank, too,
is shot but manages to get a taxi to the hotel bar where he has
arranged to meet his son and the actress, Diane. While bleeding to
death on the hotel floor, he dies happy, knowing that Diane will give

his son an "attitude to live." Each script thus concentrates on a single character, emphasizing the pathos of a rather simple situation. Neither did much to revolutionize television, or to enhance the medium's reputation, or Odets's.

On July 23, complaining of stomach pains, Odets was admitted to Cedars of Lebanon Hospital in Los Angeles to undergo tests for ulcers. His condition was diagnosed as cancer, and Odets died on August 14. His body was cremated, and a funeral service was held two days later at Forest Lawn Cemetery. Many obituaries still referred to one of America's most gifted playwrights as "promising."

Afterword
The Time is Ripe:
The 1940 Journal of Clifford
Odets (1988)

One way or another you pay for what you are.
                    —Paul Boray, *Humoresque*

In the year 1940 Odets kept a detailed daily journal. He had begun
such projects before, sometimes making regular entries for a few
months, sometimes managing only sporadic notes for a day or two at
a time, then skipping several months before providing another entry.
In 1940, however, he resolved to keep a steady record and the
result is a fascinating and revealing account of what was in many
ways a critical year in Odets's life. Recently separated from his wife,
Luise Rainer, he met Bette Grayson, whom he would marry in 1943.
Night Music was in rehearsal, eventually completing a pre-Broadway
run in Boston before opening to disastrous reviews in New York. He
also spent a few months in Hollywood, working on a film version of
Night Music (which was never made). The Group Theatre, too, was
in a time of transition, its members planning for a new season while
rethinking their philosophy; Odets himself was concerned about the
future of the Group and his relationship with them. (Soon afterward, the Group Theatre was disbanded.)

The journal reflects Odets's anxieties regarding the production of
Night Music; his mixed feelings about the actress Faye Wray, to
whom he had a very strong emotional and sexual attraction but
insisted he didn't love and didn't want to marry; his growing involvement with Bette Grayson, whom he also insisted he didn't love;

227

his agony over the failure of his marriage to Luise Rainer and his lingering attachment to her; and his love/hate association with the Group Theatre and some of its individual members, particularly Harold Clurman—their relationship approximating the intensity of a marriage—Luther Adler, and Lee Strasberg. However, the most significant insights provided here involve Odets's meditations about his recurrent thematic conundrum, the all-consuming demands of art versus the dual nature of the artist, and the important clues these reflections supply toward explaining the abrupt decline in his creative output after 1940.

Odets's major concern in the journal is the need for form, not only in his art but in his life as well. Indeed, the word "form" recurs so frequently in these pages as to suggest an obsession. Ultimately it becomes apparent that in the writing of this journal, Odets was in search of himself: locating the form of the self might perhaps resolve the questions of the proper subject and form for his art.

Odets is certain about the artist's aims and function, and, as his plays clearly demonstrate, his notions are romantic:

What is the romantic temperament? It is amazed, impressed, delighted, and enraged by the caprice of life. It is impulsive, swaggering, remonstrating, scolding, pleading, straining, sulking, appealing, denouncing the unfairness of life. It is the romantic who cries out that he is out of harmony with life— by which he means that life is not in harmony with his vision of it, the way he saw it as a youth with moral and idealistic hunger to mix his hands in it and live it fully and deeply. The classic art is to accept life, the romantic to reject it as it is and attempt to make it over as he wants it to be. The classic accepts the forms and conventions of life around it. The romantic breaks them down, rejects, and rebels against them—they do not fit him—they were made for the dead and let the dead clutch them in the graves! Yes, with the romantic it is all self-discovery and self-exploration. The injustice and coldness of life is constantly throwing him back on himself, and it is from this center of the expanding demanding growing ego that the romantic functions. The romantic's nature inwardly is one of chaos; this is because there are no accepted or standard values for him—he will not and does not accept a code made by others.[1]

This belief in the artist's need to impose and inspire a more transcendent vision of life—reflected in such protagonists as Joe Bonaparte,

Ralph Berger, Leo Gordon, Steven Takis, and Noah—is paired with a socialist idealism, dedicated to uprooting a capitalist system that destroys man's highest potential. In discussing the natures of two women who played pivotal roles in his life, Bette Grayson and Francis Farmer, Odets examines how a "fresh nature just entering the arena" is often crushed by such a society:

. . . . all of them instinctively fearful of the competitive world which kills their inner life. Horrible. Often I tell people that it is the middle class that will profit most from a revolution that brings a new and more human way of life, but most people don't understand that. Every woman, if she but realized it, would work for a socialist society and way of life. Of this I am certain, positive!

Odets expresses the belief that, unlike his revered Beethoven, who was not able to transform the world because of the hierarchical nature of his society, the twentieth-century artist does wield that potential. In this regard he even proposes Lenin as an artist.

Although Odets can thus abstract the artist's power and function as he ponders them in his journal and articulate the possibility of a better world for mankind, he is at the same time appalled by his presumption, questioning his own ability to achieve his ideals. He remains confident of his talent but not of his ability to harness that talent. The world in various manifestations, makes too many inroads on his psyche, fragmenting it into a chaos that can find no form. Among the distracting concerns elaborated here are a longing for a home, which also takes the form of a desire for a mother/wife, the price of success in the loss of privacy, and an inability to achieve the discipline and concentration necessary for sustained artistic growth. Odets broods over these problems in various ways in the journal.

Longing for the security and order of a real home, he often complains about the disorder of his life and of his apartment, which affects his ability to work. On a visit to his friend the playwright Paul Green in North Carolina, he writes with envy about Green's family life:

THURSDAY: drove out to Paul Green's house where I remarked again to myself the good normal life he leads. He has a good wife and four fine children. I spoke to them for a while and wished they were mine and the house mine and the roots mine and the whole settlement mine!

Both the failure to make a home for himself and the tendency to idealize the concept derive from the acute pain of being deprived of a secure home as a child. Odets pursues this self-examination on psychological grounds, tracing his current unhappiness to an intense fear of rejection which, perversely, frustrates his attempts to form the relationships he needs. Later in the journal he returns to this self-defeating attitude, linking it now to his inability to work:

I realized . . . that opening myself to refusal was something that I rarely permit in my life. It often accounts for the fact that I so seldom leave the house, so seldom permit myself to arrive in situations where painful refusal is possible. Pain and fear are the paralyzing agencies here, and how subtly the mechanism is set up in the self! One does not want to begin work, does not want to enter negotiations or situations in which one may be seen to be inadequate: so daring goes, inventiveness and calling on reserves are lost.

Clearly this constricting fear of failure had a profound effect on Odets's career, explaining, at least in part, his decline as an artist.

The journal reveals also how personally wounded Odets was by the failure of *Night Music*. Many entries reveal a sense of betrayal by Harold Clurman for his inadequate direction of the play and by Elia Kazan for a failure to capture the essence of Steve Takis's character:

What gets him by with any audience is his winning personality. In N.M. his characterization is very incomplete and more or less mechanical. In most places it is as if he walked out of his dressing room in his street clothes and shoes, Elia Kazan, not Steve Takis. He lacks variety of approach, variety of voice, altho his perceptions are good; he has flashes of genuine charm, too. The audiences, I think, will like him, but he is far from satisfactory to me personally. A certain uncouthness hits me, too, a sort of boisterous quality . . .

His apprehension that the play will fail builds to a cry of violent pain directed at the fabric of the American theater itself:

The whole effort now is to make the play a success, a pitiful effort. Even we forget about the charm of the play, its delicacy and poignancy. . . . Everything drives towards success. The American Theatre, excuse me, is vile and a stench hangs over it. Here is one young man who would not weep at its death!

It is revealing that Odets worries over the production and broods about Clurman and Kazan, his anxiety becomes all connected in his mind with the concepts of home and roots. In the following notation the uncertainties of life and art intertwine:

After the show, while Harold, Gadget, Kazan and I sat over drinks at the Ritz bar, I kept thinking about my real need for a certain kind of woman, one who would be able to control me and help give this blasted life of mine some kind of form. I feel sure she is hiding in an Eskimo igloo! This way, alone, half of my life is wasted, without definition and clarity. How a good woman could help me; for I seem unable to help myself.

This need for a woman to help him forms another recurring motif in the journal, a yearning for some external solution to his feelings of homelessness and incompleteness. Later he writes: "I needed a woman who will help me become more an artist, whose life is devoted to that task. No other woman. Good night."

The desire for a nurturing wife is obviously connected with his longing for the maternal care associated with childhood. He writes of losing himself in a woman's breasts, and the journal contains numerous references to his mother:

Last night I found a long letter from my dead mother. I cried twice as I read it—what did you think I would do? A lot of people would be surprised (as the little boy said) if they knew how often during a single day and night my eyes flood with tears which seem unreasonable.

Later, relating that he has reread some old journal selections, he concludes his current entry with a poignant reference: "Sleep. One old entry very touching—Mother came to my bed and kissed me good night, something she rarely did. I miss my mother always."

Despite these recurrent longings, Odets reminds himself that the emotional peace and security of a home are inimical to art, that the "normal" life must not be for him:

the simple human desire to be loved and accepted must necessarily clash
with the artist's work. I mention all of this because in the past few years the
yearning for acceptance (even by fools!) has done something to my work.
Here and there an element of truth has been lost: the truth of how one sees
the world.

He also blames "intimacy," paradoxically, for ruining his marriage to
Luise Rainer:

Intimacy of relationship is what I adore and need most in life. Yet it is
what I have had least of. With Luise I had such intimacy. And yet it is what
defeated our marriage in the end, for she would allow no larger forms,
cutting everything down to "me and thou," locked in each other's arms or in
a room.

In his entry of August 3 he proclaims a defiant philosophy of
egocentricity: "The first law of life is be thyself, baby! I never heard
of a terrier that wanted to be a bulldog—it remained for humans to
breed them together." What that self was, unfortunately, Odets
could never settle on.

Such dividedness is evident in other areas as well. On a very basic
level, Odets thoroughly enjoys the fruits of his success. During the
year of this journal he actually accomplishes very little: he thinks
about his work at great length, but spends much of his time indulging the leisure that money and celebrity afford. He meets many
friends for lengthy dinners, devotes countless hours to listening to
music, often visits Luther Adler and Sylvia Sidney at their country
home, and regularly goes out nightclubbing with the columnist
Leonard Lyons. Odets buys books and records in enormous quan-
tities and enjoys driving his Cadillac through the streets of New York
in the early hours of the morning. Raised by his father to worship at
the altar of success, Odets obviously relishes what money can buy.
Yet he remains acutely aware of its traps, as is indicated in his
account of his talk at Black Mountain College:

It was an effort to explain what happens to the talented young writer in this
country, showing how he went from maladjustment (which started him
writing to begin with) to a deeper and more horrible maladjustment which
was beyond repair. Quick and noisy success, uncritical acclaim, personal

bewilderment which becomes resentment when the first success is not followed by an even larger one; the seeking and finding of awards and regards; LACK OF REPOSE; money problems, drinking for stability; and tonic effects; Hollywood in one guise or another; looking for immediate results in every phase of the life and art . . .

Odets always hated what his father stood for, while craving the adulation and comfort derived from a success his father never came close to achieving. At some points recorded in the journal he expresses a certain satisfaction in giving money to his father, combined with a disgust at the man for needing it.

In one entry Odets half mocks himself for so thoroughly enjoying the pleasures his success affords him:

An excellent dinner and good spirits, all of which made me think that it would be a fine idea to have such parties at least once or twice a week. I am all for the spirits from the belly and the appetites, instead of the vinegary nervous spirit of the modern intellectual. What we lack today is gusto, normal and rich appetites. Let there be more suppers and more bottles of wine, say I!

Closely related to this spirit of revelry is the portrait of a man lacking in self-discipline. Odets complains repeatedly of the late hours he keeps, of his slothful life-style: staying out into the early hours of the morning, going to nightclubs, eating at Lindy's, the Stork Club and Sardi's, and then sleeping until the afternoon. As a result he is not able to concentrate for extended periods of time on his work. Aware of the need to isolate himself in order to focus on his art, he is unable to do so. Apparently unable to tolerate the quiet of his apartment for long, he finds himself telephoning friends and inviting them over or joining them for nights out on the town. Like Poe's "Man of the Crowd," Odets seems frightened by his solitude. Nevertheless, he realizes that "Hell is other people," for they pull him away from what he should be doing. His entry of October 14 reflects this dilemma:

Up late, discontent, not working well because of a distracted mind. It is necessary to say again that the artist is at a loss when the outer intensity is more dense than the inner. It is for this reason that he often tries to throw off the burden of outer connections, despite the necessity of them and the pleasure too.

In Odets's case, the "outer necessity" too often overwhelms the inner. He would later write, "You are one of the laziest men I know, you, with all your talent!!!"

Odets's mind was rather easily distracted. Sustaining the effort necessary to complete a play was a problem that plagued him through much of his career. Teeming with ideas, he would work on one briefly before shifting to another, and then another, often finishing nothing. He enjoyed the process of thinking about a play and, if necessary, researching it, but the actual composition was agony. In the journal he discusses working on at least four plays. One is a "sextette" about a group of homeless men, while another he calls "The Actress Play." He seriously attempts a play about Woodrow Wilson, buying dozens of books, commenting on some but finally despairing of having to read through all of them; eventually references to this play just disappear. The journal also records the beginnings of what he called "The Trio Play," later to become *Clash by Night*. (Some of these observations were published in "Genesis of a Play" in the *New York Times* in 1942.) The difficulty he has in concentrating on a single play, combined with his undisciplined life, undermines his ambitious plans. In one of the final entries he takes himself to task: "What worries me about this painful period in my life is that it may not be a period of mellowing but of DENATURING!"

The journal thus provides profound insight into a tormented and divided soul, while also prompting speculation about the dramatic downslide in Odets's career after 1940. Although he had struggled for many years as an actor, Odets's success as a playwright was sudden and extreme. He did work for a few years on some apprentice works, all unfinished, but he never submitted them, so he never had a series of plays rejected or produced unsuccessfully on the stage before winning the praise of critics and colleagues. *Waiting for Lefty*, his first play, was an extraordinary success, and Odets gained a major reputation on the basis of his first few efforts. No other American playwright ever produced so many important works in one year as Odets did in 1935. The combination of instant acclaim and this productive whirlwind must have been dizzying to a young man who had never had even a small taste of success before. The cumulative effect of so much frenetic achievement did not hit him until much later.

With the exception of *Paradise Lost,* Odets had not experienced a Broadway failure before *Night Music,* and while he was hurt by the adverse critical reaction to that early work, the shock of rejection must have been absorbed into the overall flurry of activity in 1935. This first setback was then followed by his biggest success, *Golden Boy,* in 1937, then *Rocket to the Moon* and a *Time* magazine cover story in 1939. In many ways, Odets's voice was perfect for his time: he spoke to the dispossessed, alienated audience of the 1930s and to forward-looking progressives who imagined a brighter future. His own inner turmoil and conflicting aspirations reflected the national mood, providing a perfect fusion of artist and audience.

However, all this personal and professional prosperity began to fall apart almost as suddenly as it had begun. Odets's first marriage, the failure of which obsessed him, is rehashed again and again in the journal, along with his concurrent need to give himself over to something or someone, be it the Group Theatre, Harold Clurman, Faye Wray, or Bette Grayson. He wrestles with this yearning, and with his inability to fulfill it, evoking a childhood fear to explain his psychological blockage:

The terror of my childhood was that either or both of my parents or my sisters might die. Many nights I stayed awake as child and boy, fearful that my parents had been killed in an auto wreck, etc. These thoughts really terrorized my youth. And that terror is one of the reasons that now I am so chary of forming permanent relationships of an intimate or personal nature. I can't face the possibilities of serious illnesses or death to others close to me; for myself I am not much mindful. This is really one of the things which makes it so difficult for me to give myself over to others.

The world situation, too, has begun to change, and the journal records Odets's fears and questions about the growing global crisis as America moves gradually toward world war.

The personal and the global chaos merge with the artistic, primarily represented in the failure of *Night Music,* which also haunts the journal. Odets seems genuinely unable to cope with this blow, even developing a fear of the Broadway process itself. This fearfulness would only increase as the Group collapsed and Odets's next play, *Clash by Night,* produced by leading Broadway impresario Billy Rose, also failed. Not surprisingly, after this reversal of fortune, Odets beat a hasty retreat to Hollywood and did not return to Broadway until 1948, then with a play focused on the success syndrome and featuring a divided protagonist who ultimately commits suicide.

The effect of Broadway acclaim and acceptance played a major role in shaping Odets's ambivalent attitude toward his career. His dividedness manifested itself in a need to yield to the lures of power and fortune (the gods of his father) and a simultaneous guilt with this yielding as a betrayal of his higher need to be true to his art. Indeed, Odets deliberately creates a rather unattractive protagonist in *The Big Knife* as a result of his self-loathing. Yet he was also so hurt by his Broadway failures as to fear trying again.

Equally influential in determining his artistic fortunes was Odets's evolving method itself. The early plays were the outpouring of a natural talent whose voice found a subject and an audience at a time that was ripe for it. Odets realized that his talent was spontaneous:

My work was instinctive, intuitive, scarcely using the conscious mind as a tool of construction. Intuition and feeling are still the prime movers of my writing.

Some years later when writing a preface (never published) to the plays of Sean O'Casey, Odets produced an analysis that could apply equally to his own early career:

The internal evidence would suggest that O'Casey in the early 1920's, swollen by the events of his times and place, was writing nevertheless out of personally emotional needs; the "affiliation" of the poet with the time, place and persons of the drama is hot headed, blind and complete.

He is no conscious poet or intellectual, the O'Casey of these early plays. He writes here almost as a workingman who has dropped his tools. . . . His sympathetic lyricism scarcely understands or hears itself, or expects to be heard beyond the street on which the poet lives. O'Casey is surely at one here with his . . . battered and trapped people. . . . The poet wants them to see the picture of waste and hear the miserably majestic music of their blasted lives.[2]

He finds that the later plays suffer from moving to "the right, away from the heart, to the manufacture of literature."

The Odets portrayed in the 1940 journal is a "burned out" writer who has experienced too much too soon. Now he is occupied with the task of regrouping, trying to find himself and his subject, preparing to face a new decade and a new world, to become a new man. Like O'Casey, Odets is no longer an impulsive artist, for he recognizes that his writing now must be the result of the "conscious mind" marching alongside "feeling and intuition." This evolution does not necessarily represent a loss, of course, though one of the principal weaknesses of *Clash by Night* is that Odets started with a thesis and tried to build a play around it rather than letting his theme emerge naturally out of a situation or a feeling.

The journal does indicate that Odets was moving into a new phase, involving a more "conscious" process, that he would need to struggle more with the problem of form in transforming his impulses into art. Henceforth he would require greater discipline and fewer distractions. Unfortunately, after 1942 this renewal of purpose would not thrive as he wished.

As he had done in 1931 and 1932, Odets anticipated his own failure in the journal:

I am a romantic, enthusiastic and moral idealist, like any young Stendhal hero. The so-called practical and realistic world has impinged itself upon my consciousness. The nature of the beast comes clearer to me each week, and one must actively take arms against it or be corrupted into a twisting cynical rascal of a diplomat. What a shock to march up a hill, banner in hand, and suddenly look down on that Hollywood in the valley! The first impact can stun you for life!

This was a subject he would return to again and again. In a television interview on February 3, 1963 (six months before his death), Herman Harvey asked him to describe the "sum and substance" of his life. Odets responded simply, "a loss of innocence," defining inno-

cence as an "uncorrupted quality with which children are born . . .
nothing outside yourself influences you."

Odets's romanticism, as revealed in the journal and in his plays,
was centered on a love of man and of the possibilities of life. His
early protagonists share a utopian vision that Odets knew was not
realizable, but he nonetheless loved his characters for dreaming the
dream. This romantic disposition accounts also for his nostalgic
bent, his need to recapture the past in an idealized childhood, like
that Jerry Wilenski could summon up from a Christmas card in *Clash
by Night*.

Because he held on to childhood dreams and adolescent fantasies,
Odets was in constant rebellion against the society and the reality
that he encountered as an adult; but his was a generalized, not a
specific mood of rejection. He did, for a time, believe in Marxism,
but it failed him, and his disillusionment—as with other fallen idols,
such as the American theater and the Group Theatre—was intense.
His penchant for despair was directed at himself as well, as can be
seen in *The Big Knife* and *The Country Girl*. Odets's disappointment,
however, was not with Marxism or the theater as such, but with
humanity for failing the ideal, which may explain his obsessive
yearning for form. In trying to express the inexpressible depth of his
disillusionment, he could find no language for it. He probably didn't
want to find it, for Odets believed that art, particularly theater,
should celebrate man and exalt his potential. Perhaps in the perver-
sity of despair he opted for a superficial success because that corruption of the artistic ideal was part of the wider betrayal he was
protesting.

Odets's fundamental miscalculation was in believing that he was
better than he was and that mankind was greater than it actually
could be. He trusted too blindly in man's capacity to believe and to
seek the ideal; he thirsted too passionately for the infinite. Odets's
art, finally, is a record of the human capacity for aspiration, his
overriding aim to compel recognition of that human potential and to
find a form that could expand to accommodate it.

Notes

Chapter 1: The Whirl and the Terror

1. I am indebted to Margaret Brenman-Gibson's biography *Clifford Odets, American Playwright: The Years from 1906–1940* (New York: Atheneum, 1981). for the biographical summary included here. Those who want to read a more detailed account of Odets's life should consult Brenman-Gibson's book. Another reliable source of biographical information is Gerald Weales, *Clifford Odets: Playwright* (New York: Pegasus, 1971).
2. Odets's typed draft, dated 1926, is in the Billy Rose Theatre Collection of the New York Public Library at Lincoln Center.
3. Harold Clurman, *The Fervent Years* (1945. Reprint. New York: DaCapo, 1975), p. 34. Clurman's is the most complete and comprehensive history of the Group Theatre.
4. Ibid., p. 43.
5. Ibid., p. 35.
6. Ibid., p. 44.
7. Quoted in Clurman, p. 35.
8. Reprinted in Clurman, p. 281.
9. Quoted in Brenman-Gibson, p. 24.
10. Clurman, p. 42.
11. Harold Clurman, "Clifford Odets," *The New York Times*, August 25, 1963, Sec. II, 1.
12. Clurman, *The Fervent Years*, p. 154.
13. Quoted in Brenman-Gibson, p. 13.

Chapter 2: Early Self-Portraits

1. All references to "910 Eden Street" are to the typed draft, dated 1931, in the Billy Rose Theatre Collection of the New York Public Library at Lincoln Center.

239

2. Harold Clurman, *The Fervent Years* (1945. Reprint. New York: DaCapo, 1975), pp. 67–68.
3. Margaret Brenman-Gibson, *Clifford Odets, American Playwright: The Years from 1906–1940* (New York: Atheneum, 1981), p. 170.
4. Ibid., p. 171.
5. Clifford Odets, "1932 Journal." This manuscript is in the Billy Rose Theatre Collection of the New York Public Library at Lincoln Center.
6. Ibid.
7. Clifford Odets, *The Time is Ripe: The 1940 Journal of Clifford Odets* (New York: Grove Press, 1988). My references are to the unbound galleys. I have therefore not used page references.
8. Clifford Odets, "Victory." All references are to Odets's typed draft, written in 1932, in the Billy Rose Theatre Collection of the New York Public Library at Lincoln Center.

Chapter 3: The Chekhovian Vision

1. Harold Clurman, *The Fervent Years* (1945. Reprint. New York: DaCapo, 1975), p. 128.
2. Ibid.
3. Ibid., p. 149.
4. Quoted in Margaret Brenman-Gibson, *Clifford Odets, American Playwright: The Years from 1906–1940* (New York: Atheneum, 1981), p. 384.
5. Clurman, pp. 150–51.
6. Ibid., p. 151.
7. Harvey Pitcher, "The Chekhov Play," in *Chekhov: New Perspectives,* ed. René and Wanda D. Wellek (Englewood Cliffs, N.J.: Prentice-Hall, 1984), p. 80.
8. Clifford Odets, *Awake and Sing!* in *Six Plays of Clifford Odets* (New York: Grove Press, 1979), p. 72. All references to the play are to this edition and are cited in the text.
9. Gerald Weales, *Clifford Odets: Playwright* (New York: Pegasus, 1971), p. 71.
10. Michael Mendelsohn, "Odets at Center Stage," *Theater Arts,* 47 (May 1963): pp. 17–18.
11. Clifford Odets, *Paradise Lost* in *Six Plays of Clifford Odets* (New York: Grove Press, 1979), p. 173. All further references to the play are to this edition and are cited in the text.

Chapter 4: The Tragic Vision

1. Quoted in Margaret Brenman-Gibson, *Clifford Odets, American Playwright: The Years from 1906–1940* (New York: Atheneum, 1981), p. 426.

2. Clifford Odets, "Democratic Vistas in Drama," *New York Times,* 21 November, 1937, sec. 11, p. 1.

3. Ibid.

4. Robert Warshaw, "The Gangster as Tragic Hero," in *The Immediate Experience* (1962. Reprint. New York: Atheneum, 1974), p. 130.

5. This early draft of *Golden Boy,* dated 1937, is in the Billy Rose Theatre Collection of the New York Public Library at Lincoln Center.

6. Clifford Odets, *Golden Boy* in *Six Plays of Clifford Odets* (New York: Grove Press, 1979), p. 247. All further references to the play are from this edition and are cited in the text.

7. Carp's quotes from Schopenhauer are more extensive in the earlier versions of the play.

8. Gerald Rabkin, *Drama and Commitment* (Bloomington: Indiana University Press, 1964), pp. 197–98.

9. Quoted in Edward Murray, *Clifford Odets: The Thirties and After* (New York: Frederick Ungar Publishing Company, 1968), pp. 160–61.

10. For a full discussion of the characteristics of Hollywood fiction, refer to Carolyn See, "The Hollywood Novel: The American Dream Cheat," in David Madden, ed., *Tough Guy Writers of the Thirties* (Carbondale: Southern Illinois University Press, 1968), pp. 197–217.

11. Clifford Odets, *The Big Knife* (New York: Random House, 1949), p. 106. All further references are to this edition and are cited in the text.

12. All quoted material not in the published version of *The Big Knife* is from "A Winter Journey, First Draft" dated 1948, in the Billy Rose Theatre Collection of the New York Public Library at Lincoln Center.

Chapter 5: Visions of Romance

1. Margaret Brenman-Gibson, *Clifford Odets, American Playwright: The Years from 1906–1940* (New York: Atheneum, 1981), p. 490.

2. Ibid., p. 509.

3. *Time,* 5 December 1938, p. 44.

4. Brenman-Gibson, p. 606.

5. Northrop Frye, *Anatomy of Criticism* (1957. Reprint. Princeton: Princeton University Press, 1973), p. 186.
6. Gillian Beer, *The Romance* (London: Methuen, 1970), p. 29.
7. Frye, pp. 186–87.
8. Gerald Weales, *Clifford Odets: Playwright* (New York: Pegasus, 1971), p. 135.
9. Harold Clurman, *The Fervent Years* (1945. Reprint. New York: DaCapo, 1975), p. 234.
10. Clifford Odets, *Golden Boy* in *Six Plays of Clifford Odets* (New York: Grove Press, 1979), p. 316.
11. Clifford Odets, *Rocket to the Moon* in *Six Plays of Clifford Odets* (New York: Grove Press, 1979), p. 416. All further references to the play cited in the text are to this edition.
12. Brenman-Gibson, p. 528.
13. Ibid., p. 670.
14. Northrop Frye, *The Secular Scripture* (1976. Reprint. Cambridge: Harvard University Press, 1982), p. 73.
15. It is interesting to note the use Odets makes of the number three in the play. Frye points out (*Anatomy of Criticism*, p. 187) that three is an important number in romance, for it corresponds with its threefold structure. In addition to the three-year anniversary of the child's death, the play has a number of three references. The play takes place over three months and there are three acts. In Stark's office there are three doctors (Cooper and Frenchy in addition to Stark), and Belle and Ben's marriage is complicated by Cleo—a love triangle. Dr. Cooper is also three months behind on his rent.
16. Brenman-Gibson, p. 527.
17. Ibid., p. 529.
18. Ibid., p. 532.
19. Clifford Odets, *Night Music* (New York: Random House, 1940), p. 160. All further references to the play cited in the text are to this edition.

Chapter 6: The Melodramatic Vision

1. Clifford Odets, "Genesis of a Play," *New York Times,* 1 February 1942, sec. 9, p. 3.
2. Robert B. Heilman, *The Iceman, the Arsonist, and the Troubled Agent* (Seattle: University of Washington Press, 1973), p. 49.
3. Heilman, p. 57.

4. Clifford Odets, *Clash by Night* (New York: Random House, 1942), p. 223. All references to the play cited in the text are to this edition.

5. Harold Clurman, *The Fervent Years* (1945. Reprint. New York: DaCapo, 1975), p. 128.

6. Rosamond Gilder, review of *Clash by Night, Theatre Arts,* March 1942, pp. 150–52.

7. Odets, "Genesis of a Play," p. 3.

8. Gerald Weales, *Clifford Odets: Playwright* (New York: Pegasus, 1971), p. 152.

9. Margaret Brenman-Gibson, *Clifford Odets, American Playwright: The Years from 1906–1940* (New York: Atheneum, 1981), p. 616.

10. "Review of *None But the Lonely Heart,*" *Time,* 20 November 1944, p. 92.

11. *Time,* 1 December 1947, p. 10.

12. Michael Mendelsohn, "Odets at Center Stage," *Theatre Arts,* May–June 1963, p. 18.

13. Armand Aulicino, "How *The Country Girl* Came About," *Theatre Arts,* May 1952, p. 55.

14. Ibid., p. 56.

15. Ibid., p. 57.

16. Ibid., p. 55.

17. Clifford Odets, *The Country Girl* (New York: Viking Press, 1951), p. 44. All references to the play are to this edition and are cited in the text.

Chapter 7: The Political Vision

1. Harold Clurman, *The Fervent Years* (1945. Reprint. New York: DaCapo, 1975), p. 142.

2. Clurman, pp. 147–48.

3. Quoted in Gerald Weales, *Clifford Odets: Playwright* (New York: Pegasus, 1971), p. 37.

4. Art Smith and Elia Kazan, "Dimitroff," *New Theatre,* July–August 1934, p. 20.

5. Ibid., p. 22.

6. Ibid., p. 24.

7. Ibid.

8. Clifford Odets, *Waiting for Lefty* in *Six Plays of Clifford Odets* (New York: Grove Press, 1979), p. 31. All references to the play are to this edition and are cited in the text.

9. Gerald Rabkin, *Drama and Commitment* (Bloomington: Indiana University Press, 1964), pp. 173–74.

10. Clifford Odets, *Waiting for Lefty and Till the Day I Die* (New York: Random House, 1935), pp. 40–41.

11. Odets, *Waiting for Lefty and Till the Day I Die*, p. 42.

12. Margaret Brenman-Gibson, *Clifford Odets, American Playwright: The Years from 1906–1940* (New York: Atheneum, 1981), p. 329.

13. Clifford Odets, *Till the Day I Die* in *Six Plays of Clifford Odets* (New York: Grove Press, 1979), p. 108. All further references to the play are to this edition and appear in the text.

14. Clifford Odets, "I Can't Sleep," *New Theatre*, 3, February 1936, pp. 8–9. Also reprinted in Margaret Brenman-Gibson, *Clifford Odets, American Playwright*, pp. 354–56. Page reference here and in following notes are to Brenman-Gibson.

15. Brenman-Gibson, p. 355.

16. Ibid., p. 356.

17. Ibid.

18. Ibid.

19. I am indebted to Margaret Brenman-Gibson's biography for information on this play.

20. I have used the typed draft of the play, dated 1935–38, in the Billy Rose Theatre Collection of the New York Public Library at Lincoln Center.

21. Clurman, *The Fervent Years*, p. 185.

22. Ibid., p. 186.

23. Michael Mendelsohn, "Odets at Center Stage," *Theatre Arts*, May–June 1963, p. 30.

24. Clifford Odets, "The Silent Partner." I have used Odets's own manuscript copy of the play dated 12 November 1936 in the Theatre Collection, New York Public Library.

Chapter 8: The Final Testament

1. Eric Bentley, ed., *Thirty Years of Treason* (New York: The Viking Press, 1971), p. 505.

2. Ibid., p. 507.

3. Ibid., p. 510.

4. Ibid., p. 517.

5. Ibid., p. 530.

6. Ibid., p. 531.

7. Murray Kempton, *Part of Our Time* (New York: Simon and Schuster, 1955), p. 208.
8. Malcolm Goldstein, "Clifford Odets and the Found Generation," in *American Drama and Its Critics,* ed. Alan S. Downer (Chicago: University of Chicago Press, 1965), p. 144.
9. Herbert Mitgang, "Odets Goes to Genesis," *New York Times,* 26 December 1954, II, p. 1.
10. Harold Clurman, *Lies Like the Truth* (New York: The Macmillan Co., 1958), p. 57.
11. André Obey, *Noah* in *Twenty Best European Plays on the American Stage,* ed. John Glassner (New York: Crown Publishers, 1957), p. 387.
12. Clifford Odets, *The Flowering Peach* (New York: Dramatists Play Service, 1954), p. 7. All references to the play are to this edition and are cited in the text.
13. Mitgang, *New York Times,* p. 3.
14. Clifford Odets, *Awake and Sing!* in *Six Plays of Clifford Odets* (New York: Grove Press, 1974), p. 50.
15. Clurman, pp. 56–57.
16. Brooks Atkinson, review of *The Flowering Peach, New York Times,* 20 December 1954.
17. Bob Thomas, *King Cohn* (1967. Reprint. New York: Bantam, 1967), pp. 317–18.
18. William Gibson, "Preface to *Golden Boy*" (1965. Reprint. New York: Bantam, 1966), p. 13.
19. "Boone, Renoir Find Common Ground," *Los Angeles Times,* 1 August 1963, IV, p. 16.
20. "Credo of a Wrong Living Man," *Time,* 14 December 1962, p. 40.

Afterword

1. Clifford Odets, *The Time is Ripe: The 1940 Journal of Clifford Odets* (New York: Grove Press, 1988). I refer throughout to the unbound galleys of the journal, which were sent to me in January 1988. I have therefore omitted page references.
2. Three copies of this typed manuscript are in the Billy Rose Theatre Collection of the New York Public Library at Lincoln Center.

Bibliography

Primary Sources

Plays

Three Plays by Clifford Odets. New York: Covici-Friede, 1935. (Includes *Waiting for Lefty, Till the Day I Die,* and *Awake and Sing!*)

Waiting for Lefty and Till the Day I Die. New York: Random House, 1935.

Paradise Lost. New York: Random House, 1936.

Golden Boy. New York: Random House, 1937.

Rocket to the Moon. New York: Random House, 1939.

Six Plays of Clifford Odets. New York: Random House, 1939. (Includes *Waiting for Lefty, Till the Day I Die, Awake and Sing!, Paradise Lost, Golden Boy,* and *Rocket to the Moon*.) Reprinted by Grove Press, 1979.

Night Music. New York: Random House, 1940.

Clash by Night. New York: Random House, 1942.

The Russian People (an adaptation of a play by Konstantin Simonov, 1943) in *Seven Soviet Plays*, ed. Henry Wadsworth Longfellow Dana (New York: Macmillan, 1946).

The Big Knife. New York: Random House, 1949.

The Country Girl. New York: Viking Press, 1951. Published as *Winter Journey*. London: French, 1955.

The Flowering Peach. New York: Dramatists Play Service, 1954.

Plays Published in Periodicals

Waiting for Lefty (Original version). *New Theatre* 2 (February 1935): 13–20.

"I Can't Sleep." *New Theatre*, vol. 3, no. 2 (February 1936): 8–9. (Also in *The Anxious Years*, ed. Louis Filler, New York: Capricorn, 1964.)

"The Silent Partner," act 2, scene 2 in *New Theatre and Film* (March 1937): 5–9.
The Country Girl. Theatre Arts (May 1952): 59–87.

Screenplays (All adapted from previously published material except for *The Story on Page One*.)

The General Died at Dawn. (Paramount). 1936. Excerpts in Sidney Kaufman, "Odets's First Film," *New Masses* 20 (July 28, 1936): 12–13.
None But the Lonely Heart (RKO), 1944. (Directed by Odets.) In: *Best Film Plays,* 1945. Ed. John Gassner and Dudley Nichols. New York: Crown, 1946.
Deadline at Dawn (RKO), 1945.
Humoresque (Warner Brothers), 1946. Coauthor, Zachary Gold.
The Sweet Smell of Success (United Artists), 1957. Coauthored by Ernst Lehman.
The Story on Page One (Twentieth Century-Fox), 1960. (Directed by Odets.)
Wild in the Country (Twentieth Century-Fox), 1961.

Musicals Based on Odets's Plays

Odets, Clifford, and Gibson, William. *Golden Boy.* New York: Atheneum, 1965. (Reprint. New York: Bantam Books, 1966). Although Odets's name appears as a coauthor, the work is primarily Gibson's.
Stone, Peter. *Two by Two,* 1970. (Based on *The Flowering Peach*.)

Articles and Essays

"Clifford Odets Capitalizes His Own Life." *New York World-Telegram* (March 19, 1935).
"Odets Tells His Own Story of Cuban Arrest." *New York Post* (July 5, 1935).
"Some Problems of the Modern Dramatist." *New York Times,* sec. 2 (December 15, 1935): 3.
Beals, Carelton, and Odets, Clifford. "Rifle Rule in Cuba." New York: Provisional Committee for Cuba (1935).
"Awakening of the American Theatre." *New Theatre* (January 1936).
"All Drama Is Propaganda." *Current Controversy* (February 1936).
"Introduction" to *Dead Souls* by Nikolay Gogol. New York: Modern Library, 1936.

"Democratic Vistas in Drama." *New York Times,* sec. 11 (November 21, 1937): 1–2.

"Critics a Mystery to Clifford Odets, So He Finds Mr. Morgan and Gives Him the Works." *New York World-Telegram* (March 2, 1940).

"Genesis of a Play." *New York Times,* sec. 9 (February 1, 1942): 3.

"On Coming Home." *New York Times,* sec. 2 (July 25, 1948): 1.

"Two Approaches to Writing a Play." *New York Times,* sec. 2 (April 22, 1951): 1–2.

"Tribute by Clifford Odets to the Late John Garfield." *New York Times,* sec. 2 (May 25, 1952).

"In Praise of a Maturing Industry." *New York Times,* sec. 2 (November 6, 1955): 5.

"When Wolfe Came Home." *New York Times,* sec. 2 (September 14, 1958): 3.

"To Whom It May Concern: Marilyn Monroe." *Show* 2 (October 1962): 67, 136.

"Willem de Kooning." *Critic* 21 (October–November 1962): 37–38.

"The Transient Olympian." *Show* 3 (April 1963): 106–7, 130–33.

"Boone, Renoir Find Common Ground." *Los Angeles Times,* sec. 4 (August 1, 1963): 16.

"How a Playwright Triumphs" (interviews and discussion with Arthur Wagner). *Harper's* 233 (September 1966): 64–70.

Journal

The Time is Ripe: The 1940 Journal of Clifford Odets. New York: Grove Press, 1988.

Selected Secondary Bibliography

Aaron, Daniel. *Writers on the Left.* New York: Harcourt, Brace and World, 1961.

Bentley, Eric. *Thirty Years of Treason*. New York: Viking Press, 1971.

Brenman-Gibson, Margaret. *Clifford Odets, American Playwright: The Years from 1906–1940*. New York: Atheneum, 1981.

Cantor, Harold. *Clifford Odets: Playwright-Poet*. Metuchen, New Jersey: Scarecrow Press, 1978.

Ciment, Michel. *Kazan on Kazan*. New York: Viking Press, 1974.

Clurman, Harold. *The Fervent Years (1945)*. Reprint. New York: DaCapo Press, 1975.

———. *Lies Like the Truth*. New York: Macmillan, 1958.

"Credo of a Wrong Living Man," *Time* (Dec. 14, 1962).

Cunningham, Frank. "Clifford Odets" in *American Writers: A Collection of Literary Biographies*. Ed. A. Walton Litz. New York: Scribners, 1981.

Fagin, N. B. "In Search of an American Cherry Orchard." *Texas Quarterly* (Summer-Autumn 1958).

Flexner, Eleanor. *American Playwrights: 1918–1938*. New York: Simon and Schuster, 1938.

Frye, Northrop. *Anatomy of Criticism (1957)*. Reprint. Princeton: Princeton University Press, 1973.

———. *The Secular Scripture: A Study of the Structure of Romance (1976)*. Reprint. Cambridge: Harvard University Press, 1982.

Goldstein, Malcolm. *The Political Stage: American Drama and the Theater of the Great Depression*. New York: Oxford University Press, 1974.

———. "Clifford Odets and the Found Generation," in *American Drama and Its Critics*. Ed. Alan S. Downer. Chicago: University of Chicago Press, 1965.

Isaacs, Edith. "Clifford Odets, First Chapters." *Theatre Arts* (April 1939).

Kempton, Murray. *Part of Our Time: Some Monuments and Ruins of the Thirties*. New York: Simon and Schuster, 1955.

Krutch, Joseph Wood. *American Drama Since 1918*. New York: George Braziller, 1957.

Lawson, John Howard. *Theory and Technique of Playwrighting and Screenwriting*. New York: Hill and Wang, 1960.

McCarten, John. "Revolution's Number One Boy." *The New Yorker* (January 22, 1938).

Mendelsohn, Michael J. *Clifford Odets: Humane Dramatist*. Deland, Florida: Evertt/Edwards, 1969.

———. "Odets at Center Stage." *Theatre Arts* (May–June 1963).

Murray, Edward. *Clifford Odets: The Thirties and After*. New York: Frederick Ungar, 1968.

Rabkin, Gerald. *Drama and Commitment: Politics in the American Theatre of the Thirties*. Bloomington: Indiana University Press, 1964.

Shuman, R. Baird. *Clifford Odets*. New York: Twayne, 1962.

———. "Clifford Odets and the Jewish Context" in *From Hester Street to Hollywood: The Jewish-American Stage and Screen*. Ed. Sarah Blacher Cohen. Bloomington: Indiana University Press, 1983.

Sugrue, Thomas. "Mr. Odets Regrets." *American Magazine* (October 1936).

Thomas, Bob. *King Cohn: The Life and Times of Harry Cohn* (1967). New York: Bantam Books, 1968.

Warshaw, Robert, *The Immediate Experience* (1962). Reprint. New York: Atheneum, 1974.

Weales, Gerald. *Clifford Odets: Playwright*. New York: Pegasus, 1971. Reprinted as *Odets: The Playwright*. New York: Methuen, 1985.

"White Hope." *Time* (December 5, 1938).

Willet, Ralph. "Clifford Odets and Popular Culture." *South Atlantic Quarterly* (1970).

Index